Access VPDN Solutions Guide

Sue Cross

Tina Fox

Mark Johnson

Ted Karakekes

Henderi (Henry) Konardi

Martina Lin

Eric Matkovich

Bruce Moon

Jeremy Pollock

Jim Rushton

Chiyu Wang

Cisco Press
201 West 103rd Street
Indianapolis, IN 46290 USA

Access VPDN Solutions Guide

Sue Cross

Tina Fox

Mark Johnson

Ted Karakekes

Henderi (Henry) Konardi

Martina Lin

Eric Matkovich

Bruce Moon

Jeremy Pollock

Jim Rushton

Chiyu Wang

Copyright© 2002 Cisco Systems, Inc.

Published by:

Cisco Press

201 West 103rd Street

Indianapolis, IN 46290 USA

Printed in the United States of America 1 2 3 4 5 6 7 8 9 0

First Printing November 2001

Library of Congress Cataloging-in-Publication Number: 2001095159

ISBN: 1-58705-064-1

Warning and Disclaimer

This book is designed to provide information about virtual private dial-up networks. Every effort has been made to make this book as complete and as accurate as possible, but no warranty or fitness is implied.

The information is provided on an "as is" basis. The author, Cisco Press, and Cisco Systems, Inc. shall have neither liability nor responsibility to any person or entity with respect to any loss or damages arising from the information contained in this book or from the use of the discs or programs that may accompany it.

The opinions expressed in this book belong to the author and are not necessarily those of Cisco Systems, Inc.

Feedback Information

At Cisco Press, our goal is to create in-depth technical books of the highest quality and value. Each book is crafted with care and precision, undergoing rigorous development that involves the unique expertise of members from the professional technical community.

Readers' feedback is a natural continuation of this process. If you have any comments regarding how we could improve the quality of this book, or otherwise alter it to better suit your needs, you can contact us through e-mail at feedback@ciscopress.com. Please make sure to include the book title and ISBN in your message.

We greatly appreciate your assistance.

Publisher	John Wait
Editor-in-Chief	John Kane
Cisco Systems Management	Michael Hakkert
	Tom Geitner
	William Warren
Managing Editor	Patrick Kanouse
Development Editor	Andrew Cupp
Project Editor	Marc Fowler
Copy Editor	Keith Cline
Technical Editors	Mark Gallo
	Bill Wagner
Team Coordinator	Tammi Ross
Book Designer	Gina Rexrode
Cover Designer	Louisa Klucznik
Production Team	Scan Communications
Indexer	Tim Wright

Trademark Acknowledgments

About the Authors

Sue Cross has 17 years of experience in developing technical information and technical training, and program management, with a primary focus on internetworking software and hardware.

Tina Fox is currently the Integration Solutions Program Manager for the Knowledge Management and Delivery group (IOS Technologies) at Cisco Systems and has been with Cisco Systems for five years. She attended the University of California at Los Angeles for both her undergraduate degree and graduate studies and completed a Certificate in Data and Telecommunications at the University of California at Irvine.

Mark Johnson is a Customer Support Escalation Engineer at Cisco Systems, where his emphasis has been access network troubleshooting for the past seven years. He received his bachelor of science degree in computer engineering from the University of Arizona.

Ted Karakekes works as a Service Provider Technical Marketing Engineer at Cisco Systems, specializing in remote access technology. He has been in this position for two+ years. Prior to joining Cisco Systems, he was a network consultant specializing in new network implementation and enhancements for remote access integration. Ted holds graduate degrees in business administration and management information systems.

Henderi (Henry) Konardi (CCIE #4976) received his bachelor of science degree in architecture from the University of Tarumanagara in Jakarta, Indonesia, and is currently working on his graduate degree in software engineering at Golden Gate University. Henry worked for three years with MCI local and data services before coming to Cisco Systems, where he worked for more than two years with the Technical Assistance Center. Henry now works with the Cisco Systems End-to-End System Test Engineering group on the ISP Team.

Martina Lin studied computer engineering at San Jose State University and for the past six years has been working as a system/software test engineer for products and technologies such as UNIX operation system, Ethernet, ATM, VoIP, Frame Relay, dial technologies, and VPN. Currently, Martina works with Cisco Systems End-to-End System Test Engineering group.

Eric Matkovich originally worked in software programming at Hewlett Packard on their remote access infrastructure, focusing on dial-up and ISDN access. He became interested in the Internet and ended up at Cisco Systems in January 1997 with the Enterprise Network Services group, where he focused on WANs and remote access technologies. Within that department, he designed and implemented networks to support both national and international 30K+ corporate telecommuters with dial, ISDN, xDSL, and VPN access.

Currently, Eric is a Technical Marketing Engineer with Cisco IOS and continues to focus on WANs, VPN, security, and broadband technologies.

Bruce Moon attended Oregon State University and Portland State University, from 1968 to 1978, and started connecting computers together in 1970 (at Oregon State University School of Oceanography; it wasn't called "networking" back then). Bruce worked as a Systems Programmer and Network Architect for Georgia-Pacific from 1978 to 1995. After working briefly with Advantis, Bruce started at Cisco Systems on April Fools Day in 1996 as a PME for the Access BU, concentrating primarily on high-end access servers (5200, 5300, 5400, 5800, AP). Bruce briefly worked on the AccessPath team as a Systems Engineer and then transferred into the Technology Center in 2000, concentrating on home network connections to the Internet. Bruce still owns his first modem (an original 300bps Hayes Smartmodem) and was a charter subscriber with GEnie, Prodigy, and AOL.

Jeremy Pollock is a Technical Writer for Cisco Systems, working on Cisco IOS software documentation. He writes feature and solution documentation, specializing in VoIP and access VPDN documentation. He received a bachelor of arts in physics from the University of California in 1997 and a Certificate in Technical Communications from San Jose State University in 1998.

Jim Rushton has worked with enterprise networking technology, in various capacities, for more than 15 years. He is currently a Cisco Systems Technical Writer in the Irvine, California office, assigned to the Knowledge Management and Delivery group (IOS Technologies).

Chiyu Wang is a Network Test Engineer at Cisco Optical Transport Interoperability Test Lab, where his work focuses on testing 10/100/1000 Ethernet IP Access over Sonet. He also worked at Cisco IOS Technology End-to-End Solutions Test Lab, where he was responsible for profiling and testing Cisco ISDN/Dialup/Access, VPDN, and IPSec solutions. He holds master's degree in computer engineering from University of Waterloo.

About the Technical Reviewers

Mark Gallo is a Technical Manager with America Online. His network certifications include Cisco CCNP and Cisco CCDP. He has led several engineering groups responsible for designing and implementing enterprise LANs and international IP networks. While working for a major international telecommunications company, his group was responsible for developing a dial solution based on L2F and L2TP. He has a bachelor of science degree in electrical engineering from the University of Pittsburgh. Mark resides in northern Virginia with his wife, Betsy, and son, Paul.

Bill Wagner works as a Cisco Certified System Instructor for Mentor Technologies. He has 22 years of computer programming and data communication experience. He has worked for corporation and companies such as Independent Computer Consultants, Numerax, McGraw-Hill/Numerax, and Standard and Poors. His teaching expertise started with the Chubb Institute, Protocol Interface, Inc., and Geotrain. Currently he teaches at Mentor Technologies.

Acknowledgments

We would like to thank the following people for their contributions to this project: Kris Thompson, Greg McMillan, Dave Phillips, Brian Adams, and Wink Schuetz for their work on the original Internetworking Solutions documentation; without their help, the original projects could not have been completed. We would also like to thank John Kane, Andrew Cupp, and Patrick Kanouse at Cisco Press for their unfailing help and support.

Contents at a Glance

Table of Contents

Introduction

Objective of This Book

The objective of the *Access VPDN Solutions Guide* is to assist network architects and operators to design and implement access VPDN services into their production network by providing end-to-end network design, network verification and troubleshooting procedures, and configuration examples.

NOTE	Access VPDNs should not be confused with dedicated virtual private networks (VPNs)—also called intranet VPNs or extranet VPNs. Dedicated VPNs connect remote offices to private networks using permanent, dedicated connections. Access VPDNs provide remote access to private networks using analog, ISDN, mobile IP, and cable technologies.

Audience

The targeted audience for the *Access VPDN Solutions Guide* is Cisco level 3 (competent), level 4 (proficient), and level 5 (expert) users. This book is intended primarily for network administrators and operations teams working for service providers that provide access VPDN services to their customers. This book also will prove useful for enterprise customers and service providers interested in leasing access VPDN services for their networks.

Book Organization

This book covers the following topics:

- Chapter 1: Access VPDN Technologies Overview
- Chapter 2: Access VPDN Dial-In Using L2F Solution
- Chapter 3: Access VPDN Dial-In Using L2TP Solution
- Chapter 4: Access VPDN Dial-In Using IPSec over L2TP Solution
- Appendix A: New Access VPDN Services: L2TP Dial-Out
- Appendix B: New Access VPDN Services: PPTP with MPPE
- Appendix C: VPDN Command Summary
- Appendix D: Debug Output

Chapter 1: Access VPDN Technologies Overview

This chapter begins with a discussion of the differences between virtual private networks (VPNs) and access virtual private dial-up network (VPDNs). It then provides an overview of access VPDN services and terminology. Finally, it includes detailed descriptions of VPDN tunneling technologies, services, encryption methods, and several related technologies.

Chapter 2: Access VPDN Dial-In Using L2F Solution

The end-to-end solution in this chapter describes how an Internet service provider (ISP) partners with an enterprise customer to design and implement an access VPDN that uses Layer 2 Forwarding (L2F). Although L2F has mostly been replaced by the Layer 2 Tunnel Protocol (L2TP), this solution is still relevant because, except for two Cisco IOS commands, this network is identical to an L2TP network.

This solution will be useful for readers with minimal experience with access VPDNs because it takes a multiphased, step-by-step approach to configuring and verifying the network. However, this solution also will be useful to more advanced readers because it includes detailed troubleshooting methodologies for identifying and solving common configuration problems.

Chapter 3: Access VPDN Dial-In Using L2TP Solution

The end-to-end solution in this chapter describes how an ISP partners with an enterprise customer and a medium-sized service provider to design and implement an access VPDN network that uses L2TP. The ISP designs the network to offer traditional VPDN service to the enterprise and wholesale dial service to the service provider.

This solution assumes that you have a basic understanding of access VPDN technologies. It is therefore more concise than the L2F solution, and includes a discussion of the ramifications of implementing such a network and possible enhancements to the network.

Chapter 4: Access VPDN Dial-In Using IPSec over L2TP Solution

The end-to-end solution in this chapter describes how an ISP partners with an enterprise customer to add Internet Protocol Security (IPSec) encryption to an existing L2TP network. It assumes you have a basic understanding of access VPDN technologies. It discusses several different ways to implement IPSec on the network and several IPSec design choices.

Appendixes

Appendixes A and B include basic information on how to configure two new access VPDN services:

- NAS-initiated L2TP dial-out
- Client-initiated PPTP dial-in with MPPE encryption

Appendix C briefly describes all the Cisco IOS commands discussed in this book.

Appendix D provides debug output for the examples used throughout the book.

CHAPTER 1

Access VPDN Technologies Overview

An access virtual private dial-up network (VPDN) is a shared network infrastructure that enables users belonging to different organizations to access their different LANs by using remote dial connections. Access VPDNs use Layer 2 tunneling technologies to create virtual point-to-point connections between remote users and resources located on an enterprise LAN. These tunneling technologies use a shared network infrastructure (such as the Internet) to provide the same direct connectivity as the expensive Public Switched Telephone Network (PSTN).

Instead of connecting directly to the network by placing expensive long-distance modem calls over the PSTN to the enterprise LAN, access VPDN users place local calls over the PSTN or Integrated Services Digital Network (ISDN) to an Internet service provider (ISP) local point of presence (PoP). Equipment at the PoP then creates a Layer 2 tunnel to forward user calls over a shared network infrastructure to the individual enterprise LANs. Forwarding calls over the Internet as opposed to making long-distance PSTN calls provides dramatic cost saving for the customer.

In addition to providing less expensive remote access, access VPDNs delegate network responsibilities between an ISP and its customers. An ISP leases VPDN service to enterprise customers who want to outsource their information technology responsibilities, and to medium-sized service providers that want to expand their geographic presence. The ISP is responsible for maintaining the modems, access servers, and internetworking expertise necessary to remotely access the network. The ISP customers are then responsible only for authenticating their users and maintaining their private networks.

Access VPDNs connect a variety of users: from a single, mobile employee to an entire branch office. Figure 1-1 shows the following methods of logging in to access VPDNs:

- Home PC by using a terminal adapter
- Small office, home office (SOHO) by using a router
- Remote office, branch office (ROBO) by using a router
- Mobile PC by using a modem

Figure 1-1 *Logging In to Access VPDNs*

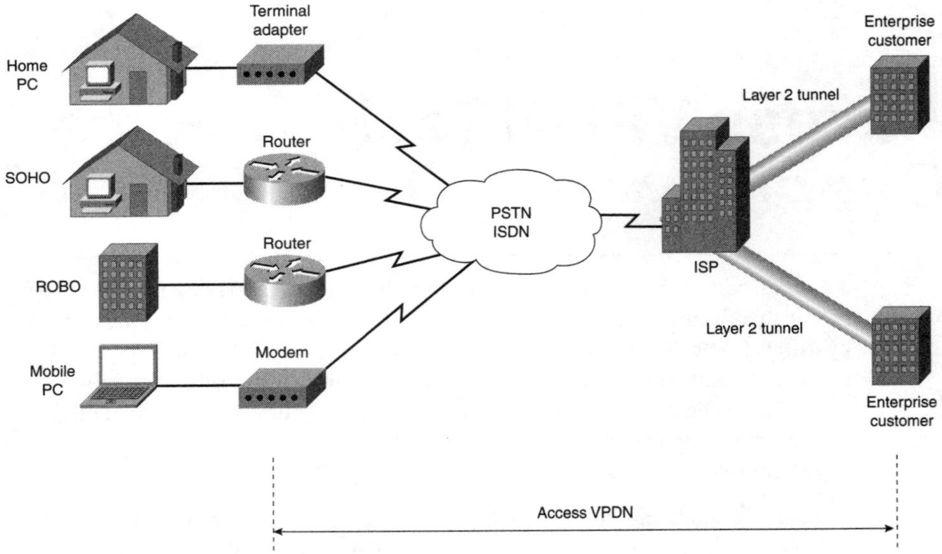

The access VPDN extends from the user to the customer network. The Layer 2 tunneling protocol (either Layer 2 Forwarding [L2F] or Layer 2 Tunneling Protocol [L2TP]) is what makes access VPDNs unique: After the tunnel has been established, the ISP is transparent to the user and the customer network. The tunnel creates a secure connection between the user and the customer network over the insecure Internet and is indistinguishable from a point-to-point connection.

This chapter contains the following sections:

- Virtual Private Networks
- Access VPDN Services
- NAS-Initiated Access VPDNs
- Client-Initiated Access VPDNs Using PPTP Dial-In
- Encryption Technologies
- Related Technologies

Virtual Private Networks

Access VPDNs are a specific type of virtual private network (VPN). VPNs create dedicated tunnels that connect remote users and sites to a single central network using a hub-and-spoke architecture. (It is generally not scalable to create dedicated tunnels connecting every site to every other site). These tunnels create a geographically dispersed virtual network that maintains the same security and management policies as a private network. VPNs are the most cost-effective way to establish point-to-point connections between remote users and central networks.

There are three main types of VPNs:

- **Access VPDNs**—Provide remote access to a customer intranet or extranet over a shared infrastructure. Access VPNs use dial, ISDN, mobile IP, and cable technologies to securely connect mobile users, telecommuters, and branch offices. The rest of this book refers to these networks by the more specific term access VPDNs.

- **Intranet VPNs**—Link customer headquarters, remote offices, and branch offices to an internal network over a shared infrastructure using dedicated connections (such as leased lines, Frame Relay, and ATM). Intranet VPNs differ from extranet VPNs in that they allow access only to the customer employees.

- **Extranet VPNs**—Link external customers, suppliers, partners, or communities of interest to a customer network over a shared infrastructure using dedicated connections. Extranet VPNs differ from intranet VPNs in that they allow access to users other than the customer employees.

This book focuses solely on access VPDNs.

Access VPDN Services

Cisco Systems offers a variety of access VPDN services. To understand a description of the specific services Cisco currently supports, you need to understand the four main criteria discussed in the following sections:

- Access VPDN Architectures
- Tunneling Protocols
- Direction of VPDN Service
- Tunnel Encryption

The following are also covered:

- Supported Access VPDN Services
- VPDN Hardware Terminology

Access VPDN Architectures

Access VPDN architectures are defined by which devices in the network initiate and terminate the Layer 2 tunnels. The two access VPDN architectural options are client-initiated or network access server- (NAS-) initiated. A NAS is an access server, maintained by the ISP, to which users dial in to and that forwards the call to the enterprise network. The options are described as follows:

- **Client-initiated access VPDNs**—Users establish an encrypted IP tunnel across the ISP shared network to the customer network. The customer manages the client software that initiates the tunnel. The main advantage of client-initiated VPDNs is that they secure the connection between the client and the ISP. However, client-initiated VPDNs are not as scalable as NAS-initiated VPDNs. The Cisco Systems implementation of client-initiated VPDNs currently supports PPTP as the tunneling protocol.

- **NAS-initiated access VPDNs**—Users dial in to the ISP NAS, which establishes a tunnel to the customer private network. NAS-initiated VPDNs are more robust than client-initiated VPDNs, allow users to connect to multiple networks by using multiple tunnels, and do not require the client to maintain the tunnel-creating software. NAS-initiated VPDNs do not encrypt the connection between the client and the ISP; however, this is not a concern for most customers because the PSTN and ISDN are much more secure than the Internet. The Cisco implementation of NAS-initiated VPDNs currently supports L2F and L2TP as the tunneling protocols.

Tunneling Protocols

Access VPDNs can use any of the following three Layer 2 tunneling protocols:

- **Layer 2 Forwarding (L2F)**—L2F is a Cisco proprietary tunneling protocol. Its main advantage is that it is a stable tunneling protocol supported by many vendors and client software applications. It is the most stable of the Layer 2 tunneling protocols. The trade-off for this stability is the fact that L2F does not scale as well as L2TP, nor does it support the advanced features L2TP does. Also, because L2F is a Cisco proprietary tunneling protocol, other vendors do not support it and all of the equipment in the VPDN must be Cisco equipment.

- **Point-to-Point Tunneling Protocol (PPTP)**—PPTP is a Microsoft proprietary tunneling protocol. It is bundled into many Microsoft Windows operating systems, which makes it an easily deployable solution for many enterprises.

- **Layer 2 Tunneling Protocol (L2TP)**—L2TP is the Internet Engineering Task Force (IETF) standard Layer 2 tunneling protocol that was designed to merge the best features of L2F and PPTP. L2TP offers the best performance and scalability of the three. L2TP is supported by many other networking vendors, and recent releases of Cisco IOS software have greatly improved the stability of L2TP tunnels.

Direction of VPDN Service

Cisco Systems access VPDNs now support service across both directions of the network, dial-in and dial-out:

- **Access VPDN dial-in**—Connects remote users to enterprise LANs. This service is useful for providing remote users and branch offices access to the central network.
- **Access VPDN dial-out**—Enables enterprise LANs to initiate calls to remote sites. This service is useful when central networks need to distribute information (such as price lists) to branch offices.

Tunnel Encryption

You can configure access VPDNs to encrypt sensitive traffic using one of the following two encryption technologies:

- **Internet Protocol Security (IPSec)**—IPSec ensures data confidentiality, integrity, and authenticity. The Cisco implementation of IPSec gives users flexibility by offering several encryption algorithms, hash algorithms, and authentication methods.
- **Microsoft Point-to-Point Encryption (MPPE)**—MPPE provides 40-bit or 128-bit RC4 encryption. It is bundled into many Microsoft Windows operating systems, which makes it an easily deployable solution for many enterprises.

Supported Access VPDN Services

Now that you are familiar with the basic criteria that define an access VPDN, you are ready to learn about the specific access VPDN services Cisco currently supports. The following supported combinations of the access VPDN criteria define the Cisco access VPDN services:

- NAS-initiated L2F dial-in
- NAS-initiated L2F dial-in with IPSec encryption

- NAS-initiated L2TP dial-in
- NAS-initiated L2TP dial-in with IPSec encryption
- NAS-initiated L2TP dial-out
- NAS-initiated L2TP dial-out with IPSec encryption
- Client-initiated PPTP dial-in
- Client-initiated PPTP dial-in with MPPE encryption

VPDN Hardware Terminology

As new tunneling protocols have been developed for VPDNs, new terminology has been created to describe the hardware involved in VPDNs. Fundamentally, two routers are needed for a VPDN:

- **NAS**—The NAS receives incoming calls for dial-in VPDNs and places outgoing calls for dial-out VPDNs. Typically it is maintained by an ISP that wants to provide VPDN services to its customers.
- **Home gateway**—The home gateway terminates dial-in VPDNs and initiates dial-out VPDNs. Typically it is maintained by the ISP customer and is the contact point for the customer network.

Table 1-1 lists the generic terms and the technology-specific terms that are often used for these devices.

Table 1-1 *VPDN Hardware Terminology*

L2F Term	L2TP Term	PPTP Term
Home gateway	L2TP network server (LNS)	PPTP network server (PNS)
NAS	L2TP access concentrator (LAC)	PPTP access concentrator (PAC)

In dial-in scenarios, users dial in to the NAS, and the NAS forwards the call to the home gateway using a VPDN tunnel. In dial-out scenarios, the home gateway initiates a VPDN tunnel to the NAS, and the NAS dials out to the clients.

NAS-Initiated Access VPDNs

Figure 1-2 shows the connection between a client (the user hardware and software) and the home gateway. The NAS and home gateway establish a Layer 2 tunnel that the NAS uses to forward the PPP link to the home gateway. The access VPDN then extends from the client to the home gateway. The tunnel creates a virtual point-to-point connection between the client and the home gateway.

Figure 1-2   *End-to-End Access VPDN Protocol Flow*

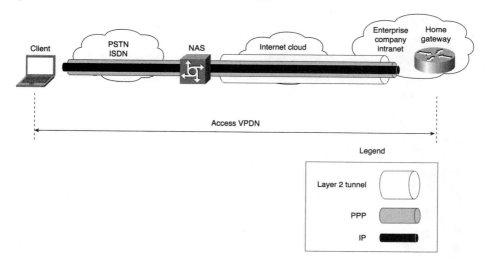

The following sections provide a functional description of the sequence of events that establish an access VPDN:

- **Protocol Negotiation Overview**—Provides an overview of the negotiation events that take place as the access VPDN is established.

- **L2F Tunnel and Session Authentication Process**—Describes how the NAS and home gateway establish L2F tunnels and L2F user sessions.

- **L2TP Tunnel Negotiation Process**—Describes how the NAS and home gateway establish L2TP tunnels.

- **L2TP Session Establishment Process**—Describes how the LAC and LNS establish L2TP dial-in and dial-out sessions.

Protocol Negotiation Overview

A user that wants to connect to the enterprise customer home gateway first establishes a PPP connection to the ISP NAS. The NAS then establishes a Layer 2 tunnel with the home gateway. Finally, the home gateway authenticates the client username and password, and establishes the PPP connection with the client. Figure 1-3 shows the sequence of protocol negotiation events between the ISP NAS and the enterprise customer home gateway.

Figure 1-3   *Protocol Negotiation Events Between Access VPDN Devices*

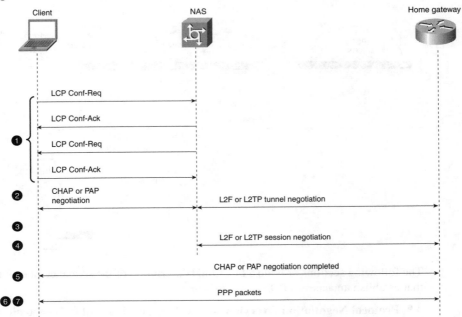

Table 1-2 explains the sequence of events shown in Figure 1-3.

Table 1-2   *Protocol Negotiation Event Descriptions*

Event	Description
1	The user client and the NAS conduct a standard PPP link control protocol (LCP) negotiation.
2	The NAS and client begin PPP authentication by using one of the following PPP authentication protocols: • Challenge Handshake Authentication Protocol (CHAP) • Password Authentication Protocol (PAP) • Microsoft CHAP (MS-CHAP) See the "CHAP, MS-CHAP, and PAP Authentication Processes" section later in this chapter for more details.

Table 1-2   *Protocol Negotiation Event Descriptions (Continued)*

Event	Description
3	The NAS identifies that the call is a VPDN session by comparing the call characteristics to a configuration on either a local database or on its authentication, authorization, and accounting (AAA) server.
	If the NAS is configured for Dialed Number Identification Service (DNIS)-based tunneling, it matches the phone number from which the user dialed in. If the NAS is configured for domain name–based tunneling, it matches the user domain name.
	Thus the NAS associates the call with the proper VPDN group, and initiates a VPDN session to forward the call to the home gateway by using either an L2F or L2TP tunnel.
	Because this is the first VPDN session with the home gateway, the NAS and the home gateway negotiate a VPDN tunnel. See the "L2F Tunnel and Session Authentication Process" and "L2TP Tunnel Negotiation Process" sections later in this chapter for more details.
4	After the tunnel has been opened, the NAS forwards the user information to the home gateway, which then negotiates the user VPDN session. See the "L2F Tunnel and Session Authentication Process" and "L2TP Session Establishment Process" sections later in this chapter for more details. The home gateway then creates a virtual access interface for the client based on the user information the NAS forwards.
5	When using CHAP or MS-CHAP authentication, the home gateway authenticates the challenge and response (using either local or remote AAA) and sends an Auth-OK packet to the client, which completes the three-way authentication.
	When using PAP authentication, the home gateway authenticates the forwarded client PAP request and sends a PAP acknowledgment to the client, which completes the two-way authentication.
	The home gateway can renegotiate CHAP, MS-CHAP, or PAP with the client.
6	After the home gateway has authenticated the client, the client and the home gateway can exchange I/O PPP-encapsulated packets. The NAS acts as a transparent PPP frame forwarder.
7	Subsequent incoming VPDN sessions (designated for the same home gateway using the same tunneling protocol) do not repeat the tunnel negotiation because the tunnel is already open.

L2F Tunnel and Session Authentication Process

When the NAS receives a call from a client that instructs it to create an L2F tunnel with the home gateway, it first sends a challenge to the home gateway. The home gateway then sends a combined challenge and response to the NAS. Finally, the NAS responds to the home gateway challenge, and the two devices open the L2F tunnel.

Before the NAS and home gateway can authenticate the tunnel, they must have a common "tunnel secret." A tunnel secret is a pair of usernames with the same password that is configured on both the NAS and the home gateway. By combining the tunnel secret with random value algorithms, which are used to encrypt to the tunnel secret, the NAS and home gateway authenticate each other and establish the L2F tunnel.

Figure 1-4 shows the L2F tunnel authentication process.

Figure 1-4   *L2F Tunnel Authentication Process*

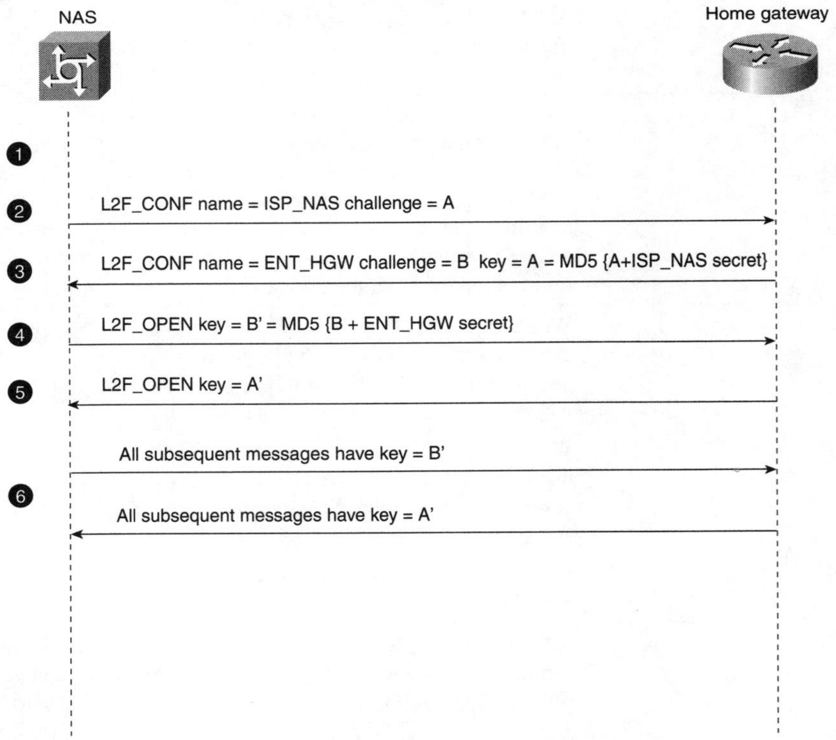

Table 1-3 explains the sequence of events shown in Figure 1-4.

Table 1-3   *L2F Tunnel Authentication Event Descriptions*

Event	Description
1	Before the NAS and home gateway open an L2F tunnel, both devices must have a common tunnel secret in their configurations.
2	The NAS sends an L2F_CONF packet that contains the NAS name and a random challenge value, A.
3	After the home gateway receives the L2F_CONF packet, it sends an L2F_CONF packet back to the NAS with the home gateway name and a random challenge value, B. This message also includes a key containing A' (the MD5 of the NAS secret and the value A).
4	When the NAS receives the L2F_CONF packet, it compares the key A' with the MD5 of the NAS secret and the value A. If the key and value match, the NAS sends an L2F_OPEN packet to the home gateway with a key containing B' (the MD5 of the home gateway secret and the value B).
5	When the home gateway receives the L2F_OPEN packet, it compares the key B' with the MD5 of the home gateway secret and the value B. If the key and value match, the home gateway sends an L2F_OPEN packet to the NAS with the key A'.
6	All subsequent messages from the NAS include key=B'; all subsequent messages from the home gateway include key=A'.

For more information on L2F, see RFC 2341, "Cisco Layer Two Forwarding Protocol (L2F)."

L2TP Tunnel Negotiation Process

Establishing an L2TP session is a two-part process: First, the LAC and LNS establish an L2TP tunnel. Second, the LAC and LNS establish the user session that is to be tunneled.

Before an L2TP tunnel can be established, the LAC and LNS must determine the following:

- The identity (tunnel name) of the other tunnel endpoint
- The framing capabilities (either synchronous or asynchronous)
- The shared tunnel secret
- The bearer capabilities (either digital or analog)

The LAC and LNS determine this information by using a three-message exchange. These messages are called L2TP control connection messages.

Figure 1-5 shows the L2TP tunnel negotiation process.

Figure 1-5 *L2TP Tunnel Negotiation Process*

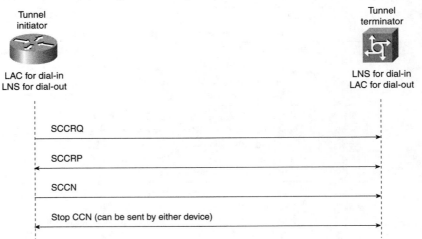

Table 1-4 describes the packets shown in Figure 1-5.

Table 1-4 *L2TP Tunnel Control Connection Messages*

Abbreviation	Message Name	Message Purpose
SCCRQ	Start-Control-Connection-Request	Initializes a tunnel between a LAC and an LNS, and is sent by the tunnel initiator, which is the LAC for dial-in and the LNS for dial-out.
SCCRP	Start-Control-Connection-Reply	Replies to a received SCCRQ message, and indicates that the SCCRQ was accepted.

Table 1-4   *L2TP Tunnel Control Connection Messages (Continued)*

Abbreviation	Message Name	Message Purpose
SCCN	Start-Control-Connection-Connected	Replies to a received SCCRP message, and completes the L2TP tunnel establishment process.
Stop CCN	Stop-Control-Connection-Connected	Indicates that the tunnel is being shut down and that the control connection should be closed. It can be sent by either the LAC or LNS.

L2TP Session Establishment Process

There are two types of L2TP sessions: dial-in sessions and dial-out sessions.

L2TP sessions are established with a three-message exchange similar to L2TP tunnel establishment. Dial-in sessions are initiated by the LAC, and dial-out sessions are initiated by the LNS.

Figure 1-6 shows the L2TP dial-in session establishment process.

Figure 1-6   *L2TP Dial-In Session Establishment Process*

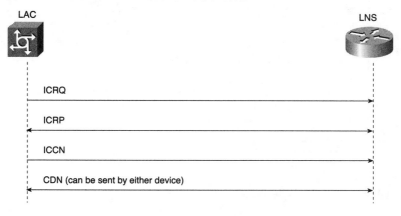

Table 1-5 describes the packets shown in Figure 1-6.

Table 1-5   *L2TP Dial-In Session Control Connection Messages*

Abbreviation	Message Name	Message Purpose
ICRQ	Incoming-Call-Request	Sent from the LAC to the LNS. Indicates that the LAC has received an incoming call that requires an L2TP session be established to the LNS.
ICRP	Incoming-Call-Reply	Sent from the LNS to the LAC. Indicates that the ICRQ was accepted.
ICCN	Incoming-Call-Connected	Sent from the LAC to the LNS. Completes the session establishment.
CDN	Call-Disconnect-Notify	Sent by either the LAC or LNS. Requests that the specific session within the L2TP tunnel be shut down.

Figure 1-7 shows the L2TP dial-out session establishment process.

Figure 1-7   *L2TP Dial-Out Session Establishment Process*

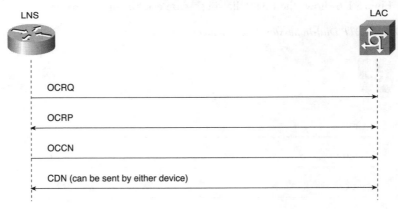

Table 1-6 describes the packets shown in Figure 1-7.

Table 1-6   *L2TP Dial-Out Session Control Connection Messages*

Abbreviation	Message Name	Message Purpose
OCRQ	Outgoing-Call-Request	Sent from the LNS to the LAC. Indicates that the LNS has received an outgoing call that requires an L2TP session be established to the LAC.
OCRP	Outgoing-Call-Reply	Sent from the LAC to the LNS. Indicates that the OCRQ was accepted.
OCCN	Outgoing-Call-Connected	Sent from the LNS to the LAC. Completes the session establishment.
CDN	Call-Disconnect-Notify	Sent by either the LAC or LNS. Requests that the specific session within the L2TP tunnel be shut down.

Client-Initiated Access VPDNs Using PPTP Dial-In

PPTP is a network protocol that enables the secure transfer of data from a remote client to a private server by creating a VPDN across TCP/IP-based data networks. PPTP supports on-demand, multiprotocol, virtual private networking over public networks, such as the Internet.

Cisco Systems supports client-initiated VPDNs using PPTP. Therefore only the client and the tunnel server need to be configured. The client first establishes basic connectivity by dialing in. After the client has established a PPP session, it initiates a PPTP tunnel to the tunnel server. The tunnel server is configured to terminate PPTP tunnels and clone virtual-access interfaces from virtual templates.

MPPE is an outcropping technology that can be used to encrypt PPTP VPDNs. It encrypts the entire session from the client to the tunnel server. For more information on MPPE, see the "Encryption Technologies" section later in this chapter.

Aspects of PPTP are described in the following sections:

- PPTP Negotiation
- Flow Control Alarm

PPTP Negotiation

The following sequence describes the protocol negotiation events that establish a PPTP tunnel and session:

1   The client dials in to an ISP and establishes a PPP session.

2   The client establishes a TCP connection with the tunnel server.

3   The tunnel server accepts the TCP connection.

4   The client sends a PPTP SCCRQ message to the tunnel server.

5   The tunnel server establishes a new PPTP tunnel and replies with an SCCRP message.

6   The client initiates the session by sending an OCRQ message to the tunnel server.

7   The tunnel server creates a virtual access interface.

8   The tunnel server replies with an OCRP message.

Flow Control Alarm

The flow control alarm is a new function that indicates if PPTP detects congestion or lost packets. When a flow control alarm goes off, PPTP reduces volatility and additional control traffic by establishing an accompanying stateful MPPE session.

For more information, see the **pptp flow-control static-rtt** VPDN configuration command and the output from the **show vpdn session window** user EXEC command in Appendix B, "New Access VPDN Services: PPTP with MPPE." The **pptp flow-control static-rtt** command is in the "PPTP with MPPE Configuration Tasks" section, and the **show vpdn session window** command output is in the "Verifying a PPTP Connection" section.

Encryption Technologies

Because VPDN traffic travels over the public Internet, it is subject to security threats such as loss of privacy, loss of data integrity, identity spoofing, and denial-of-service. The goal of encryption in an access VPDN network to is to address all of these threats in the software itself, without requiring expensive host and application modifications.

Cisco currently supports two encryption technologies for access VPDN networks, which are described in the following sections:

- **IPSec Encryption**—Used in NAS-initiated access VPDNs.
- **MPPE Encryption**—Used in client-initiated access VPDNs.

IPSec Encryption

IPSec is a framework of open standards for ensuring secure private communications over IP networks. IPSec ensures confidentiality, integrity, and authenticity of data communications across a public IP network. IPSec provides IP network layer encryption. It defines several packet formats: the authentication header (AH) to provide data integrity, and the encapsulating security payload (ESP) to provide confidentiality and data integrity. Key management and security associations (SAs), the IPSec parameters between two devices, are negotiated with the Internet Key Exchange (IKE). IKE can use digital certificates for device authentication to enable the creation of large encryption networks.

The three possible IPSec tunnel architectures are described in the following sections:

- IPSec Tunnel Between the LAC and LNS
- IPSec Tunnel Between the Peer and LNS
- IPSec Tunnel Between the Client and LNS

The following topics are also covered:

- IPSec Negotiation Process
- IPSec Design Considerations

IPSec Tunnel Between the LAC and LNS

The client initiates a PPP session to the LAC. The LAC negotiates an L2TP tunnel with the LNS and forwards the client PPP session to the LNS. The LAC and LNS then negotiate an IPSec tunnel to encrypt the client PPP session. The session is encrypted between the LAC and LNS, which is the segment of the network most susceptible to attack, but it is not encrypted between the client and the LAC.

IPSec Tunnel Between the Peer and LNS

The client connects to the peer, and the peer initiates a PPP session to the LAC. A peer is a small router in the remote office that connects the office to the Internet. The LAC negotiates an L2TP tunnel with the LNS and forwards the client PPP session to the LNS. The peer and LNS then negotiate an IPSec tunnel to encrypt the client PPP session. In this solution, the only segment of the network that is not encrypted is the connection between the client and the peer. However, because the client and peer are typically in the same office, this solution usually is not a security risk.

IPSec Tunnel Between the Client and LNS

The client initiates a PPP session (either by itself or by using a peer) to the LAC. The LAC negotiates an L2TP tunnel with the LNS and forwards the client PPP session to the LNS. The client and LNS then negotiate an IPSec tunnel to encrypt the client PPP session. In this solution, the entire network is encrypted. This solution is useful when different parties share a peer. It is also useful for mobile users who do not have access to a peer but still need a secure remote connection. The disadvantages of this solution are that it requires that every client must be configured for IPSec (rather than just the single peer), and that IPSec negotiation may take longer on clients than on the peer.

IPSec Negotiation Process

IPSec negotiation is processed by the three software components IPSec, IKE, and the crypto engine, as follows:

- **IPSec**—Initiates IPSec negotiation, and then verifies and implements the IKE negotiations.
- **IKE**—Negotiates the security policies and SAs.
- **Crypto engine**—Performs the actual encryption tasks.

Figure 1-8 shows a summary of how an IPSec session is negotiated by these three software components. The session is created in two phases.

The following sequence describes the events shown in Figure 1-8:

1 The VPDN tunnel and session are established.

2 Traffic on the peer matches the crypto access list, triggering the peer to initiate IPSec negotiation. This begins phase 1 of IKE.

3 Because no existing SA is currently in place, IKE on the peer begins negotiating with IKE on the LNS.

Figure 1-8   *IPSec Negotiation Process*

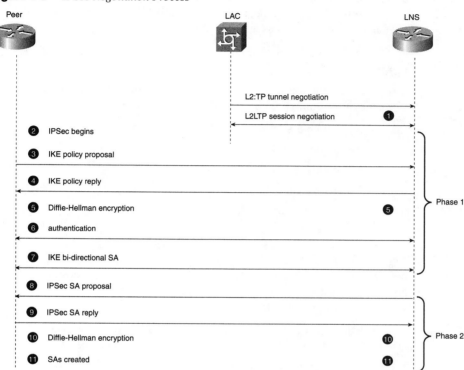

4 The LNS sends its IKE phase 1 proposals to the peer according to the configured IKE policy.

5 When the devices agree on an IKE policy, they perform Diffie-Hellman encryption on the session key, which now protects the communication.

6 The devices authenticate each other as configured in the IKE policy using one of the following methods:

— Preshared keys

— Rivest, Shamir, and Adelman (RSA) signatures

— RSA-encrypted nonces

7 The devices create the IKE bidirectional SA, which concludes phase 1 of IKE.

8 IKE on the LNS sends an IPSec SA proposal to the peer, which begins phase 2.

9 The peer compares the LNS SA proposal to its own configured policies (transforms, PFS, lifetime, and so on), and selects the most preferential match, which it sends as an SA reply to the LNS.

10 The devices again perform Diffie-Hellman encryption to generate the session key.

11 IKE creates the following four IPSec SAs according to the agreed-upon match of the configured policies of the two devices:

— AH inbound SA

— AH outbound SA

— ESP inbound SA

— ESP outbound SA

IPSec negotiation is now complete.

IPSec Design Considerations

When designing an IPSec network, you will make a number of decisions. Most decisions involve choosing between increased performance and increased security. The following list provides details on these decisions:

- **Authentication, or authentication and encryption**—IPSec can be configured to perform authentication only, or both authentication and encryption.

- **Encryption algorithm**—IPSec offers the choice of two encryption algorithms: 56-bit DES-CBC or 168-bit DES. 168-bit DES is the more secure of the two encryption algorithms, but it requires more time and processing power than 56-bit DES-CBC. Also, there are international restrictions on 168-bit encryption.

- **Hash algorithm**—IPSec offers the choice of two hash algorithms: SHA-1 and MD5. MD5 is slightly faster. There has been a demonstrated successful (but extremely difficult) attack against MD5; however, the HMAC variant used by IKE prevents this attack.

- **Authentication method**—IPSec offers three authentication methods, as follows:

    — RSA signatures—The most secure and the most scalable authentication method. However, RSA signatures require the use of a certification authority, which makes them the most difficult option to configure.

> — RSA encrypted nonces—Do not require that the peers possess the public keys of each other, and do not require the use of a certification authority. They are easier to configure in a small network, but do not scale well for large-scale networks.

> — Preshared keys—The simplest authentication method. Preshared keys do not scale well for large-scale networks, and are not as secure as RSA encrypted nonces.

- **Diffie-Hellman group identifier options**—The Diffie-Hellman identifier is used for deriving key materials between peers. IPSec offers the choice of 768-bit or 1024-bit Diffie-Hellman groups. The 1024-bit Diffie-Hellman group is more secure, but requires more CPU time to execute.

- **Security association lifetimes**—The lifetimes of IKE security associations can be configured to any desired value. The default value is 86,400 seconds, or one day. When the first IKE negotiation begins, SAs are negotiated. Each peer retains the SAs until the SA lifetime expires. Any subsequent IKE negotiations can reuse these SAs, which speeds future negotiations. Therefore, longer lifetimes can increase performance, but they also increase SAs exposure to attack. The longer an SA is used, the more encrypted traffic can be gathered by an attacker and used in an attack.

MPPE Encryption

MPPE is an encryption technology developed by Microsoft to encrypt point-to-point links. These PPP connections can be over a dialup line or over a VPDN tunnel. MPPE works as a subfeature of Microsoft Point-to-Point Compression (MPPC).

MPPC is a scheme used to compress PPP packets between Cisco and Microsoft client devices. The MPPC algorithm is designed to optimize bandwidth utilization in order to support multiple simultaneous connections.

MPPE is negotiated using bits in the MPPC option within the Compression Control Protocol (CCP) MPPC configuration option (CCP configuration option number 18).

MPPE uses the RC4 algorithm with either 40- or 128-bit keys. All keys are derived from the clear-text authentication password of the user. RC4 is stream cipher; therefore, the sizes of the encrypted and decrypted frames are the same size as the original frame. The Cisco implementation of MPPE is fully interoperable with that of Microsoft and uses all available options, including historyless mode. Historyless mode can increase throughput in lossy environments such as VPDNs, because neither side needs to send CCP Resets Request packets to synchronize encryption contexts when packets are lost.

MPPE Encryption Types

The two modes of MPPE encryption offered are described in the following sections:

- Stateful MPPE Encryption
- Stateless MPPE Encryption

Stateful MPPE Encryption

Stateful MPPE encryption provides better performance than stateless MPPE encryption, but may be adversely affected by networks that experience substantial packet loss. If you choose stateful encryption, you also should configure flow control to minimize the detrimental effects of this lossiness.

Because of the way that the RC4 tables are reinitialized during stateful synchronization, two packets may be encrypted using the same key. For this reason, stateful encryption may not be appropriate for lossy network environments (such as Layer 2 tunnels on the Internet).

Stateless MPPE Encryption

Stateless MPPE encryption provides a lower level of performance than stateful MPPE encryption, but will be more reliable in a lossy network environment.

If you choose stateless encryption, you *should not* configure flow control.

Related Technologies

The rest of this chapter discusses technologies that are not strictly VPDN technologies, but that are essential elements of a VPDN network. These technologies are described in the following sections:

- CHAP, MS-CHAP, and PAP Authentication Processes
- Virtual Access Interfaces and Virtual Templates
- IP Address Pools

CHAP, MS-CHAP, and PAP Authentication Processes

To authenticate a user for a VPDN session, the NAS and home gateway use one of the PPP-supported authentication protocols: CHAP, MS-CHAP, or PAP. CHAP and PAP are described in RFC 1334. Both are supported on synchronous and asynchronous interfaces.

The main difference between CHAP and PAP is that CHAP sends an encrypted password and uses a three-way handshake authentication method. PAP sends the user password over the network unencrypted, and uses a two-way handshake. For this reason, CHAP is a more secure, standalone authentication method. Generally, PAP should be used only with one-time passwords. One-time passwords expire after a short period of time, so they cannot be reused if they are intercepted.

The following sections explain CHAP, MS-CHAP, and PAP authentication in an access VPDN.

CHAP Authentication Process

CHAP is a three-way process in which the user password is sent as a 64-bit signature rather than as plain text. This encryption enables the secure exchange of the user password between the user client and the home gateway.

The NAS first challenges the client, and the client responds. The NAS then forwards this CHAP information to the home gateway, which authenticates the client and sends a third CHAP message (either a success or failure message) to the client.

NOTE   The CHAP password *must be* at least one octet long. The CHAP password *should be* at least 16 octets long (the length of the hash value for the MD5 algorithm). This password length ensures a sufficiently large range for the secret to provide protection against exhaustive search attacks.

Figure 1-9 shows the three-way CHAP authentication process.

Figure 1-9 *Three-Way CHAP Authentication Process*

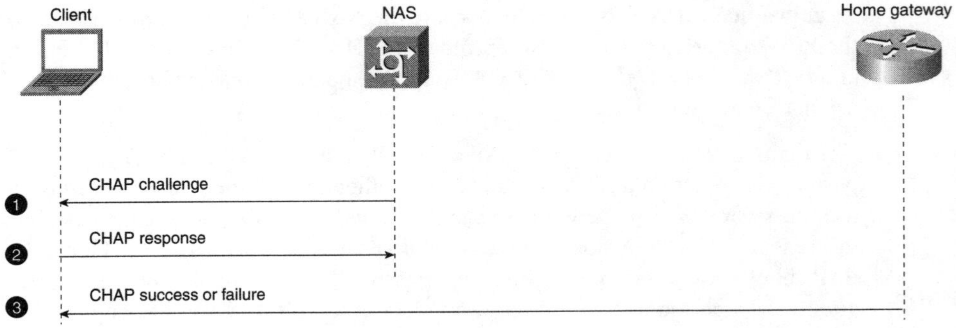

Table 1-7 explains the sequence of events shown in Figure 1-9.

Table 1-7 *CHAP Event Descriptions*

Event	Description
1	When the user initiates a PPP session with the NAS, the NAS sends a CHAP challenge to the client. The challenge packet contains a tunnel ID, a random number, and the host name of the NAS.
2	When the client receives the CHAP challenge, it concatenates the ID, the password, and the random number using MD5. It then sends this encrypted password along with the username as the CHAP response.
	The NAS uses either the phone number from which the user dialed in (when using DNIS-based authentication) or the user domain name (when using domain name–based authentication) to determine the IP tunnel endpoint information.
	At this point, PPP negotiation is suspended, and the NAS asks its AAA server for IP tunnel information. The AAA server supplies the information needed to authenticate the tunnel between the NAS and the home gateway.
	Next, the NAS and the home gateway authenticate each other and establish a VPDN tunnel. Then the NAS forwards the PPP negotiation—along with the CHAP response—to the home gateway.
3	When the home gateway receives the CHAP response, it authenticates the response by retrieving the password associated with the user username and concatenating the ID, password, and random number. If this MD5 matches the MD5 in the CHAP response, the home gateway sends a CHAP success to the client. If the MD5s do not match, the home gateway sends a CHAP failure message to the client.

MS-CHAP Authentication

MS-CHAP operates in essentially the same way as CHAP. The main differences between MS-CHAP and standard CHAP are as follows:

- MS-CHAP is enabled by negotiating CHAP Algorithm 0x80 in LCP option 3, Authentication Protocol.

- The MS-CHAP Response packet is in a format designed for compatibility with Microsoft Windows NT 4.0, 3.5, and 3.51; Microsoft Windows 95, 98, and 2000; and Microsoft LAN Manager 2.x networking products. The MS-CHAP format does not require the authenticator to store a clear or reversibly encrypted password.

- MS-CHAP provides an authenticator-controlled authentication retry mechanism and an authenticator-controlled change password mechanism.

- MS-CHAP defines a set of reason-for-failure codes returned in the Failure packet Message field.

When using PPTP in your access VPDN, you must use MS-CHAP.

PAP Authentication Process

PAP is simpler and less secure than the CHAP authentication methods. PAP is a two-way authentication process in which the user password is sent in clear text. Because of this insecure exchange, you should use PAP only with one-time passwords.

Figure 1-10 shows the two-way PAP authentication process.

Figure 1-10 *Two-Way PAP Authentication Process*

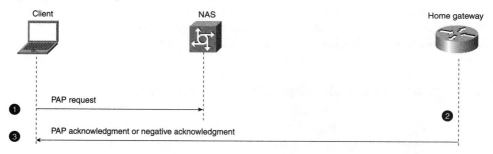

Table 1-8 explains the sequence of events shown in Figure 1-10.

Table 1-8   *PAP Event Descriptions*

Event	Description
1	When the client and NAS have completed LCP negotiation, the client sends a PAP request to the NAS that contains the username and password.
2	When the NAS receives the PAP request, it uses either the phone number from which the user dialed in (when using DNIS-based authentication) or the user domain name (when using domain name–based authentication) to determine the IP tunnel endpoint information.
	At this point, PPP negotiation is suspended, and the NAS asks its AAA server for IP tunnel information. The AAA server supplies the information needed to authenticate the tunnel between the NAS and the home gateway.
	Next, the NAS and the home gateway authenticate each other and establish a VPDN tunnel. Then the NAS forwards the PPP negotiation—along with the PAP request—to the home gateway.
3	When the home gateway receives the PAP request, it authenticates the username and password, and sends a PAP acknowledgment or PAP negative acknowledgment depending on the validity of the username and password.

After the home gateway has authenticated the client, the access VPDN is established. The VPDN tunnel creates a virtual point-to-point connection between the client and the home gateway. The NAS acts as a transparent packet forwarder.

When subsequent clients dial in to the NAS to be forwarded to the home gateway, the NAS and home gateway need not repeat the VPDN session negotiation because the VPDN tunnel is already open.

Virtual Access Interfaces and Virtual Templates

After the VPDN tunnel and user session have been established and the user authenticated, the home gateway needs to supply the client with an interface and IP address. The home gateway clones a virtual access interface from a virtual template and assigns the interface an IP address from an IP address pool.

A virtual access interface is a temporary interface that is created to terminate incoming PPP sessions that do not have physical connections, such as VPDN sessions. Virtual access interfaces are not directly user configurable, and they last only as long as the session is active. They are configured according to a virtual template.

A virtual template consists of the configuration information that is used to configure virtual access interfaces. Typically a virtual template contains the following elements:

- The physical interface that is used to send traffic and identify the virtual access interface

- The IP address pool that is used to assign an IP address to the virtual access interface

- The authentication method

IP Address Pools

An IP address pool is a range of IP addresses that are dynamically assigned to virtual access interfaces. The client that is connected to the virtual access interface then uses the assigned IP address to communicate with the customer network. When the client terminates the session, the IP address is returned to the IP address pool, where it can be reassigned to a new session.

CHAPTER 2

Access VPDN Dial-In Using L2F Solution

This solution describes how an Internet service provider (ISP) partners with an enterprise customer to design, implement, and troubleshoot a test lab version of an access VPDN network that uses Layer 2 Forwarding (L2F) as the tunneling protocol.

In an access VPDN, an ISP maintains an extended WAN, including core routers; many geographically dispersed points of presence (PoPs), including network access servers (NASs); all the circuits, modems, and phone lines necessary to connect the network; and all the networking expertise necessary to maintain the network. The ISP leases VPDN service to enterprise customers. The employees of the enterprise customer dial in to the local ISP NAS (multiple enterprises can dial in to the same NAS), which then creates a Layer 2 tunnel to the network of the enterprise customer and forwards the employee's call. This tunnel creates a secure, virtual point-to-point connection from the employee computer to the enterprise network and provides employees with inexpensive remote access to the intranet resources of the enterprise customer from remote locations.

Access VPDNs involve the cooperation of two partners: an ISP and an enterprise customer. The responsibilities of each partner are as follows:

- **ISP**—Responsible for maintaining an extended WAN including core routers; many geographically dispersed PoPs including NASs; all the circuits, modems, and phone lines necessary to connect the network, and all the networking expertise necessary to maintain the network. Optionally, the ISP also may maintain a AAA server for its access VPDN customers Often, the ISP will lease its IT infrastructure to smaller ISPs that want to cost-effectively increase the coverage area they offer to their customers. This access VPDN solution is primarily intended for network administrators and operations teams working for ISPs who provide access VPDN services to enterprise customers.

- **Enterprise customer**—Responsible for maintaining its user database and enterprise network. Often, the enterprise customer is a smaller ISP that does not want to take on the expense and commitment of establishing its own IT infrastructure. This solution also is useful to enterprise customers that want to establish access VPDNs.

In this chapter, ISP refers to the partner that is responsible for the IT infrastructure, and enterprise customer (or enterprise, for short) refers to the partner that leases the IT infrastructure.

This chapter contains the following sections:

- Business Objectives
- Proposed Solution: NAS-Initiated Access VPDN Using L2F
- Implementation
- Phase 1: Configuring the NAS for Basic Dial Access
- Phase 2: Configuring the Access VPDN to Work with Local AAA
- Phase 3: Configuring the Access VPDN to Work with Remote AAA

Business Objectives

ISPs need to offer value-added services to their customers to differentiate themselves in increasingly competitive markets. ISPs want to expand beyond traditional Internet access service and offer IT outsourcing to enterprises, but they do not want to take on the added responsibilities of maintaining enterprise user databases. Access VPDNs enable ISPs to offer IT outsourcing in which enterprises can either maintain their own user databases or contract with the ISP to have the ISP maintain user information.

Enterprises need to enable their employees to access their private networks from remote locations. Traditionally, meeting this need requires the purchase of expensive NASs, the hiring of network administrators to maintain the NASs, purchasing or leasing WAN connections, and expensive long-distance and 800 number phone bills. Access VPDNs offer a simpler and less expensive alternative.

Original Network Topology

Initially, the ISP offers only traditional Internet access service to individual customers. The enterprise customer must maintain its own access server to allow remote employees to access the enterprise network. This need requires the enterprise customer to maintain its own IT infrastructure and expertise. When employees need to access the network from remote locations, the enterprise must pay for expensive long-distance phone calls. Figure 2-1 shows the original separate ISP and enterprise networks.

Figure 2-1   *Original Network Topology*

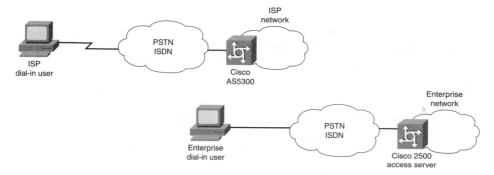

Business Drivers

The ISP has the following motivations for establishing the access VPDN:

- It needs to differentiate itself in the competitive ISP market.

- It wants to offer IT outsourcing service to enterprise customers.

- It wants to focus on maintaining its own network while limiting added responsibilities for maintaining the networks of its customers.

The enterprise customer has the following motivations for establishing the access VPDN:

- As the enterprise grows, it is forced to purchase additional access servers and lease additional phone lines to allow its employees remote access.

- As the enterprise IT infrastructure increases, it has to hire additional network administrators.

- The increasing complexity of the enterprise IT infrastructure causes increased network delays and failures.

- As the enterprise territory expands, costs of long-distance and 800 number phone bills from employees accessing the enterprise network increase.

Proposed Solution: NAS-Initiated Access VPDN Using L2F

Figure 2-2 shows a basic diagram of the completed access VPDN solution. The enterprise employees now have dialup modem access to intranet resources through the Public Switched Telephone Network (PSTN). The ISP is responsible for the required dial hardware and WAN services. The ISP and enterprise customer decide to use L2F because it is a stable tunneling protocol.

An enterprise employee that needs to connect to the enterprise network dials in to the ISP NAS. The NAS then negotiates an L2F tunnel with the enterprise home gateway, and forwards the employee call to the home gateway.

Figure 2-2   *End-to-End Access VPDN Solution*

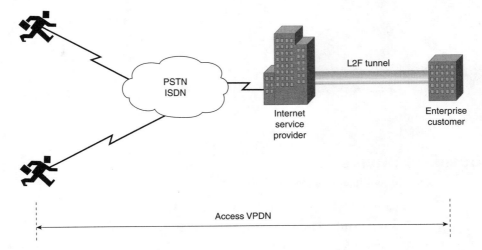

Strategy

This section describes the strategy that the ISP and enterprise customer use to design the access VPDN network. The ISP responsibilities are as follows:

- Purchase, configure, and maintain the Cisco AS5300 NAS. The NAS is located at the PoP and is used to forward PPP sessions to the enterprise customer network.

- Maintain a Cisco Secure Access Control System (ACS) UNIX server that authenticates the IP tunnel endpoint and domain name assigned to the enterprise customer home gateway.

- Maintain an edge router that connects the ISP network to the enterprise customer network.

The enterprise customer responsibilities are as follows:

- Purchase, configure, and maintain a Cisco Systems home gateway and the clients that are used by employees to connect to the enterprise network. In this solution, a Cisco 7206 router is used for the home gateway. The enterprise could use another platform, but the home gateway must be a Cisco router to support L2F.

- Maintain a Cisco Secure ACS NT server that authenticates and authorizes the enterprise employee usernames and passwords. In some environments, the ISP maintains the enterprise user information on its AAA server, but in this solution, the enterprise decides to maintain its own AAA server.

Because the partners will design and implement this network from scratch, they decide to use a three-phase approach to creating the access VPDN. Table 2-1 describes the configuration phases, which partners are responsible for the configurations, and shows which devices will be configured. The illustrations in the Devices column of Table 2-1 show the devices that will be configured in black. This chapter does not describe how to configure the devices in gray.

Table 2-1   *Configuration Phases and Devices*

Phase	Description	Devices
1	Configuring the NAS for Basic Dial Access The ISP configures the NAS.	
2	Configuring the Access VPDN to Work with Local AAA The ISP configures the NAS. The enterprise customer configures the home gateway.	

continues

Table 2-1 *Configuration Phases and Devices (Continued)*

Phase	Description	Devices
3	Configuring the Access VPDN to Work with Remote AAA The ISP configures the NAS and the Cisco Secure ACS UNIX server. The enterprise customer configures the home gateway and the Cisco Secure ACS NT server.	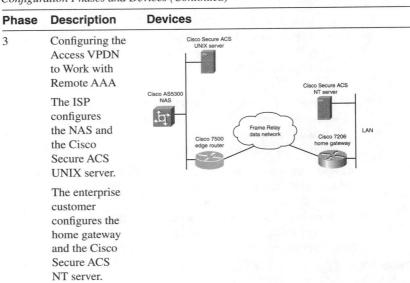

A user named Jeremy with the username jeremy@hgw.com appears in many configurations, illustrations, and examples in this solution. The goal of the solution is to give Jeremy basic IP and modem services by forwarding his PPP session from the NAS to the home gateway. To help you understand how the various hardware and software components work together to forward the PPP session, follow Jeremy through the solution.

If you use this information to configure your own network, be sure to substitute your own IP addresses, passwords, usernames, host names, and telephone numbers.

Design Considerations

Table 2-2 describes the design options that ISP and enterprise consider to develop their network design strategy.

Table 2-2 *Access VPDN Design Considerations*

Design Consideration	Design Decision
What services do the ISP customers require?	Basic dial-in access using L2F tunneling.
What platform(s) will the ISP use for the NASs?	Cisco AS5300.

Table 2-2   *Access VPDN Design Considerations (Continued)*

Design Consideration	Design Decision
Will the ISP use Multilink Point-to-Point (ML-PPP)? If so, will the ISP use an offload router?	No.
What platform will the customers use for tunnel servers?	Cisco 7206 router.
Will the partners use local or remote AAA?	Both the ISP and enterprise will use remote AAA.
If remote, what AAA protocol will the partners use?	Both the ISP and enterprise will use RADIUS.
If remote, what AAA software will the partners use?	The ISP will use Cisco Secure ACS UNIX, and the enterprise will use the Cisco Secure ACS NT platform.
Which IP addressing scheme will the different partner use?	The entire network except for the enterprise IP address pool will be on the 172.22.66.0 255.255.255.192 subnet, which is owned by the ISP. The devices will be assigned the following addresses: • NAS: 172.22.66.23 • Home gateway: 172.22.66.25 • Cisco Secure ACS UNIX server: 172.22.66.18 • Cisco Secure ACS NT server: 172.22.66.13 The enterprise will assign IP addresses to remote clients from the following address pool: 172.30.2.1 to 172.30.2.96
What deployment strategy will the partners use to implement the network?	See the section "Implementation" for details.

NOTE   This solution describes how the ISP and enterprise implement the access VPDN in a test lab environment. Therefore, all the devices use the 172.22.66.0/26 subnet. Only the IP address pool on the home gateway uses a different subnet (the 172.30.2.0/24 subnet). In an actual production environment, the ISP and enterprise would most likely use their own separate subnets.

Network Topology

Figure 2-3 shows the specific network devices used to build the access VPDN in this solution. In this network, the two partners are responsible for the following devices:

- The ISP is responsible for a Cisco AS5300 NAS, a Cisco Secure ACS UNIX server, and a Cisco 7500 series edge router (the configuration of which is not described in this solution).

- The enterprise customer is responsible for a Cisco 7206 home gateway, a Cisco Secure ACS NT server, and the remote clients using modems.

Figure 2-3   *Access VPDN Solution Network Topology*

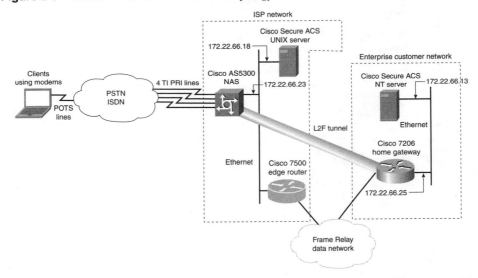

The L2F tunnel runs between the Cisco AS5300 NAS and Cisco 7206 router. The L2F tunnel is forwarded across a Frame Relay network, which is not described in this book.

NOTE   This solution does not describe how to configure the edge router or the Frame Relay data network on the home gateway. Although these components are shown in Figure 2-3, they are not critical in understanding how to build an access VPDN solution and are beyond the scope of this solution. Besides Frame Relay, the partners could use any of a number of WAN connections, including leased line or ATM. For more information about how to configure Frame Relay and serial interfaces, refer to the *Cisco IOS Wide-Area Networking Configuration Guide.*

Benefits

Access VPDNs benefit both ISPs and enterprise customers.

The benefits to ISPs are as follows:

- Offers end-to-end custom solutions that help differentiate the ISP in an increasingly competitive market
- Eliminates responsibility of managing the enterprise customer user database
- Allows expansion to broadband technologies (such as DSL, cable, and wireless) as they become available

The benefits to enterprise customers are as follows:

- Allows enterprise customers to focus on their core business responsibilities
- Minimizes equipment costs
- Simplifies complexity of upgrading technology
- Eliminates need to maintain internetworking expertise
- Reduces long-distance and 800 number costs
- Increases flexibility and scalability of connecting and disconnecting branch offices, users, and external partners
- Prioritizes traffic to ensure bandwidth for critical applications

Ramifications

After the ISP and enterprise establish the access VPDN, they might face the following challenges:

- The enterprise might outgrow the network and need to expand the access VPDN.
- The enterprise might want to encrypt the VPDN sessions to keep company confidential information secure.
- The enterprise might want to enable small offices to connect to the network using ISDN.
- The enterprise might require more sophisticated user segmentation to differentiate between employees from different departments, outside vendors, and other network users.

After this test access VPDN network has been established, the ISP and enterprise will want to consider the following possible enhancements:

- Adding devices to expand to a large-scale VPDN network
- Supporting other Layer 2 tunneling protocols such as L2TP or PPTP

- Supporting client-initiated VPDNs
- Supporting ISDN dial-in
- Supporting dial-out
- Configuring advanced user segmentation using remote AAA
- Configuring accounting
- Configuring Link Control Protocol (LCP) renegotiation
- Supporting one-time (token) passwords

Implementation

To build the access VPDN, the ISP and enterprise customer divide the configurations into three major phases, which are described in the following sections:

- Phase 1: Configuring the NAS for Basic Dial Access
- Phase 2: Configuring the Access VPDN to Work with Local AAA
- Phase 3: Configuring the Access VPDN to Work with Remote AAA

Device Characteristics

Table 2-3 provides a detailed description of the hardware and software components used in the solution.

Table 2-3 *Hardware and Software Used in the Solution*

	NAS	Home Gateway	Cisco Secure ACS UNIX Server	Cisco Secure ACS NT Server	Client
Chassis type	Cisco AS5300 NAS	Cisco 7206 router	Sun workstation	PC workstation	PC laptop
Physical interfaces	1 Ethernet interface 4 T1 PRI ports 96 terminal lines	1 Fast Ethernet interface 4 serial interfaces	1 Fast Ethernet interface	1 Fast Ethernet interface	1 RJ-11 port

Table 2-3 *Hardware and Software Used in the Solution (Continued)*

	NAS	Home Gateway	Cisco Secure ACS UNIX Server	Cisco Secure ACS NT Server	Client
Hardware components	Cisco AS5300 NAS 96 MICA technologies modems, 2 MICA CC, and 1 Quad T1/PRI T1 cable RJ45 to RJ45	Cisco 7206 router, 6-slot chassis Cisco 7200 series input/output controller with Fast Ethernet 4-port serial port adapter, enhanced V.35 cable, DTE, male, 10 feet	1 Ethernet card	1 Ethernet card	1 internal modem

continues

Table 2-3   *Hardware and Software Used in the Solution (Continued)*

	NAS	Home Gateway	Cisco Secure ACS UNIX Server	Cisco Secure ACS NT Server	Client
Software loaded	Cisco IOS Release 11.3(7) AA Cisco AS5300 series IP	Cisco IOS Release 12.0(2)T Cisco 7200 series IP	Cisco Secure ACS UNIX version 2.3.1 Solaris 2.6	Cisco Secure ACS NT version 2.1 Windows NT 4.0	Windows 95
Telephone number or username	510555-0945[1] —	—	—	—	jeremy@hgw.com password = subaru
Memory	Cisco AS5300 main DRAM, 64 MB Cisco AS5300 system Flash, 16 MB Cisco AS5300 boot Flash, 8 MB	Cisco 7200 I/O PCMCIA Flash memory, 20 MB Cisco 7200 NPE DRAM, 64 MB	128 MB RAM 128 MB swap space	128 MB RAM	64 MB RAM

Table 2-3   *Hardware and Software Used in the Solution (Continued)*

	NAS	**Home Gateway**	**Cisco Secure ACS UNIX Server**	**Cisco Secure ACS NT Server**	**Client**
Ethernet IP Address	172.22.66.23 255.255.255.192	172.22.66.25 255.255.255.192	172.22.66.18 255.255.255.192	172.22.66.13 255.255.255.192	172.30.2.1[2]

[1]This is the PRI telephone number assigned to the central site (NAS). The PRI number is often called the hunt group number, which distributes calls among the available B channels. Make sure your PRI provider assigns all four PRI trunks on the Cisco AS5300 NAS to this number.

[2]The home gateway dynamically assigns this IP address to the client in this solution.

Phase 1: Configuring the NAS for Basic Dial Access

In this first phase, the ISP responsibilities are as follows:

- Configure the Cisco AS5300 NAS to support basic IP and modem services
- Verify that basic dial access works before the ISP starts forwarding PPP sessions to the enterprise customer home gateway
- Troubleshoot the NAS if there are problems

Figure 2-4 shows the ISP basic dial access topology. Clients using modems dial in to the NAS over four T1 PRI lines that are assigned to 555-0945.

Figure 2-4   *Basic Dial Access Network Topology*

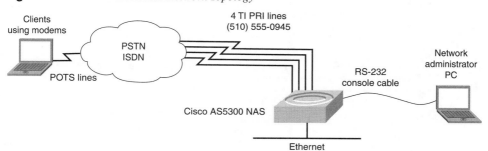

After the ISP completes this phase, basic dial access will function as follows:

1 The client dials in to the NAS.

2 The client and the NAS complete PPP negotiation.

3 The NAS assigns an IP address to the client.

4 The client and NAS now bidirectionally support IP services.

Configuring the NAS

To configure the NAS for basic dial access, the ISP performs the configuration steps described in the following sections:

Step 1   Configure Basic Settings

Step 2   Configure Local AAA

Step 3   Configure the LAN Interface

Step 4   Commission the T1 Controllers

Step 5   Configure the Serial Channels to Receive Modem Calls

Step 6   Configure the Modems and Asynchronous Lines

Step 7   Specify the IP Address Pool and DNS Servers

Step 8   Configure the Group-Async Interface

Step 1: Configure Basic Settings

In this step, the ISP configures the host name, enable password, and service time stamps:

```
!Apply millisecond time stamping to debug output.
!These time stamps help identify debug output when there is
!a lot of activity on the router.
service timestamps debug datetime msec
!Apply millisecond time stamping to logging output.
service timestamps log datetime msec
!Encrypt passwords in the configuration file.
service password-encryption
!
!Assign a host name to the access server.
!A host name distinguishes the NAS from other devices on the network.
hostname ISP_NAS
!
!Enter a secret enable password, which secures privileged EXEC mode.
!An enable password allows you to prevent unauthorized configuration
!changes. Be sure to change letmein to your own secret password.
enable secret 5 letmein
```

Step 2: Configure Local AAA

In this step, the ISP enables the AAA access control system and configures usernames for the network administrator and dial-in user. AAA provides the primary framework through which the ISP sets up access control on the NAS. Authentication identifies the client; authorization tells the client what it can do; accounting records what the client did do.

```
!Initiate the AAA access control system.
aaa new-model
!Configure PPP authentication to use the local database.
aaa authentication ppp default local
!
!Create a local login username for the client.
!The username jeremy and password subaru are locally authenticated by
!the NAS.
!Later in the case study, jeremy is authenticated
!by the home gateway Cisco Secure AAA server (not the NAS).
username jeremy password 7 021511590A141A
!Create a local login database and username for the network
!administrator.
username jane-admin password 7 0501090A6C5C4F1A0A1218000F
```

Step 3: Configure the LAN Interface

In this step, the ISP assigns an IP address to the Ethernet interface and brings up the interface:

```
interface Ethernet0
!Configure the IP address and subnet mask on the Ethernet interface.
!Be sure to use your own IP address and subnet mask.
 ip address 172.22.66.23 255.255.255.192
!Brings up the interface.
!This command does not appear in the running configuration, but
!it is necessary for you to issue this command to make the interface
!active.
no shutdown
```

Step 4: Commission the T1 Controllers

In this step, the ISP defines the ISDN switch type and commissions the T1 controllers to allow modem calls to come into the NAS. The ISP must specify the following information for each controller:

- Framing type
- Line code type
- Clock source
- Time slot assignments

Commissioning the T1 controllers is configured as follows:

```
!Enter the telco switch type, which is 5ESS in this solution.
!An ISDN switch type that is specified in global configuration mode is
!automatically propagated into the individual serial interfaces (for
!example, interface serial 0:23, 1:23, 2:23, and 3:23).
isdn switch-type primary-5ess
!
controller T1 0
!Enter the T1 framing type, which is extended super frame (ESF) in this
!solution.
 framing esf
!Configure the access server to get its primary clocking from the T1
!line assigned to controller 0. Line clocking comes from the remote
!switch.
 clock source line primary
!Enter the T1 line code type, which is B8ZS in this solution.
 linecode b8zs
!Assign all 24 T1 timeslots as ISDN PRI channels. After you enter this
!command, a D-channel serial interface is instantly created
!(for example S0:23) as well as individual B-channel serial interfaces
!(for example S0:0, S0:1, S0:2, S0:3, and so on.). The D-channel
!interface functions like a dialer for all the 23 B channels using
!the controller. If this was an E1 interface, the PRI group range would
!be 1 to 31. The D-channel serial interfaces would be S0:15, S1:15,
!S2:15, and S3:15. The framing and line code would also likely be
!different for an E1 interface.
pri-group timeslots 1-24
!
!Apply the same configuration to the other three controllers.
controller T1 1
 framing esf
 clock source line secondary
 linecode b8zs
 pri-group timeslots 1-24
!
controller T1 2
 framing esf
 clock source internal
 linecode b8zs
 pri-group timeslots 1-24
!
controller T1 3
 framing esf
 clock source internal
 linecode b8zs
 pri-group timeslots 1-24
```

Step 5: Configure the Serial Channels to Receive Modem Calls

In this step, the ISP configures the D channels to allow incoming voice calls to be routed to the integrated MICA modems and uses the D channel to control the behavior of individual B channels:

```
!Access configuration mode for the D-channel serial interface that
!corresponds to controller T1 0.
!The behavior of serial 0:0 through !serial 0:22 is controlled by the
!configuration instructions provided !for serial 0:23. This concept is
!also true for the other remaining D-channel configurations.
interface Serial0:23
 no ip address
 isdn switch-type primary-5ess
!Enable analog modem voice calls coming in through the B channels to be
!connected to the integrated modems.
 isdn incoming-voice modem
 no cdp enable
!
!Apply the same configuration to the other D-channel serial interfaces.
interface Serial1:23
 no ip address
 isdn switch-type primary-5ess
 isdn incoming-voice modem
 no cdp enable
!
interface Serial2:23
 no ip address
 isdn switch-type primary-5ess
 isdn incoming-voice modem
 no cdp enable
!
interface Serial3:23
 no ip address
 isdn switch-type primary-5ess
 isdn incoming-voice modem
 no cdp enable
```

Step 6: Configure the Modems and Asynchronous Lines

In this step, the ISP defines a range of modem lines and enables PPP clients to dial in, bypass the EXEC facility, and automatically start PPP. The ISP should configure the modems and lines after the ISDN channels are operational. Each modem corresponds with a dedicated asynchronous line inside the access server. The modem speed of 115200 bps and hardware flow control are default values for integrated modems.

```
!Enter the range of modem lines that you want to configure.
!The NAS used in this case study has 96 integrated MICA modems.
line 1 96
!These two autoselect commands enable EXEC (shell) and PPP services
!on the same lines.
!Enable PPP clients to dial in, bypass the EXEC facility, and
!automatically start PPP on the lines.
```

continues

(Continued)

```
autoselect ppp
!Displays the username:password prompt as the modems connect.
autoselect during-login
!Support incoming and outgoing modem calls.
modem inout
```

Step 7: Specify the IP Address Pool and DNS Servers

In this step, the ISP creates an IP addresses pool that contains one IP address and specifies a primary and secondary Domain Name System (DNS) server. In the following phases of this solution, the client is assigned an IP address from the local IP pool configured on the home gateway. The NAS, which is maintained by the ISP, does not assign IP addresses to the enterprise customer clients when the network is configured as an access VPDN.

```
!Specify the domain name servers on the network, which can be used for
!clients dialing in with PPP.
async-bootp dns-server 171.68.10.70 171.68.10.140
!Create an IP pool containing one IP address to assign to one client.
ip local pool default 1.1.1.1
```

Step 8: Configure the Group-Async Interface

In this step, the ISP creates a group-async interface and projects protocol characteristics to the 96 asynchronous interfaces. The group-async interface is a template that controls the configuration of all the asynchronous interfaces inside the NAS. Asynchronous interfaces are lines running in PPP mode. An asynchronous interface uses the same number as its corresponding line. Configuring all the asynchronous interfaces as an async group saves the ISP time by reducing the number of configuration steps.

```
!Create the group-async interface.
interface Group-Async1
!Use the IP address defined on the Ethernet interface.
 ip unnumbered Ethernet0
!Enable PPP.
 encapsulation ppp
!Configure interactive mode on the asynchronous interfaces.
!Interactive mode means that clients can dial in to the NAS and get a
!router prompt or PPP session.
!Dedicated mode (the other available option) means that only PPP
!sessions can be established on the NAS. Clients cannot dial in and get
!an EXEC (shell) session.
 async mode interactive
!Assign IP addresses to clients from the default IP address pool.
 peer default ip address pool default
!Configure CHAP and PAP authentication to be used on the interface
!during LCP !negotiation. The access server first authenticates with
```

(Continued)

```
!CHAP. If CHAP is rejected by the client, PAP authentication is used.
 ppp authentication chap pap
!Specify the range of asynchronous interfaces to include in the group,
!which is usually equal to the number of modems in the access server.
 group-range 1 96
```

Verifying Basic Dial Access

This section describes how to verify that clients can dial in to the NAS as shown in Figure 2-4:

Step 1   Verify the NAS Running Configuration

Step 2   Dial In to the NAS

Step 3   Ping the NAS

Step 4   Display Active Call Statistics on the NAS

Step 5   Ping the Client

Step 6   Verify That the Asynchronous Interface Is Up and That LCP Is Open

After you successfully test these connections, go to the section "Phase 2: Configuring the Access VPDN to Work with Local AAA." If you experience problems, see the section "Troubleshooting Basic Dial Access" later in this chapter.

Step 1: Verify the NAS Running Configuration

In this step, enter the **show running-config** privileged EXEC command to make sure that the NAS accepted the commands you entered. Commands in the following configuration that were not discussed in the preceding text do not directly pertain to the access VPDN and are therefore beyond the scope of this book.

```
ISP_NAS# show running-config

Building configuration...

Current configuration:
!
version 11.3
service timestamps debug datetime msec
service timestamps log datetime msec
service password-encryption
!
```

continues

(Continued)

```
hostname ISP_NAS
!
aaa new-model
aaa authentication ppp default local
enable secret 5 $1$AXl/$27hOM6j51a5P76Enq.LCf0
!
!
username jeremy password 7 021511590A141A
username jane-admin password 7 0501090A6C5C4F1A0A1218000F
!
async-bootp dns-server 171.68.10.70 171.68.10.140
isdn switch-type primary-5ess
!
controller T1 0
 framing esf
 clock source line primary
 linecode b8zs
 pri-group timeslots 1-24
!
controller T1 1
 framing esf
 clock source line secondary
 linecode b8zs
 pri-group timeslots 1-24
!
controller T1 2
 framing esf
 clock source internal
 linecode b8zs
 pri-group timeslots 1-24
!
controller T1 3
 framing esf
 clock source internal
 linecode b8zs
 pri-group timeslots 1-24
!
!
interface Ethernet0
 ip address 172.22.66.23 255.255.255.192
!
interface Serial0:23
 no ip address
 isdn switch-type primary-5ess
 isdn incoming-voice modem
 no cdp enable
!
interface Serial1:23
 no ip address
 isdn switch-type primary-5ess
 isdn incoming-voice modem
 no cdp enable
!
interface Serial2:23
 no ip address
 isdn switch-type primary-5ess
 isdn incoming-voice modem
 no cdp enable
!
interface Serial3:23
 no ip address
 isdn switch-type primary-5ess
```

(Continued)

```
        isdn incoming-voice modem
        no cdp enable
        !
       interface FastEthernet0
        no ip address
        shutdown
        !
       interface Group-Async1
        ip unnumbered Ethernet0
        encapsulation ppp
        async mode interactive
        peer default ip address pool default
        ppp authentication chap pap
        group-range 1 96
        !
       ip local pool default 1.1.1.1
       ip classless
       ip route 0.0.0.0 0.0.0.0 172.22.66.1
       !
       line con 0
        transport input none
       line 1 96
        autoselect during-login
        autoselect ppp
        modem inout
       line aux 0
       line vty 0 4
       !
       end
```

Step 2: Dial In to the NAS

In this step, from the client, dial in to the NAS. Use the PRI telephone number assigned to the NAS T1 trunks. (Sometimes the PRI telephone is called the hunt group number.) Figure 2-5 shows the username, password, and PRI telephone entered in the Windows 95 dialup networking utility.

Figure 2-5   *Windows 95 Dialup Networking Utility*

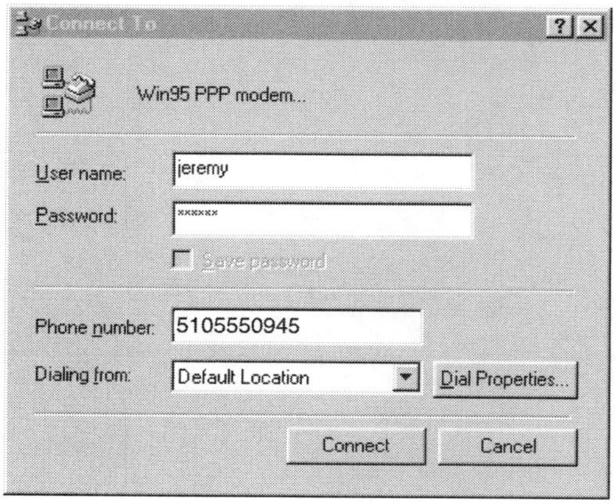

As the call comes into the NAS, the following LINK-3-UPDOWN message automatically appears on the NAS terminal screen. In this example, the call comes in to the NAS on asynchronous interface 47. The asynchronous interface is up.

```
*Jan  1 21:22:18.410: %LINK-3-UPDOWN: Interface Async47, changed state
to up
```

NOTE No **debug** commands are turned on to display this log message. If you are using Telnet to access the NAS instead of the NAS console port, you will need to enable the **terminal monitor** user EXEC command to display these log messages. Start troubleshooting the NAS if this message does not display within 30 seconds of the client initiating the call.

Step 3: Ping the NAS

In this step, ping the NAS from the client. On the desktop of the client, perform the following steps:

Step 1 Click Start.

Step 2 Select Run.

Step 3 Enter **ping 172.22.66.23** (see Figure 2-6).

Step 4 Click OK.

Step 5 Look at the ping terminal screen and verify that the NAS is sending ping reply packets to the client (see Figure 2-7).

Figure 2-6 *Windows 95 Ping Utility*

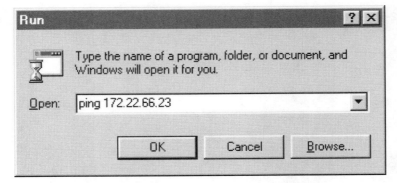

Figure 2-7   *Ping Reply Packets Sent from the NAS to the Client*

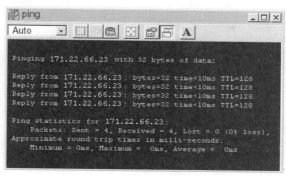

Step 4: Display Active Call Statistics on the NAS

In this step, from the NAS, enter the **show caller** user EXEC command and **show caller user jeremy** command to verify that the client received an IP address. This example shows that jeremy is using TTY line 47, asynchronous interface 47, and IP address 1.1.1.1. The network administrator jane-admin is using console 0.

```
ISP_NAS# show caller

     Line       User          Service    Active
     con 0      jane-admin      TTY        01:54:15
     tty 47     jeremy         Async       00:00:54
     As47       jeremy          PPP        00:00:50

ISP_NAS# show caller user jeremy

    User: jeremy, line tty 47, service Async, active 00:01:49
    TTY: Line 47, running PPP on As47, idle 00:00:00
    Line: Baud rate (TX/RX) is 115200/115200, no parity, 1 stopbits, 8
     databits
    Status: Ready, Active, No Exit Banner, Async Interface Active
     HW PPP Support Active
    Capabilities: Hardware Flowcontrol In, Hardware Flowcontrol Out
                  Modem Callout, Modem RI is CD,
                  Line is permanent async interface, Integrated Modem
    Modem State: Ready
    Timeouts: Idle EXEC   Idle Session  Modem Answer  Session   Dispatch
              00:10:00       never           -         never    not set

    User: jeremy, line As47, service PPP, active 00:01:45
    PPP: LCP Open, CHAP (<- AAA), IPCP
    IP: Local 172.22.66.23, remote 1.1.1.1
    Counts: 29 packets input, 1690 bytes, 0 no buffer
            0 input errors, 0 CRC, 0 frame, 0 overrun
            12 packets output, 255 bytes, 0 underruns
            0 output errors, 0 collisions, 0 interface resets
```

NOTE   The **show caller** command was added to the Cisco IOS software in Release
11.3(5)AA. If your version of software does not support the **show caller**
command, use the **show user** user EXEC command instead.

Step 5: Ping the Client

In this step, from the NAS, ping the client at IP address 1.1.1.1:

```
ISP_NAS# ping 1.1.1.1

Type escape sequence to abort.
Sending 5, 100-byte ICMP Echos to 1.1.1.1, timeout is 2 seconds:
!!!!!
Success rate is 100 percent (5/5), round-trip min/avg/max = 128/136/160
  ms
```

Step 6: Verify That the Asynchronous Interface Is Up and That LCP Is Open

In this step, from the NAS, enter the **show interface async 47** privileged EXEC
command to verify that the interface is up, LCP is open, and no errors are reported:

```
ISP_NAS# show interface async 47

Async47 is up, line protocol is up
Async47 is up, line protocol is up
  modem(slot/port)=1/46, state=CONNECTED
  dsx1(slot/unit/channel)=0/0/0,
    status=VDEV_STATUS_ACTIVE_CALL.VDEV_STATUS_ALL.
  Hardware is Async Serial
  Interface is unnumbered. Using address of Ethernet0 (172.22.66.23)
  MTU 1500 bytes, BW 115 Kbit, DLY 100000 usec,
    reliability 255/255, txload 1/255, rxload 1/255
  Encapsulation PPP, loopback not set, keepalive not set
  DTR is pulsed for 5 seconds on reset
  LCP Open
  Open: IPCP
  Last input 00:00:46, output 00:02:42, output hang never
  Last clearing of "show interface" counters never
  Queueing strategy: fifo
Output queue 0/10, 0 drops; input queue 1/10, 0 drops
  5 minute input rate 0 bits/sec, 0 packets/sec
  5 minute output rate 0 bits/sec, 0 packets/sec
    37 packets input, 2466 bytes, 0 no buffer
    Received 0 broadcasts, 0 runts, 0 giants, 0 throttles
    0 input errors, 0 CRC, 0 frame, 0 overrun, 0 ignored, 0 abort
    12 packets output, 255 bytes, 0 underruns
    0 output errors, 0 collisions, 0 interface resets
    0 output buffer failures, 0 output buffers swapped out
    0 carrier transitions
```

Troubleshooting Basic Dial Access

This section provides the ISP with a methodology for troubleshooting basic dial access as described in Figure 2-8. Perform the following steps to perform basic dialup fault isolation. The shaded lines of output indicate important information.

Step 1   Check the ISDN Status

Step 2   Troubleshoot PPP Negotiation

Step 3   Troubleshoot ISDN

Step 4   Check the Error Status of the T1 Controllers

Step 5   Troubleshoot the Modem Call State Machine

Figure 2-8   *Troubleshooting Flow Diagram for Basic Dial Access*

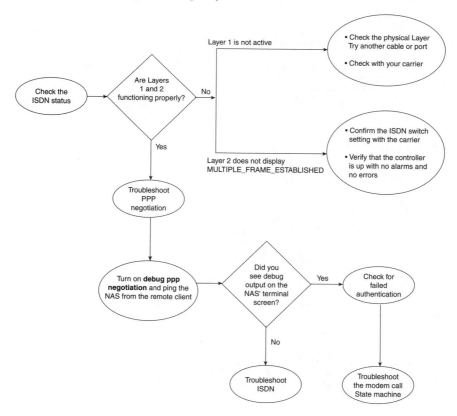

If you use a Telnet session to connect to the NAS, enable the **terminal monitor** EXEC command, which ensures that your EXEC session is receiving the logging and debug output from the NAS.

When you finish troubleshooting, enter the **undebug all** or **no debug all** privileged EXEC commands to turn off all **debug** commands. Isolating debug output helps you efficiently build a network.

Step 1: Check the ISDN Status

In this step, enter the **show isdn status** privileged EXEC command to confirm that Layer 1 is active and the display field MULTIPLE_FRAME_ESTABLISHED appears at Layer 2. This example shows that each serial interface is functioning properly:

```
ISP_NAS# show isdn status

Global ISDN Switchtype = primary-5ess
ISDN Serial0:23 interface
        dsl 0, interface ISDN Switchtype = primary-5ess
    Layer 1 Status:
        ACTIVE
    Layer 2 Status:
        TEI = 0, Ces = 1, SAPI = 0, State = MULTIPLE_FRAME_ESTABLISHED
    Layer 3 Status:
        1 Active Layer 3 Call(s)
    Activated dsl 0 CCBs = 1
        CCB:callid=11E, sapi=0, ces=0, B-chan=12, calltype=DATA
ISDN Serial1:23 interface
        dsl 1, interface ISDN Switchtype = primary-5ess
    Layer 1 Status:
        ACTIVE
    Layer 2 Status:
        TEI = 0, Ces = 1, SAPI = 0, State = MULTIPLE_FRAME_ESTABLISHED
    Layer 3 Status:
        1 Active Layer 3 Call(s)
    Activated dsl 1 CCBs = 1
        CCB:callid=12A, sapi=0, ces=0, B-chan=2, calltype=VOICE
ISDN Serial2:23 interface
        dsl 2, interface ISDN Switchtype = primary-5ess
    Layer 1 Status:
        ACTIVE
    Layer 2 Status:
        TEI = 0, Ces = 1, SAPI = 0, State = MULTIPLE_FRAME_ESTABLISHED
    Layer 3 Status:
        1 Active Layer 3 Call(s)
    Activated dsl 2 CCBs = 1
        CCB:callid=143, sapi=0, ces=0, B-chan=7, calltype=DATA
ISDN Serial3:23 interface
        dsl 3, interface ISDN Switchtype = primary-5ess
```

```
Layer 1 Status:
    ACTIVE
Layer 2 Status:
    TEI = 0, Ces = 1, SAPI = 0, State = MULTIPLE_FRAME_ESTABLISHED
Layer 3 Status:
    4 Active Layer 3 Call(s)
Activated dsl 3 CCBs = 4
    CCB:callid=160, sapi=0, ces=0, B-chan=14, calltype=VOICE
    CCB:callid=162, sapi=0, ces=0, B-chan=17, calltype=VOICE
    CCB:callid=167, sapi=0, ces=0, B-chan=22, calltype=VOICE
    CCB:callid=168, sapi=0, ces=0, B-chan=23, calltype=VOICE
Total Allocated ISDN CCBs = 7
```

If Layer 1 is not active, perform the following steps:

Step 1   Check the physical layer connectivity. Try using another port or cable.

Step 2   Check with your PRI provider.

If the display field MULTIPLE_FRAME_ESTABLISHED does not appear at Layer 2, perform the following steps:

Step 3   Verify that the ISDN switch setting is correct.

Step 4   Enter the **show controller** privileged EXEC command to verify that the controller is up without any alarms or errors. For an example, see the section "Step 4: Checking the Error Status of the T1 Controllers."

NOTE   If you isolated the problem to Layers 1 or 2 and you think that it has been corrected, return to the verification steps and confirm that the problem is resolved. If the client still cannot dial in to the NAS, go to Step 2.

Step 2: Troubleshoot PPP Negotiation

In this step, troubleshoot PPP negotiation by performing the following steps:

1   Turn on the **debug ppp negotiation** privileged EXEC command.

2   Ping the NAS from the client.

3   Observe the debug output messages that appear on the NAS terminal screen. If you do not see debug output, turn off the **debug ppp negotiation** command and go to Step 3.

Successful PPP Negotiation

It is important to understand what a successful debug PPP sequence looks like before you troubleshoot PPP negotiation. In this way, comparing a faulty PPP debug session against a successfully completed debug PPP sequence saves you time and effort.

Following is an example of a successful PPP sequence. The most important lines are first described, and then are indicated with shading.

```
ISP_NAS# debug ppp negotiation
PPP protocol negotiation debugging is on
ISP_NAS# show debug

PPP:
    PPP protocol negotiation debugging is on

ISP_NAS#
Mar 13 10:57:13.415: %LINK-3-UPDOWN: Interface Async1, changed state to
    up
```

Outgoing configuration request (O CONFREQ). The NAS sends an outgoing PPP configuration request packet to the client.

```
Mar 13 10:57:15.415: As1 LCP: O CONFREQ [ACKrcvd] id 2 len 25
Mar 13 10:57:15.415: As1 LCP:    ACCM 0x000A0000 (0x0206000A0000)
Mar 13 10:57:15.415: As1 LCP:    AuthProto CHAP (0x0305C22305)
Mar 13 10:57:15.415: As1 LCP:    MagicNumber 0x1084F0A2
    (0x05061084F0A2)
Mar 13 10:57:15.415: As1 LCP:    PFC (0x0702)
Mar 13 10:57:15.415: As1 LCP:    ACFC (0x0802)
```

Incoming configuration acknowledgment (I CONFACK). The client acknowledges the NAS PPP request.

```
Mar 13 10:57:15.543: As1 LCP: I CONFACK [REQsent] id 2 len 25
Mar 13 10:57:15.543: As1 LCP:    ACCM 0x000A0000 (0x0206000A0000)
Mar 13 10:57:15.543: As1 LCP:    AuthProto CHAP (0x0305C22305)
Mar 13 10:57:15.543: As1 LCP:    MagicNumber 0x1084F0A2
    (0x05061084F0A2)
Mar 13 10:57:15.543: As1 LCP:    PFC (0x0702)
Mar 13 10:57:15.547: As1 LCP:    ACFC (0x0802)
```

Incoming configuration request (I CONFREQ). The client wants to negotiate the callback protocol.

```
Mar 13 10:57:16.919: As1 LCP: I CONFREQ [ACKrcvd] id 4 len 23
Mar 13 10:57:16.919: As1 LCP:    ACCM 0x000A0000 (0x0206000A0000)
Mar 13 10:57:16.919: As1 LCP:    MagicNumber 0x001327B0
    (0x0506001327B0)
Mar 13 10:57:16.919: As1 LCP:    PFC (0x0702)
Mar 13 10:57:16.919: As1 LCP:    ACFC (0x0802)
Mar 13 10:57:16.919: As1 LCP:    Callback 6  (0x0D0306)
```

Outgoing configuration reject (O CONFREJ). The NAS rejects the callback option.

```
Mar 13 10:57:16.919: As1 LCP: O CONFREJ [ACKrcvd] id 4 len 7
Mar 13 10:57:16.919: As1 LCP:    Callback 6  (0x0D0306)
```

Incoming configuration request (I CONFREQ). The client requests a new set of options. Notice that Microsoft Callback is not requested this time.

```
Mar 13 10:57:17.047: As1 LCP: I CONFREQ [ACKrcvd] id 5 len 20
Mar 13 10:57:17.047: As1 LCP:    ACCM 0x000A0000 (0x0206000A0000)
Mar 13 10:57:17.047: As1 LCP:    MagicNumber 0x001327B0
  (0x0506001327B0)
Mar 13 10:57:17.047: As1 LCP:    PFC (0x0702)
Mar 13 10:57:17.047: As1 LCP:    ACFC (0x0802)
```

Outgoing configuration acknowledgment (O CONFACK). The NAS accepts the new set of options.

```
Mar 13 10:57:17.047: As1 LCP: O CONFACK [ACKrcvd] id 5 len 20
Mar 13 10:57:17.047: As1 LCP:    ACCM 0x000A0000 (0x0206000A0000)
Mar 13 10:57:17.047: As1 LCP:    MagicNumber 0x001327B0
  (0x0506001327B0)
Mar 13 10:57:17.047: As1 LCP:    PFC (0x0702)
Mar 13 10:57:17.047: As1 LCP:    ACFC (0x0802)
```

PPP LCP negotiation is completed successfully (LCP: State is Open). Each side has acknowledged (CONFACK) the other side's configuration request (CONFREQ).

```
Mar 13 10:57:17.047: As1 LCP: State is Open
Mar 13 10:57:17.047: As1 PPP: Phase is AUTHENTICATING, by this end
```

PPP authentication is completed successfully. After LCP negotiates, authentication starts. Authentication must take place before any network protocols, such as IP, are delivered. Both sides authenticate with the method negotiated during LCP. The NAS is authenticating the client using CHAP.

```
Mar 13 10:57:17.047: As1 CHAP: O CHALLENGE id 1 len 28 from "ISP_NAS"
Mar 13 10:57:17.191: As1 CHAP: I RESPONSE id 1 len 30 from "jeremy"
Mar 13 10:57:17.191: As1 CHAP: O SUCCESS id 1 len 4
Mar 13 10:57:17.191: As1 PPP: Phase is UP
Mar 13 10:57:17.191: As1 IPCP: O CONFREQ [Closed] id 1 len 10
Mar 13 10:57:17.191: As1 IPCP:    Address 172.22.66.23
  (0x0306AC164217)
Mar 13 10:57:17.303: As1 IPCP: I CONFREQ [REQsent] id 1 len 40
Mar 13 10:57:17.303: As1 IPCP:    CompressType VJ 15 slots
  CompressSlotID (0x020
```

continues

(Continued)

```
6002D0F01)
Mar 13 10:57:17.303: As1 IPCP:    Address 0.0.0.0 (0x030600000000)
Mar 13 10:57:17.303: As1 IPCP:    PrimaryDNS 0.0.0.0 (0x810600000000)
Mar 13 10:57:17.303: As1 IPCP:    PrimaryWINS 0.0.0.0 (0x820600000000)
Mar 13 10:57:17.303: As1 IPCP:    SecondaryDNS 0.0.0.0 (0x830600000000)
Mar 13 10:57:17.303: As1 IPCP:    SecondaryWINS 0.0.0.0 (0x840600000000)
Mar 13 10:57:17.303: As1 IPCP: O CONFREJ [REQsent] id 1 len 22
Mar 13 10:57:17.303: As1 IPCP:    CompressType VJ 15 slots
  CompressSlotID (0x020 6002D0F01)
Mar 13 10:57:17.303: As1 IPCP:    PrimaryWINS 0.0.0.0 (0x820600000000)
Mar 13 10:57:17.303: As1 IPCP:    SecondaryWINS 0.0.0.0 (0x840600000000)
Mar 13 10:57:17.319: As1 CCP: I CONFREQ [Not negotiated] id 1 len 15
Mar 13 10:57:17.319: As1 CCP:    MS-PPC supported bits 0x00000001
  (0x120600000001)
Mar 13 10:57:17.319: As1 CCP:    Stacker history 1 check mode EXTENDED
  (0x1105000104)
Mar 13 10:57:17.319: As1 LCP: O PROTREJ [Open] id 3 len 21 protocol CCP
Mar 13 10:57:17.319: As1 LCP: (0x80FD0101000F1206000000000111050001)
Mar 13 10:57:17.319: As1 LCP: (0x04)
Mar 13 10:57:17.319: As1 IPCP: I CONFACK [REQsent] id 1 len 10
Mar 13 10:57:17.319: As1 IPCP:    Address 172.22.66.23 (0x0306AC164217)
Mar 13 10:57:18.191: %LINEPROTO-5-UPDOWN: Line protocol on Interface
  Async1,
changed state to up
.
.
.
Mar 13 10:57:20.543: As1 IPCP: I CONFREQ [ACKrcvd] id 4 len 22
Mar 13 10:57:20.543: As1 IPCP:    Address 1.1.1.1 (0x030601010101)
Mar 13 10:57:20.547: As1 IPCP:    PrimaryDNS 171.68.10.70
  (0x8106AB440A46)
Mar 13 10:57:20.547: As1 IPCP:    SecondaryDNS 171.68.10.140
  (0x8306AB440A8C)
Mar 13 10:57:20.547: As1 IPCP: O CONFACK [ACKrcvd] id 4 len 22
Mar 13 10:57:20.547: As1 IPCP:    Address 1.1.1.1 (0x030601010101)
Mar 13 10:57:20.547: As1 IPCP:    PrimaryDNS 171.68.10.70
  (0x8106AB440A46)
Mar 13 10:57:20.547: As1 IPCP:    SecondaryDNS 171.68.10.140
  (0x8306AB440A8C)
```

The state is open for IP Control Protocol (IPCP). A route is negotiated and installed for the IPCP peer, which is assigned IP address 1.1.1.1.

```
Mar 13 10:57:20.547: As1 IPCP: State is Open
Mar 13 10:57:20.551: As1 IPCP: Install route to 1.1.1.1
```

Unsuccessful PPP Negotiation

Failed authentication is a common occurrence. Misconfigured or mismatched usernames and passwords create error messages in debug output.

The following example shows that the username sam-admin does not have permission to dial in to the NAS, which does not have a local username configured for this user. To correct the problem, use the **username** *name* **password** *password* global configuration command to add the username sam-admin to the local AAA database of the NAS.

```
Mar 13 11:01:42.399: As2 LCP: State is Open
Mar 13 11:01:42.399: As2 PPP: Phase is AUTHENTICATING, by this end
Mar 13 11:01:42.399: As2 CHAP: O CHALLENGE id 1 len 28 from "ISP_NAS"
Mar 13 11:01:42.539: As2 CHAP: I RESPONSE id 1 len 30 from "sam-admin"
Mar 13 11:01:42.539: As2 CHAP: Unable to validate Response. Username
   sam-admin not found
Mar 13 11:01:42.539: As2 CHAP: O FAILURE id 1 len 26 msg is
   "Authentication failure"
Mar 13 11:01:42.539: As2 PPP: Phase is TERMINATING
```

The following example shows that the username sam-admin is configured on the NAS. However, the password comparison failed. To correct this problem, use the **username** *name* **password** *password* command to specify the correct login password for sam-admin:

```
Mar 13 11:04:06.843: As3 LCP: State is Open
Mar 13 11:04:06.843: As3 PPP: Phase is AUTHENTICATING, by this end
Mar 13 11:04:06.843: As3 CHAP: O CHALLENGE id 1 len 28 from "ISP_NAS"
Mar 13 11:04:06.987: As3 CHAP: I RESPONSE id 1 len 30 from "sam-admin"
Mar 13 11:04:06.987: As3 CHAP: O FAILURE id 1 len 25 msg is "MD/DES
   compare failed"
Mar 13 11:04:06.987: As3 PPP: Phase is TERMINATING
```

NOTE   If you isolated the problem to PPP negotiation and you think that it has been corrected, return to the verification steps and confirm that the problem is resolved. If you are still having problems, go to Step 3.

Step 3: Troubleshoot ISDN

In this step, troubleshoot ISDN if no debug output appeared when you tried debugging PPP negotiation. Turn on ISDN Q.931 debugging by enabling the **debug isdn q931** privileged EXEC command and verify that no other **debug** commands are enabled:

```
ISP_NAS# debug isdn q931

ISDN Q931 packets debugging is on
ISP_NAS# show debug

ISDN:
  ISDN Q931 packets debugging is on
```

Send a PPP modem call into the NAS. As the call enters the access server, the following successful call setup messages appear on the NAS terminal screen.

```
ISP_NAS#
```

The NAS receives (RX) the ISDN setup message for an incoming call. Call characteristics appear.

```
Mar 13 11:06:01.715: ISDN Se0:23: RX <- SETUP pd = 8  callref = 0x02AD
Mar 13 11:06:01.715:          Bearer Capability i = 0x8090A2
Mar 13 11:06:01.719:          Channel ID i = 0xA98381
Mar 13 11:06:01.719:          Progress Ind i = 0x8283 - Origination
                                address is no
n-ISDN
Mar 13 11:06:01.719:          Calling Party Number i = '!', 0x83,
                                '4089548021'
Mar 13 11:06:01.719:          Called Party Number i = 0xC1, '5550945'
```

The NAS sends (TX) a call-proceeding message. The NAS has not answered the call as yet.

```
Mar 13 11:06:01.719: ISDN Se0:23: TX -> CALL_PROC pd = 8  callref =
  0x82AD
Mar 13 11:06:01.719:          Channel ID i = 0xA98381
Mar 13 11:06:01.719: ISDN Se0:23: TX -> ALERTING pd = 8  callref =
  0x82AD
```

The NAS sends a connect message and answers the call.

```
Mar 13 11:06:01.867: ISDN Se0:23: TX -> CONNECT pd = 8  callref = 0x82AD
```

The NAS receives a connect acknowledgment, and the connection is established.

```
Mar 13 11:06:01.895: ISDN Se0:23: RX <- CONNECT_ACK pd = 8  callref =
  0x02AD
Mar 13 11:06:33.619: %LINK-3-UPDOWN: Interface Async4, changed state
  to up
Mar 13 11:06:38.903: %LINEPROTO-5-UPDOWN: Line protocol on Interface
  Async4, changed state to up
```

If this debug output does not display on your terminal screen, confirm that the client is dialing the correct telephone number. If the number is correct, troubleshoot the problem with your PRI provider. If you are still having problems, go to Step 4.

Step 4: Check the Error Status of the T1 Controllers

In this step, enter the **show controller t1** privileged EXEC command to display the error status of the T1 controllers. A properly functioning T1 0 controller displays "T1 0 is up" and "No alarms detected." The following example shows four T1 controllers in good working condition:

```
ISP_NAS# show controller t1

T1 0 is up.
 Applique type is Channelized T1
No alarms detected.
 Version info of slot 0:  HW: 4, Firmware: 16, PLD Rev: 0

Manufacture Cookie Info:
 EEPROM Type 0x0001, EEPROM Version 0x01, Board ID 0x42,
 Board Hardware Version 1.32, Item Number 800-2540-2,
 Board Revision A0, Serial Number 11488142,
 PLD/ISP Version 0.0, Manufacture Date 10-Nov-1998.

 Framing is ESF, Line Code is B8ZS, Clock Source is Line Primary.
 Data in current interval (748 seconds elapsed):
    0 Line Code Violations, 0 Path Code Violations
    0 Slip Secs, 0 Fr Loss Secs, 0 Line Err Secs, 0 Degraded Mins
    0 Errored Secs, 0 Bursty Err Secs, 0 Severely Err Secs, 0 Unavail
      Secs
 Total Data (last 30 15 minute intervals):
    0 Line Code Violations, 0 Path Code Violations,
    0 Slip Secs, 0 Fr Loss Secs, 0 Line Err Secs, 0 Degraded Mins,
    0 Errored Secs, 0 Bursty Err Secs, 0 Severely Err Secs, 0 Unavail
      Secs
T1 1 is up.
 Applique type is Channelized T1
No alarms detected.
 Version info of slot 0:  HW: 4, Firmware: 16, PLD Rev: 0

Manufacture Cookie Info:
 EEPROM Type 0x0001, EEPROM Version 0x01, Board ID 0x42,
 Board Hardware Version 1.32, Item Number 800-2540-2,
 Board Revision A0, Serial Number 11488142,
 PLD/ISP Version 0.0, Manufacture Date 10-Nov-1998.

 Framing is ESF, Line Code is B8ZS, Clock Source is Line Secondary
.
 Data in current interval (751 seconds elapsed):
    0 Line Code Violations, 0 Path Code Violations
    0 Slip Secs, 0 Fr Loss Secs, 0 Line Err Secs, 0 Degraded Mins
```

continues

(Continued)

```
    0 Errored Secs, 0 Bursty Err Secs, 0 Severely Err Secs, 0 Unavail
      Secs
Total Data (last 30 15 minute intervals):
    0 Line Code Violations, 0 Path Code Violations,
    0 Slip Secs, 0 Fr Loss Secs, 0 Line Err Secs, 0 Degraded Mins,
    0 Errored Secs, 0 Bursty Err Secs, 0 Severely Err Secs, 0 Unavail
      Secs
T1 2 is up.
Applique type is Channelized T1
No alarms detected.
Version info of slot 0:  HW: 4, Firmware: 16, PLD Rev: 0

Manufacture Cookie Info:
 EEPROM Type 0x0001, EEPROM Version 0x01, Board ID 0x42,
 Board Hardware Version 1.32, Item Number 800-2540-2,
 Board Revision A0, Serial Number 11488142,
 PLD/ISP Version 0.0, Manufacture Date 10-Nov-1998.

Framing is ESF, Line Code is B8ZS, Clock Source is Internal.
Data in current interval (755 seconds elapsed):
    0 Line Code Violations, 0 Path Code Violations
    0 Slip Secs, 0 Fr Loss Secs, 0 Line Err Secs, 0 Degraded Mins
    0 Errored Secs, 0 Bursty Err Secs, 0 Severely Err Secs, 0 Unavail
      Secs
Total Data (last 30 15 minute intervals):
    0 Line Code Violations, 0 Path Code Violations,
    0 Slip Secs, 0 Fr Loss Secs, 0 Line Err Secs, 0 Degraded Mins,
    0 Errored Secs, 0 Bursty Err Secs, 0 Severely Err Secs, 0 Unavail
      Secs
T1 3 is up.
Applique type is Channelized T1
No alarms detected.
Version info of slot 0:  HW: 4, Firmware: 16, PLD Rev: 0

Manufacture Cookie Info:
 EEPROM Type 0x0001, EEPROM Version 0x01, Board ID 0x42,
 Board Hardware Version 1.32, Item Number 800-2540-2,
 Board Revision A0, Serial Number 11488142,
 PLD/ISP Version 0.0, Manufacture Date 10-Nov-1998.

Framing is ESF, Line Code is B8ZS, Clock Source is Internal.
Data in current interval (757 seconds elapsed):
    0 Line Code Violations, 0 Path Code Violations
    0 Slip Secs, 0 Fr Loss Secs, 0 Line Err Secs, 0 Degraded Mins
    0 Errored Secs, 0 Bursty Err Secs, 0 Severely Err Secs, 0 Unavail
      Secs
Total Data (last 30 15 minute intervals):
    0 Line Code Violations, 0 Path Code Violations,
    0 Slip Secs, 0 Fr Loss Secs, 0 Line Err Secs, 0 Degraded Mins,
    0 Errored Secs, 0 Bursty Err Secs, 0 Severely Err Secs, 0 Unavail
      Secs
```

If counters increase on a specific T1 controller, look closely at the error statistics. Focus on the current interval that is indented under the display field "Data in current interval."

Error counters are recorded over a 24-hour period in 15-minute intervals. You must specify a specific controller number to see this detailed information. Enter the **clear controller t1** *number* privileged EXEC command before you look for current error statistics. Error counters stop increasing when the controller is configured correctly.

Step 5: Troubleshoot the Modem Call State Machine

In this step, troubleshoot the modem call state machine (CSM) by using the **debug modem csm** privileged EXEC command. You should troubleshoot the CSM if you have verified the following:

- The **show isdn status** privileged EXEC command demonstrates good working status as shown in Step 1.
- You do not see PPP debug output as shown in Step 2.
- The ISDN debug output demonstrates good working status as shown in Step 3.

Send a PPP modem call into the NAS. Transition states in the debug output signify that everything is operating properly. If you do not see transition states, look at the disconnect reason for the modem. For example, enter the **show modem log 1/4** user EXEC command.

See the following example of successful debug output for the **debug modem csm** command:

```
ISP_NAS#
Mar 13 11:13:12.487: EVENT_FROM_ISDN::dchan_idb=0x60EA108C,
    call_id=0x1D, ces=0x
1bchan=0x0, event=0x1, cause=0x0
Mar 13 11:13:12.487: VDEV_ALLOCATE: slot 1 and port 4 is allocated.
Mar 13 11:13:12.487: EVENT_FROM_ISDN:(001D): DEV_INCALL at slot 1 and
    port 4
Mar 13 11:13:12.487: CSM_PROC_IDLE: CSM_EVENT_ISDN_CALL at slot 1,
    port 4
Mar 13 11:13:12.487: Mica Modem(1/4): Configure(0x1 = 0x0)
Mar 13 11:13:12.487: Mica Modem(1/4): Configure(0x23 = 0x0)
Mar 13 11:13:12.487: Mica Modem(1/4): Call Setup
Mar 13 11:13:12.611: Mica Modem(1/4): State Transition to Call Setup
Mar 13 11:13:12.611: Mica Modem(1/4): Went offhook
Mar 13 11:13:12.611: CSM_PROC_IC1_RING: CSM_EVENT_MODEM_OFFHOOK at slot
    1, port 4
Mar 13 11:13:12.631: EVENT_FROM_ISDN::dchan_idb=0x60EA108C, call
id=0x1D,
ces=0x1 bchan=0x0, event=0x4, cause=0x0
Mar 13 11:13:12.631: EVENT_FROM_ISDN:(001D): DEV_CONNECTED at slot 1 and
    port 4
```

continues

```
Mar 13 11:13:12.631: CSM_PROC_IC4_WAIT_FOR_CARRIER: CSM_EVENT_ISDN
  CONNECTED at slot 1, port 4
Mar 13 11:13:12.631: Mica Modem(1/4): Link Initiate
Mar 13 11:13:13.751: Mica Modem(1/4): State Transition to Connect
Mar 13 11:13:18.903: Mica Modem(1/4): State Transition to Link
Mar 13 11:13:37.051: Mica Modem(1/4): State Transition to Trainup
Mar 13 11:13:38.731: Mica Modem(1/4): State Transition to EC Negotiating
Mar 13 11:13:39.387: Mica Modem(1/4): State Transition to Steady State
Mar 13 11:13:42.007: %LINK-3-UPDOWN: Interface Async5, changed state to
  up
Mar 13 11:13:46.751: %LINEPROTO-5-UPDOWN: Line protocol on Interface
  Async5, changed state to up
Mar 13 11:14:41.803: Mica Modem(1/4): State Transition to Steady State
  Speedshifting
Mar 13 11:14:44.139: Mica Modem(1/4): State Transition to Steady State
Mar 13 11:17:30.475: %SYS-5-CONFIG_I: Configured from console by vty0
  (171.68.201.22)
```

Phase 2: Configuring the Access VPDN to Work with Local AAA

In this second phase, the ISP and enterprise customer perform the following tasks:

- Configure their network devices to work as an access VPDN.
- Use local AAA to authenticate the tunnel and the users.
- Verify that the access VPDN works properly.
- Troubleshoot the access VPDN if there are problems.

The ISP configures the NAS, and the enterprise customer configures the home gateway.

After the ISP and enterprise customer verify that their access VPDN works by using local AAA, they reconfigure their devices to use remote AAA servers. See the section "Phase 3: Configuring the Access VPDN to Work with Remote AAA" for details.

Figure 2-9 shows the access VPDN network topology. The tunnel and user authentication occurs locally between the Cisco AS5300 NAS and the Cisco 7206 home gateway.

After the ISP and enterprise customer have completed this phase, the network will function as follows:

1 When the user wants to connect to the enterprise customer network, the user dials in to the NAS by using the username jeremy@hgw.com.

2 The NAS and the client perform LCP negotiation.

3 The NAS authenticates the domain name, hgw.com, and determines the tunnel endpoint information.

Figure 2-9 *Access VPDN Topology Using Local AAA*

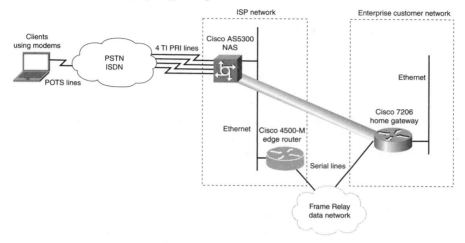

4 The NAS negotiates an L2F tunnel with the home gateway. Once the tunnel is established, the NAS forwards the call to the home gateway.

5 The home gateway authenticates the username and assigns the client an IP address. (It can optionally assign IP addresses for DNS and WINS servers.)

6 The client and the home gateway can now exchange PPP packets. The NAS now acts as a transparent PPP frame forwarder.

Configuring the NAS

The ISP now reconfigures the NAS for VPDN using local AAA and L2F as the tunneling protocol by performing the following configuration steps:

Step 1 Configure VPDN to Initiate L2F Tunnels

Step 2 Authenticate and Authorize the Tunnel

Step 3 Remove Unnecessary Commands

Step 1: Configure VPDN to Initiate L2F Tunnels

In this step, the ISP enables VPDN, configures a VPDN group, and configures VPDN to tunnel users based on their domain name:

```
!Enable VPDN.
vpdn enable
!
!Instructs the NAS to only look for tunnel information based on the user
!domain name. This reduces connectivity time, because by default, the
!NAS first looks for tunnel information based on the user DNIS. If DNIS
```

continues

(Continued)

```
!is not found, the software searches for a domain name. Reducing the
!connectivity time can reduce the number of system timeouts.
vpdn search-order domain dnis
Creates VPDN group 1.
vpdn-group 1
!Creates a request dialin subgroup.
 request dialin
!Specifies that this subgroup will only create L2F tunnels.
  protocol l2f
!Configures this subgroup to tunnel users with the domain name hgw.com.
  domain hgw.com
!Configures this subgroup to initiate L2F tunnels to IP address
!172.22.66.25.
   initiate-to ip 172.22.66.25
!Configures this VPDN group to identify itself as ISP_NAS for tunnel
!authentication.
  local name ISP_NAS
```

Step 2: Authenticate and Authorize the Tunnel

In this step, the ISP adds local usernames for bidirectional authentication between the NAS and home gateway and configures AAA for authentication and authorization:

```
!Configures local usernames with the same password that are used for
!bidirectional tunnel authentication between the NAS and the home
!gateway.
!These usernames and password are called the tunnel secret. The NAS and
!the home gateway must both have the same usernames with the same
!password. These usernames are not related to client authentication.
username ISP_NAS password cisco
username ENT_HGW password cisco
!
!Configures AAA to authenticate and authorize VPDN tunnels using the
!local username database.
aaa authentication ppp default local
aaa authorization network default local
```

Step 3: Remove Unnecessary Commands

In this step, the ISP removes the local IP address pool from the NAS and deletes the client username and password from the local database:

```
!Removes the local IP address pool from the NAS because the client will
!now be assigned an IP address from the home gateway local IP address
!pool.
no ip local pool default 1.1.1.1
interface group-async 1
 no peer default ip address pool default
!
!Removes the client username and password from the local AAA database
!because the home gateway will now perform user authentication.
no username jeremy password subaru
```

Home Gateway Running Configuration

The enterprise customer configures the home gateway for VPDN using local AAA and L2F as the tunneling protocol by performing the following configuration steps:

Step 1   Configure Basic Settings

Step 2   Configure Local AAA

Step 3   Enable VPDN to Accept L2F Tunnel

Step 4   Create the Virtual Template

Step 5   Specify the IP Address Pool and BOOTP Servers

Step 1: Configure Basic Settings

In this step, the enterprise configures the host name, enable password, service time stamps, and the Fast Ethernet interface that is used for VPDN traffic:

```
!Set debug time stamps to include millisecond dating.
service timestamps debug datetime msec
!Encrypt passwords that appear as part of the configuration.
service password-encryption
!
hostname ENT_HGW
!
enable secret 5 $1$44oH$gZlAZLwylZJSNKGDk.BKb0
!
!Set the default domain name that the Cisco IOS software will use to
!complete unqualified host names.
ip domain-name cisco.com
!Set the IP address of the host that will supply Domain Name System (DNS)
!information.
ip name-server 171.68.10.70
!
interface FastEthernet0/0
!Assign an IP address to the FastEthernet 0/0 interface.
 ip address 172.22.66.25 255.255.255.192
```

Step 2: Configure Local AAA

In this step, the enterprise adds the usernames needed to authenticate the user and the tunnel and configures local AAA for authentication and authorization:

```
!Enable the AAA access control system. This step immediately locks down
!login and PPP authentication.
aaa new-model
!Specify that login users will be authenticated using the local
!database.
aaa authentication login default local
!Specify that PPP users will be authenticated using the local database.
aaa authentication ppp default local
!Specify that network-related service requests will be authorized by
!using the local database.
```

continues

(Continued)

```
aaa authorization network default local
!
!Set the username and password for the administrator.
username jane-admin password 7 00001C05
!Add the local username that is used to authenticate the remote user.
username jeremy@hgw.com password 7 140407090D163F
!Add local usernames and passwords for bidirectional tunnel
!authentication between the NAS and the home gateway. These usernames
!are called the tunnel secret. The NAS and the home gateway must both
!have the same usernames with the same password. These usernames
!authenticate the tunnel, not !the user.
username ISP_NAS password 7 070C285F4D06
username ENT_HGW password 7 107249D900E4
```

Step 3: Enable VPDN to Accept L2F Tunnel

In this step, the enterprise enables and configures VPDN using L2F tunnels:

```
!Enable VPDN.
vpdn enable
!
!Create VPDN group 1.
vpdn-group 1
!Create an accept dialin subgroup.
 accept-dialin
!Specify that this subgroup use L2F.
  protocol l2f
!Instructs the subgroup to clone virtual access interfaces from virtual
!template 1.
   virtual-template 1
!Specifies that this VPDN group will negotiate VPDN tunnels with LACs
!that identify themselves with the local name ISP_NAS.
 terminate-from hostname ISP_NAS
!Configures the local name that the VPDN group will use to identify
!itself for tunnel authentication.
 local name ENT_HGW
```

Step 4: Create the Virtual Template

In this step, the enterprise creates the virtual template that is used to clone virtual access interfaces:

```
!Create virtual template 1 that is used to clone virtual-access
!interfaces.
interface Virtual-Template1
!Specify that the virtual-access interfaces use the IP address of the
!Fast Ethernet 0/0 interface.
 ip unnumbered FastEthernet0/0
!Return an IP address from the default pool to the client.
 peer default ip address pool default
!Enable CHAP authentication using the local username database.
 ppp authentication chap
```

Step 5: Specify the IP Address Pool and BOOTP Servers

In this step, the enterprise specifies the IP address pool and the BOOTP servers. The IP address pool is the addresses that the home gateway assigns to clients. You must configure an IP address pool. You also can provide BOOTP servers. DNS servers translate host names to IP addresses. WINS servers, which are specified using the **async-bootp nbns-server** global configuration command, provide dynamic NetBIOS names that Windows devices use to communicate without IP addresses.

```
!Return the configured addresses of Domain Name Servers in response to
!BOOTP requests.
async-bootp dns-server 172.23.1.10 172.23.2.10
!Return the configured addresses of Windows NT servers in response to
!BOOTP requests.
async-bootp nbns-server 172.23.1.11 172.23.2.11
!Configure the default local pool of IP address that will be used by
!clients.
ip local pool default 172.30.2.1 172.30.2.96
```

Verifying the Access VPDN

This section describes how to verify that the access VPDN functions as shown in Figure 2-9:

Step 1 Check the NAS Running Configuration

Step 2 Check the Home Gateway Running Configuration

Step 3 Dial In to the NAS

Step 4 Ping the Home Gateway

Step 5 Display Active Call Statistics on the Home Gateway

Step 6 Ping the Client

Step 7 Verify That the Virtual Access Interface Is Up and That LCP Is Open

Step 8 Display Active L2F Tunnel Statistics

After you successfully test these connections, go to the section "Phase 3: Configuring the Access VPDN to Work with Remote AAA." If you experience problems, see the section "Troubleshooting the Access VPDN."

Step 1: Check the NAS Running Configuration

In this step, enter the **show running-config** privileged EXEC command to make sure that the NAS accepted the commands you entered. Commands in the following configuration that were not discussed in the preceding text do not directly pertain to the access VPDN and are therefore beyond the scope of this book.

```
ISP_NAS# show running-config

Building configuration...

Current configuration:
!
version 11.3
service timestamps debug datetime msec
service timestamps log datetime msec
service password-encryption
!
hostname ISP_NAS
!
aaa new-model
aaa authentication ppp default local
aaa authorization network default local
enable secret 5 $1$AXl/$27hOM6j51a5P76Enq.LCf0
!
username jane-admin password 7 0501090A6C5C4F1A0A1218000F
username ENT_HGW password 7 104D000A0618
username ISP_NAS password 7 13061E010803
vpdn enable
!
vpdn search-order domain dnis
vpdn-group 1
 request dialin
  protocol l2f
  domain hgw.com
  initiate-to ip 172.22.66.25
 local name ISP_NAS
!
async-bootp dns-server 171.68.10.70 171.68.10.140
isdn switch-type primary-5ess
!
!
controller T1 0
 framing esf
 clock source line primary
 linecode b8zs
 pri-group timeslots 1-24
!
controller T1 1
 framing esf
 clock source line secondary
 linecode b8zs
 pri-group timeslots 1-24
!
controller T1 2
 framing esf
 clock source internal
 linecode b8zs
 pri-group timeslots 1-24
!
```

(Continued)

```
controller T1 3
 framing esf
 clock source internal
 linecode b8zs
 pri-group timeslots 1-24
!
!
interface Ethernet0
 ip address 172.22.66.23 255.255.255.192
!
interface Serial0:23
 no ip address
 isdn switch-type primary-5ess
 isdn incoming-voice modem
 no cdp enable
!
interface Serial1:23
 no ip address
 isdn switch-type primary-5ess
 isdn incoming-voice modem
 no cdp enable
!
interface Serial2:23
 no ip address
 isdn switch-type primary-5ess
 isdn incoming-voice modem
 no cdp enable
!
interface Serial3:23
 no ip address
 isdn switch-type primary-5ess
 isdn incoming-voice modem
 no cdp enable
!
interface FastEthernet0
 no ip address
 shutdown
!
interface Group-Async1
 ip unnumbered Ethernet0
 encapsulation ppp
 async mode interactive
 no peer default ip address
 ppp authentication chap pap
 group-range 1 96
!
ip classless
ip route 0.0.0.0 0.0.0.0 172.22.66.1
!
!
line con 0
 transport input none
line 1 96
 autoselect during-login
 autoselect ppp
 modem inout
line aux 0
line vty 0 4
!
end
```

Step 2: Check the Home Gateway Running Configuration

In this step, enter the **show running-config** privileged EXEC command to make
sure that the home gateway accepted the commands you entered. Commands in the
following configuration that were not discussed in the preceding text do not directly
pertain to the access VPDN and are therefore beyond the scope of this book.

```
ENT_HGW# show running-config

Building configuration...

Current configuration:
!
version 12.0
service timestamps debug datetime msec
service timestamps log uptime
service password-encryption
!
hostname ENT_HGW
!
aaa new-model
aaa authentication login default local
aaa authentication ppp default local
aaa authorization network default local
enable secret 5 $1$44oH$gZlAZLwylZJSNKGDk.BKb0
!
username jane-admin password 7 00001C05
username ISP_NAS password 7 070C285F4D06
username ENT_HGW password 7 107249D900E4
username jeremy@hgw.com password 7 140407090D163F
ip subnet-zero
ip domain-name cisco.com
ip name-server 171.68.10.70
!
vpdn enable
!
vpdn-group 1
 accept dialin
  protocol l2f
  virtual-template 1
 terminate-from hostname ISP_NAS
 local name ENT_HGW
!
async-bootp dns-server 172.23.1.10 172.23.2.10
async-bootp nbns-server 172.23.1.11 172.23.2.11
!
!
!
interface FastEthernet0/0
 ip address 172.22.66.25 255.255.255.192
 no ip directed-broadcast
!
.
.
.
!
interface Virtual-Template1
 ip unnumbered FastEthernet0/0
 peer default ip address pool default
```

(Continued)

```
  ppp authentication chap
 !
 ip local pool default 172.30.2.1 172.30.2.96
 ip classless
 ip route 0.0.0.0 0.0.0.0 172.22.66.1
 !
 !
 line con 0
  transport input none
 line aux 0
 line vty 0 4
  password 7 045F0405
  login local
 !
 end
```

Step 3: Dial In to the NAS

In this step, from the client, dial in to the NAS by using the PRI telephone number assigned to the NAS T1 trunks. Sometimes the PRI telephone number is called the hunt group number.

As the call comes into the NAS, a LINK-3-UPDOWN message automatically appears on the NAS terminal screen. In this example, the call comes in to the NAS on asynchronous interface 14. The asynchronous interface is up.

```
*Jan  1 21:22:18.410: %LINK-3-UPDOWN: Interface Async14, changed state
  to up
```

NOTE	No **debug** commands are turned on to display this log message. Start troubleshooting the NAS if this message does not display within 30 seconds of the client initiating the call.

Step 4: Ping the Home Gateway

In this step, from the client, ping the home gateway. On the desktop of the client, perform the following steps:

Step 1   Click Start.

Step 2   Select Run.

Step 3   Enter **ping 172.22.66.25**.

Step 4   Click OK.

Step 5   Look at the terminal screen and verify that the home gateway is sending ping reply packets to the client.

Step 5: Display Active Call Statistics on the Home Gateway

In this step, from the home gateway, enter the **show caller** privileged EXEC command and **show caller user jeremy@hgw.com** user EXEC command to verify that the client received an IP address. This example shows that Jeremy is using interface virtual access 1 and is assigned IP address 172.30.2.1. The network administrator jane-admin is using console 0.

```
ENT_HGW# show caller

    Line       User               Service       Active
    con 0      jane-admin           TTY          00:00:25
    Vi1        jeremy@hgw.com     PPP    L2F      00:01:28

ENT_HGW# show caller user jeremy@hgw.com

    User: jeremy@hgw.com, line Vi1, service PPP L2F, active 00:01:35
    PPP: LCP Open, CHAP (<- AAA), IPCP
    IP: Local 172.22.66.25, remote 172.30.2.1
    VPDN: NAS ISP_NAS, MID 1, MID open
          HGW  ENT_HGW, NAS CLID 36, HGW CLID 1, tunnel open
    Counts: 105 packets input, 8979 bytes, 0 no buffer
            0 input errors, 0 CRC, 0 frame, 0 overrun
            18 packets output, 295 bytes, 0 underruns
            0 output errors, 0 collisions, 0 interface resets
```

NOTE   The **show caller** command was introduced in Cisco IOS Release 11.3(5)AA. If your Cisco IOS software does not include the **show caller** command, use the **show user** command instead.

Step 6: Ping the Client

In this step, from the home gateway, ping the client at IP address 172.30.2.1:

```
ENT_HGW# ping 172.30.2.1

Type escape sequence to abort.
Sending 5, 100-byte ICMP Echos to 172.30.2.1, timeout is 2 seconds:
!!!!!
Success rate is 100 percent (5/5), round-trip min/avg/max = 128/132/152
  ms
```

Step 7: Verify That the Virtual Access Interface Is Up and That LCP Is Open

In this step, from the home gateway, enter the **show interfaces virtual-access 1** privileged EXEC command to verify that the interface is up, LCP is open, and no errors are reported:

```
ENT_HGW# show interfaces virtual-access 1

Virtual-Access1 is up, line protocol is up
  Hardware is Virtual Access interface
  Interface is unnumbered. Using address of FastEthernet0/0
    (172.22.66.25)
  MTU 1500 bytes, BW 115 Kbit, DLY 100000 usec,
     reliabilility 255/255, txload 1/255, rxload 1/255
Encapsulation PPP, loopback not set, keepalive set (10 sec)
  DTR is pulsed for 5 seconds on reset
  LCP Open
  Open: IPCP
  Last input 00:00:02, output never, output hang never
  Last clearing of "show interface" counters 3d00h
  Queueing strategy: fifo
Output queue 1/40, 0 drops; input queue 0/75, 0 drops
  5 minute input rate 0 bits/sec, 0 packets/sec
  5 minute output rate 0 bits/sec, 0 packets/sec
     114 packets input, 9563 bytes, 0 no buffer
     Received 0 broadcasts, 0 runts, 0 giants, 0 throttles
     0 input errors, 0 CRC, 0 frame, 0 overrun, 0 ignored, 0 abort
     27 packets output, 864 bytes, 0 underruns
     0 output errors, 0 collisions, 0 interface resets
     0 output buffer failures, 0 output buffers swapped out
     0 carrier transitions
```

Step 8: Display Active L2F Tunnel Statistics

In this step, from the home gateway, display active tunnel statistics by entering the **show vpdn** user EXEC command and **show vpdn tunnel all** user EXEC command:

```
ENT_HGW# show vpdn

% No active L2TP tunnels

L2F Tunnel and Session

 NAS CLID HGW CLID NAS Name        HGW Name       State
 36        1        ISP_NAS         ENT_HGW        open
                    172.22.66.23    172.22.66.25
```

continues

(Continued)

```
        CLID   MID    Username                Intf   State
        36     1      jeremy@hgw.com          Vi1    open

        ENT_HGW# show vpdn tunnel all

        % No active L2TP tunnels

        L2F Tunnel
        NAS name: ISP_NAS
        NAS CLID: 36
        NAS IP address 172.22.66.23
        Gateway name: ENT_HGW
        Gateway CLID: 1
        Gateway IP address 172.22.66.25
        State: open
        Packets out: 52
        Bytes out: 1799
        Packets in: 100
        Bytes in: 7143
```

Troubleshooting the Access VPDN

This section provides the ISP and enterprise customer with a methodology for troubleshooting the access VPDN as described in Figure 2-10. Step 1 shows debug output from a successful call. If your debug output does not match the successful output, perform the remaining steps to begin troubleshooting the network. The shaded lines of debug output indicate important information.

Step 1   Compare Your Debug Output to the Successful Debug Output

Step 2   Troubleshoot L2F Negotiation

Step 3   Troubleshoot PPP Negotiation

Step 4   Troubleshoot AAA Negotiation

Figure 2-10 shows the methodology used to troubleshoot the access VPDN.

If you use a Telnet session to connect to the NAS and home gateway, enable the **terminal monitor** global configuration command, which ensures that your EXEC session is receiving the logging and debug output from the devices.

When you finish troubleshooting, use the **undebug all** privileged EXEC command to turn off all **debug** commands. Isolating **debug** output helps you efficiently build a network.

Figure 2-10 *Troubleshooting Flow Diagram for Access VPDN with Local AAA*

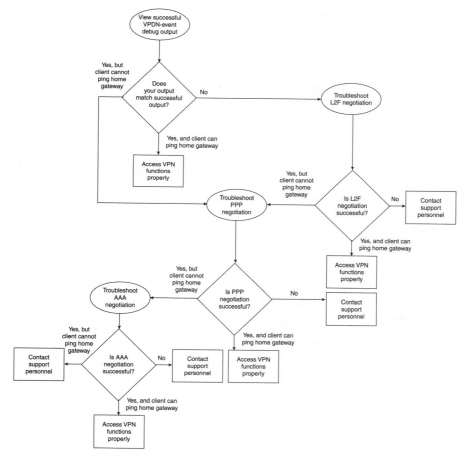

Step 1: Compare Your Debug Output to the Successful Debug Output

In this step, enable the **debug vpdn-event** privileged EXEC command on both the NAS and the home gateway. The following debug output shows successful VPDN negotiation on the NAS and home gateway:

```
ISP_NAS#
Jan  7 00:19:35.900: %LINK-3-UPDOWN: Interface Async9, changed state to
  up
```

continues

(Continued)

```
Jan  7 00:19:39.532: sVPDN: Got DNIS string As9
Jan  7 00:19:39.532: As9 VPDN: Looking for tunnel -- hgw.com --
Jan  7 00:19:39.540: As9 VPDN: Get tunnel info for hgw.com with NAS
  ISP_NAS,
IP172.22.66.25
Jan  7 00:19:39.540: As9 VPDN: Forward to address 172.22.66.25
Jan  7 00:19:39.540: As9 VPDN: Forwarding...
Jan  7 00:19:39.540: As9 VPDN: Bind interface direction=1
Jan  7 00:19:39.540: As9 VPDN: jeremy@hgw.com is forwarded
Jan  7 00:19:40.540: %LINEPROTO-5-UPDOWN: Line protocol on Interface
  Async9,
changed state to up
ISP_NAS#

ENT_HGW#
Jan  7 00:19:39.967: VPDN: Chap authentication succeeded for ISP_NAS
Jan  7 00:19:39.967: Vi1 VPDN: Virtual interface created for
  jeremy@hgw.com
Jan  7 00:19:39.967: Vi1 VPDN: Set to Async interface
Jan  7 00:19:39.971: Vi1 VPDN: Clone from Vtemplate 1 filterPPP=0
  blocking
6w5d: %LINK-3-UPDOWN: Interface Virtual-Access1, changed state to up
Jan  7 00:19:40.051: Vi1 VPDN: Bind interface direction=2
Jan  7 00:19:40.051: Vi1 VPDN: PPP LCP accepted rcv CONFACK
Jan  7 00:19:40.051: Vi1 VPDN: PPP LCP accepted sent CONFACK
6w5d: %LINEPROTO-5-UPDOWN: Line protocol on Interface Virtual-Access1,
changed state to up
```

If you see this debug output but cannot ping the home gateway, go to the section "Step 3: Troubleshooting PPP Negotiation."

If you do not see this debug output, go to the section "Step 2: Troubleshooting L2F Negotiation."

Step 2: Troubleshoot L2F Negotiation

This step describes several common misconfigurations that prevent successful L2F negotiation:

- Misconfigured NAS Tunnel Secret
- Misconfigured Home Gateway Tunnel Secret
- Misconfigured Tunnel Name

Misconfigured NAS Tunnel Secret

The NAS and the home gateway must both have the same usernames with the same password to authenticate the L2F tunnel. These usernames are called the tunnel secret. In this solution, these usernames are ISP_NAS and ENT_HGW. The password is "cisco" for both usernames on both devices.

If one of the tunnel secrets on the NAS is incorrect, you will see the following debug output when you dial in to the NAS and the **debug vpdn l2x-errors** privileged EXEC command is enabled on the NAS and home gateway:

```
ISP_NAS#
Jan  1 00:26:49.899: %LINK-3-UPDOWN: Interface Async3, changed state to
   up
Jan  1 00:26:54.643: %LINEPROTO-5-UPDOWN: Line protocol on Interface
   Async3, changed state to up
Jan  1 00:27:00.559: L2F: Resending L2F_OPEN, time #1
Jan  1 00:27:05.559: L2F: Resending L2F_ECHO, time #1
Jan  1 00:27:05.559: L2F: Resending L2F_OPEN, time #2
Jan  1 00:27:10.559: L2F: Resending L2F_ECHO, time #2
Jan  1 00:27:10.559: L2F: Resending L2F_OPEN, time #3
Jan  1 00:27:15.559: L2F: Resending L2F_ECHO, time #3
Jan  1 00:27:15.559: L2F: Resending L2F_OPEN, time #4
Jan  1 00:27:20.559: L2F: Resending L2F_ECHO, time #4
Jan  1 00:27:20.559: L2F: Resending L2F_OPEN, time #5
Jan  1 00:27:25.559: L2F: Resending L2F_ECHO, time #5
Jan  1 00:27:25.559: L2F: Resend packet (type 2) around too long,
   time to kill off the tunnel
ISP_NAS#

ENT_HGW#
Jan  1 00:26:53.645: L2F: Packet has bogus2 key C8353FAB B6369121
5w6d: %VPDN-6-AUTHENFAIL: L2F HGW , authentication failure for  tunnel
   ISP_NAS;
Invalid key
5w6d: %VPDN-5-UNREACH: L2F NAS 172.22.66.23 is unreachable
Jan  1 00:27:00.557: L2F: Gateway received tunnel OPEN while in state
   closed
ENT_HGW#
```

The phrase "time to kill off the tunnel" in the NAS debug output indicates that the tunnel was not opened. The phrase "Packet has bogus2 key" in the home gateway debug output indicates that the NAS has an incorrect tunnel secret.

To avoid this problem, make sure that you configure both the NAS and home gateway for the same two usernames with the same password.

Misconfigured Home Gateway Tunnel Secret

If one of the tunnel secrets on the home gateway is incorrect, you will see the following debug output when you dial in to the NAS and the **debug vpdn l2x-errors** privileged EXEC command is enabled on the NAS and home gateway:

```
ISP_NAS#
Jan  1 00:45:27.123: %LINK-3-UPDOWN: Interface Async7, changed state
   to up
Jan  1 00:45:30.939: L2F: Packet has bogus1 key B6C656EE 5FAC6B3
```

continues

(Continued)

```
Jan  1 00:45:30.939: %VPDN-6-AUTHENFAIL: L2F NAS ISP_NAS,
  authentication failure
 for  tunnel ENT_HGW; Invalid key
Jan  1 00:45:31.935: %LINEPROTO-5-UPDOWN: Line protocol on Interface
  Async7, changed state to up
Jan  1 00:45:35.559: L2F: Resending L2F_OPEN, time #1
Jan  1 00:45:35.559: L2F: Packet has bogus1 key B6C656EE 5FAC6B3
ISP_NAS#

ENT_HGW#
Jan  1 00:45:30.939: L2F: Tunnel authentication succeeded for ISP_NAS
Jan  1 00:45:35.559: L2F: Gateway received tunnel OPEN while in state
  open
Jan  1 00:45:40.559: L2F: Gateway received tunnel OPEN while in state
  open
Jan  1 00:45:45.559: L2F: Gateway received tunnel OPEN while in state
  open
Jan  1 00:45:50.559: L2F: Gateway received tunnel OPEN while in state
  open
```

Notice how this output is similar to the debug output you see when the NAS has a misconfigured tunnel secret username. This time you see the phrase "Packet has bogus1 key" on the NAS rather than on the home gateway. This message tells you that the home gateway has an incorrect tunnel secret.

To avoid this problem, make sure that you configure both the NAS and home gateway for the same two usernames with the same password.

Misconfigured Tunnel Name

If the NAS and home gateway do not have matching tunnel names, they cannot establish an L2F tunnel. These tunnel names are configured under the **vpdn-group 1** global configuration command on both the NAS and the home gateway by using the **local name** VPDN group configuration command.

The home gateway must be configured to accept tunnels from the name the NAS sends it. This is done by configuring a VPDN group using the following commands:

```
vpdn-group 1
 accept dialin
  protocol l2f
  virtual-template 1
 terminate-from hostname ISP_NAS
 local name ENT_HGW
```

The home gateway is thus configured to accept tunnels from a NAS identifying itself as ISP_NAS. The name the home gateway returns to the NAS is configured by using the **local name ENT_HGW** VPDN group configuration command where ENT_HGW is the name.

In the following debug output, the NAS attempted to open a tunnel by using the name "isp". Because the home gateway did not know this name, it did not open the tunnel. To see the following debug output, enable the **debug vpdn l2x-events** and **debug vpdn l2x-errors** privileged EXEC commands on the home gateway:

```
ENT_HGW#
Jan  1 01:28:54.207: L2F: L2F_CONF received
Jan  1 01:28:54.207: L2X: Never heard of isp
Jan  1 01:28:54.207: L2F: Couldn't find tunnel named isp
```

To avoid this problem, make sure that the tunnel names match on the home gateway and on the NAS.

If you corrected the problem in your configuration, return to the section "Verifying Basic Dial Access."

If your call still cannot successfully complete L2F negotiation, contact your support personnel.

Step 3: Troubleshoot PPP Negotiation

In this step, enable the **debug ppp negotiation** privileged EXEC command on the home gateway and dial in to the NAS. You should not need to enable this command on the NAS because you already verified dialup connectivity to the NAS in the section "Phase 1: Configuring the NAS for Basic Dial Access."

The following debug output shows successful PPP negotiation on the home gateway:

```
1d02h: %LINK-3-UPDOWN: Interface Virtual-Access1, changed state to up
*Feb  4 14:14:40.505: Vi1 PPP: Treating connection as a dedicated line
*Feb  4 14:14:40.505: Vi1 PPP: Phase is ESTABLISHING, Active Open
*Feb  4 14:14:40.505: Vi1 PPP: Treating connection as a dedicated line
*Feb  4 14:14:40.505: Vi1 PPP: Phase is AUTHENTICATING, by this end
*Feb  4 14:14:40.509: Vi1 PPP: Phase is UP
```

If your call successfully completed PPP negotiation but you still cannot ping the home gateway, go on to the section "Step 4: Troubleshooting AAA Negotiation."

If your call cannot successfully complete PPP negotiation, contact your support personnel.

Step 4: Troubleshoot AAA Negotiation

The following section shows debug output of successful AAA negotiation and then explains a common misconfiguration that prevents successful AAA negotiation.

Successful AAA Negotiation

Enable the **debug aaa authentication** and **debug aaa authorization** privileged EXEC commands on the home gateway and dial in to the NAS.

The following debug output shows successful AAA negotiation on the home gateway. This output has been edited to exclude repetitive lines.

```
Jan 15 21:35:10.902: AAA/AUTHEN: create_user (0x612C5DE4)
    user='ENT_HGW' ruser='
' port='' rem_addr='' authen_type=CHAP service=PPP priv=1
Jan 15 21:35:10.902: AAA/AUTHEN/START (1765780899): port=''
    list='default' action=SENDAUTH service=PPP
Jan 15 21:35:10.902: AAA/AUTHEN/START (1765780899): found list default
Jan 15 21:35:10.902: AAA/AUTHEN/START (1765780899): Method=LOCAL
Jan 15 21:35:10.902: AAA/AUTHEN (1765780899): status = PASS
Jan 15 21:35:10.902: AAA/AUTHEN: create_user (0x612C5DE4)
    user='ISP_NAS' ruser='
' port='' rem_addr='' authen_type=CHAP service=PPP priv=1
Jan 15 21:35:10.906: AAA/AUTHEN/START (990949917): port=''
    list='default' action
=SENDAUTH service=PPP
Jan 15 21:35:10.906: AAA/AUTHEN/START (990949917): found list default
Jan 15 21:35:10.906: AAA/AUTHEN/START (990949917): Method=LOCAL
Jan 15 21:35:10.906: AAA/AUTHEN (990949917): status = PASS
8w0d: %LINK-3-UPDOWN: Interface Virtual-Access1, changed state to up
Jan 15 21:35:10.994: AAA/AUTHEN: create_user (0x612E4234)
    user='jeremy@hgw.com'
ruser='' port='Virtual-Access1' rem_addr='408/5550945'
    authen_type=CHAP service=
PPP priv=1
Jan 15 21:35:10.994: AAA/AUTHEN/START (2063987649): port='Virtual
    Access1' list=
'' action=LOGIN service=PPP
Jan 15 21:35:10.994: AAA/AUTHEN/START (2063987649): using "default"
    list
Jan 15 21:35:10.994: AAA/AUTHEN/START (2063987649): Method=LOCAL
Jan 15 21:35:10.994: AAA/AUTHEN (2063987649): status = PASS
Jan 15 21:35:10.994: Vi1 AAA/AUTHOR/LCP: Authorize LCP
Jan 15 21:35:10.994: AAA/AUTHOR/LCP Vi1 (2975944584): Port='Virtual
    Access1' list='' service=NET
Jan 15 21:35:10.994: AAA/AUTHOR/LCP: Vi1 (2975944584)
    user='jeremy@hgw.com'
```

(Continued)

```
Jan 15 21:35:10.998: AAA/AUTHOR/LCP: Vi1 (2975944584) send AV
   service=ppp
Jan 15 21:35:10.998: AAA/AUTHOR/LCP: Vi1 (2975944584) send AV
   protocol=lcp
Jan 15 21:35:10.998: AAA/AUTHOR/LCP (2975944584) found list "default"
Jan 15 21:35:10.998: AAA/AUTHOR/LCP: Vi1 (2975944584) Method=LOCAL
Jan 15 21:35:10.998: AAA/AUTHOR (2975944584): Post authorization
   status=
PASS_REPL
Jan 15 21:35:10.998: Vi1 AAA/AUTHOR/FSM: We can start IPCP
8w0d: %LINEPROTO-5-UPDOWN: Line protocol on Interface Virtual-Access1,
   changed state to up
Jan 15 21:35:14.094: Vi1 AAA/AUTHOR/IPCP: Start.  Her address
   0.0.0.0, we want 1
72.30.2.1
```

If this debug output appears, but you still cannot ping the home gateway, contact your support personnel and troubleshoot your network backbone.

If you do not see this debug output, you need to troubleshoot AAA negotiation.

Incorrect User Password

If the user password is incorrect (or it is incorrectly configured), the tunnel will be established, but the home gateway will not authenticate the user. If the user password is incorrect, the following debug output appears on the NAS and home gateway when you dial in to the NAS and the **debug vpdn l2x-errors** and **debug vpdn l2x-events** privileged EXEC commands are enabled:

```
ISP_NAS#
Jan  1 01:00:01.555: %LINK-3-UPDOWN: Interface Async12, changed state
   to up
Jan  1 01:00:05.299:  L2F: Tunnel state closed
Jan  1 01:00:05.299:  L2F: MID  state closed
Jan  1 01:00:05.299: L2F: Open UDP socket to 172.22.66.25
Jan  1 01:00:05.299:  L2F: Tunnel state opening
Jan  1 01:00:05.299: As12 L2F: MID jeremy@hgw.com state
   waiting_for_tunnel
Jan  1 01:00:05.303: L2F: L2F_CONF received
Jan  1 01:00:05.303: L2F: Removing resend packet (L2F_CONF)
Jan  1 01:00:05.303: ENT_HGW L2F: Tunnel state open
Jan  1 01:00:05.307: L2F: L2F_OPEN received
Jan  1 01:00:05.307: L2F: Removing resend packet (L2F_OPEN)
Jan  1 01:00:05.307: L2F: Building nas2gw_mid0
Jan  1 01:00:05.307: L2F: L2F_CLIENT_INFO: CLID/DNIS 4089548021/
   5550945
Jan  1 01:00:05.307: L2F: L2F_CLIENT_INFO: NAS-Port Async12
Jan  1 01:00:05.307: L2F: L2F_CLIENT_INFO: Client-Bandwidth-Kbps 115
Jan  1 01:00:05.307: L2F: L2F_CLIENT_INFO: NAS-Rate L2F/26400/28800
Jan  1 01:00:05.307: As12 L2F: MID jeremy@hgw.com state opening
```

continues

(Continued)

```
Jan  1 01:00:05.307: L2F: Tunnel authentication succeeded for ENT_HGW
Jan  1 01:00:05.391: L2F: L2F_OPEN received
Jan  1 01:00:05.391: L2F: Got a MID management packet
Jan  1 01:00:05.391: L2F: Removing resend packet (L2F_OPEN)
Jan  1 01:00:05.391: As12 L2F: MID jeremy@hgw.com state open
Jan  1 01:00:05.391: As12 L2F: MID synced NAS/HG Clid=47/12 Mid=1
Jan  1 01:00:05.523: L2F: L2F_CLOSE received
Jan  1 01:00:05.523: %VPDN-6-AUTHENERR: L2F HGW ENT_HGW cannot locate
a AAA server for As12 user jeremy@hgw.com; Authentication failure

ENT_HGW#
Jan  1 01:00:05.302: L2F: L2F_CONF received
Jan  1 01:00:05.302: L2F: Creating new tunnel for ISP_NAS
Jan  1 01:00:05.302:  L2F: Tunnel state closed
Jan  1 01:00:05.302: L2F: Got a tunnel named ISP_NAS, responding
Jan  1 01:00:05.302: L2F: Open UDP socket to 172.22.66.23
Jan  1 01:00:05.302: ISP_NAS L2F: Tunnel state opening
Jan  1 01:00:05.306: L2F: L2F_OPEN received
Jan  1 01:00:05.306: L2F: Removing resend packet (L2F_CONF)
Jan  1 01:00:05.306: ISP_NAS L2F: Tunnel state open
Jan  1 01:00:05.306: L2F: Tunnel authentication succeeded for ISP_NAS
Jan  1 01:00:05.310: L2F: L2F_OPEN received
Jan  1 01:00:05.310: L2F: L2F_CLIENT_INFO: CLID/DNIS 4089548021/
  5550945
Jan  1 01:00:05.310: L2F: L2F_CLIENT_INFO: NAS-Port Async12
Jan  1 01:00:05.310: L2F: L2F_CLIENT_INFO: Client-Bandwidth-Kbps 115
Jan  1 01:00:05.310: L2F: L2F_CLIENT_INFO: NAS-Rate L2F/26400/28800
Jan  1 01:00:05.310: L2F: Got a MID management packet
Jan  1 01:00:05.310:  L2F: MID  state closed
Jan  1 01:00:05.310: L2F: Start create mid intf process for
  jeremy@hgw.com
5w6d: %LINK-3-UPDOWN: Interface Virtual-Access1, changed state to up
Jan  1 01:00:05.390: Vi1 L2X: Discarding packet because of no mid
  session
Jan  1 01:00:05.390: Vi1 L2F: Transfer NAS-Rate L2F/26400/28800
  to LCP
Jan  1 01:00:05.390: Vi1 L2F: Finish create mid intf for
  jeremy@hgw.com
Jan  1 01:00:05.390: Vi1 L2F: MID jeremy@hgw.com state open
5w6d: %VPDN-6-AUTHENERR: L2F HGW ENT_HGW cannot locate a AAA server for
  Vi1
user jeremy@hgw.com; Authentication failure
```

Phase 3: Configuring the Access VPDN to Work with Remote AAA

In this third phase, the ISP and the enterprise customer perform the following tasks:

- Reconfigure the NAS and home gateway to work as an access VPDN using remote AAA. To ensure that the access VPDN is using remote AAA, the ISP and enterprise customer modify the AAA and VPDN configurations on the NAS and home gateway.

- Configure Cisco Secure ACS on the UNIX and NT servers. The NAS uses Cisco Secure UNIX to authenticate the user domain name and to determine the IP tunnel endpoint information. The home gateway uses Cisco Secure NT to authenticates the user username and password. The NAS and home gateway continue to use their local username databases to authenticate the tunnel.

- Verify that the access VPDN works properly.

- Troubleshoot the access VPDN if problems exist.

The ISP configures the NAS and Cisco Secure UNIX. The enterprise customer configures the home gateway and Cisco Secure NT. Figure 2-11 shows the access VPDN network topology.

Figure 2-11 *Access VPDN Topology Using Remote AAA*

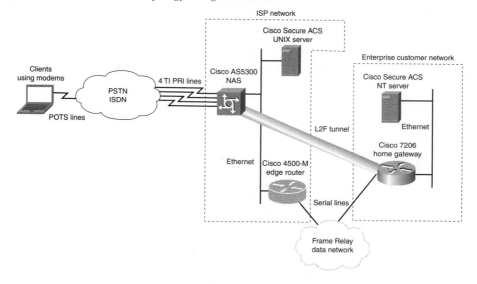

After the ISP and enterprise customer have completed this phase, the network will function as follows:

1 When the user wants to connect to the enterprise customer network, the user dials in to the NAS by using the username jeremy@hgw.com.

2 The NAS and the client perform LCP negotiation.

3 The Cisco Secure UNIX server authenticates the domain name, hgw.com, and supplies the NAS with the tunnel endpoint information.

4 The NAS negotiates an L2F tunnel with the home gateway. The NAS and home gateway authenticate the tunnel by using their local username databases, which contain the tunnel secret. After the tunnel has been established, the NAS forwards the call to the home gateway.

5 The Cisco Secure NT server authenticates the username and assigns the client an IP address. (It also can assign IP addresses for DNS and WINS servers.)

6 The client and the home gateway can now exchange PPP packets. The NAS now acts as a transparent PPP frame forwarder.

Configuring the NAS

To reconfigure the NAS to use remote AAA for VPDN tunneling, the ISP makes the following changes to the NAS configuration:

```
!Instructs AAA to first use the local database and then use the RADIUS
!server for PPP and VPDN authentication. The order of authentication
!methods is local
!first and RADIUS second because the tunnel is authenticated locally
!and the user domain name is authenticated by the RADIUS server.
 aaa authentication ppp default local radius
!Instructs AAA to use the Cisco Secure UNIX server to authorize network
!related service requests.
 aaa authorization network default radius
!
!Configures the Cisco Secure UNIX server IP address.
 radius-server host 172.22.66.18
!Defines a key to decrypt the data that runs between the NAS and the
!RADIUS server.
!This key must be configured as cisco because Cisco implementation of
!RADIUS has a hard-coded password of cisco. This is separate from the
!NAS and home gateway passwords used to authenticate each other.
 radius-server key cisco
!
!Removes the VPDN group because all tunneling information is now stored
!on the RADIUS server.
 no vpdn-group 1
```

Configuring the Home Gateway

To reconfigure the home gateway to use remote AAA for VPDN tunneling, the enterprise customer makes the following changes to the home gateway configuration:

```
!Instructs AAA to first use the local database and then use the RADIUS
!server for PPP and VPN authentication. The order of authentication
!methods is local first and RADIUS second because the tunnel is
```

(Continued)

```
!authenticated locally, and the user username and password are
!authenticated by the RADIUS server.
aaa authentication ppp default local radius
!Instructs AAA to use the RADIUS server to authorize network-related
!service requests.
aaa authorization network default radius
!Enables AAA accounting that sends a stop accounting notice at the end
!of the requested user process.
aaa accounting network default start-stop radius
!
!Specifies the RADIUS server IP address and the ports to be used for
!authentication and !accounting requests.
radius-server host 172.22.66.13 auth-port 1645 acct-port 1646
!Sets the authentication key and encryption key to cisco for all
!RADIUS communication.
radius-server key cisco
!
!Removes the jeremy@hgw.com username from the local database.This
!ensures that the home !gateway uses RADIUS instead of the local
!username database to authenticate the username.
no username jeremy@hgw.com
```

Configuring the Cisco Secure ACS UNIX Server

The ISP configures a RADIUS server to authenticate users' domain names and determine tunnel endpoint information. The ISP uses Cisco Secure ACS UNIX software for its RADIUS server. The following "vpdn" file contains all the VPDN RADIUS authentication and authorization attributes needed for the home gateway user:

```
vi vpdn

radius=Cisco11.3 {
check_items= {
2=cisco
6=5
}
reply_attributes= {
9,1="vpdn:gw-password=cisco"
9,1="vpdn:nas-password=cisco"
9,1="vpdn:tunnel-id=ISP_NAS"
9,1="vpdn:ip-addresses=172.22.66.25"
}
```

The following "ENT_HGW" file contains the password for the home gateway user:

```
vi ENT_HGW

radius=Cisco11.3 {
check_items= {
2=cisco
}
}
```

The following "ISP_NAS" file contains the password for the user created by the tunnel-id attribute:

```
vi ISP_NAS

radius=Cisco11.3 {
check_items= {
2=cisco
}
}
```

The following "nas_list" file configures the NAS at 172.22.66.23 as the only NAS:

```
vi nas_list

NAS.172.22.66.23
```

The following "nas1" file identifies the RADIUS dictionary that the NAS uses, the NAS IP address, the applicable vendor, and the shared secret key:

```
vi nas1

NASName="172.22.66.23"
SharedSecret="cisco"
RadiusVendor="Cisco"
Dictionary="DICTIONARY.Cisco11.3"
```

The following command deletes the default NAS list:

```
./DeleteProfile -p 9900 -u NAS_LIST
```

The following commands add the necessary profiles for the NAS, home gateway, and tunnel authentication:

```
./AddProfile -p 9900 -u NAS_LIST -s nas_list
./AddProfile -p 9900 -u NAS.172.22.66.23 -s nas1
./AddProfile -p 9900 -g NAS_Group
./AddProfile -p 9900 -u hgw.com -pr NAS_Group -s vpdn
./AddProfile -p 9900 -u ENT_HGW -pr NAS_Group -s ENT_HGW
./AddProfile -p 9900 -u ISP_NAS -pr NAS_Group -s ISP_NAS
```

The following command changes to the config working directory and modifies the CSU.cfg file to support VPDN accounting records:

```
cd /cs/config
vi CSU.cfg
DOMAIN config_local_domain =
        {
                {
                "hgw.com",
                "@",
                suffix
                }
        };
```

The following commands shut down and restart the Cisco Secure UNIX server, so that the new configuration will by active:

```
/etc/rc0.d/K80CiscoSecure
/etc/rc2.d/S80CiscoSecure
```

Configuring the Cisco Secure ACS NT Server

The enterprise configures a Cisco Secure ACS NT server to authenticate and authorize its users. The enterprise uses the Cisco Secure graphical user interface (GUI) to configure the server. Table 2-4 shows screen captures from the configuration process and describes the appropriate configuration selections.

Table 2-4   *Cisco Secure ACS NT Server Configuration*

Use This Display	To Do This
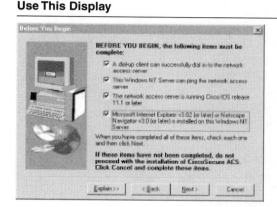	Install Cisco Secure NT. Before you can successfully install Cisco Secure NT, make sure the network meets the following criteria: • A client can successfully dial in to the NAS. If you have successfully configured the access VPDN to work with local AAA, you have met this criterion. • This Windows NT server can ping the NAS. If you have configured the access VPDN to work with local AAA, you have met this criterion. • The NAS is running Cisco IOS Release 11.1 or later release. • A compatible browser is installed on the Windows NT server. • On the Before You Begin screen, check all the corresponding boxes when the requirements are met. • Click Next.

continues

Table 2-4 *Cisco Secure ACS NT Server Configuration (Continued)*

Use This Display	To Do This
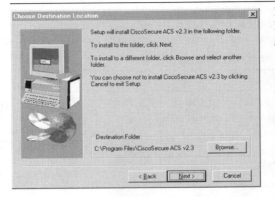	In the Choose Destination Location screen: <ul><li>Select the folder where Setup will install Cisco Secure NT.</li><li>Click Next.</li></ul>
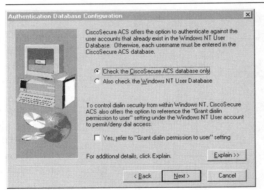	In the Authentication Database Configuration screen, define the database where Cisco Secure NT authenticates users. You have the option to use either the local Cisco Secure database or the local Cisco Secure database and the Windows NT user database. In this scenario, only the local Cisco Secure database is queried for user accounts. <ul><li>Click Check the CiscoSecure ACS database only.</li><li>Click Next.</li></ul>

Table 2-4   *Cisco Secure ACS NT Server Configuration (Continued)*

Use This Display	To Do This
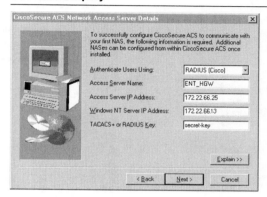	In the Cisco Secure ACS Network Access Server Details screen, select the security protocol. Remember that Cisco Secure NT calls the home gateway the network access server. • Select RADIUS (Cisco) in the security protocol box. • Type ENT_HGW in the Access Server Name box. • Type 172.22.66.25 in the Access Server IP Address box. • Type 172.22.66.13 in the Windows NT Server IP Address box. • Click Next.

continues

Table 2-4 *Cisco Secure ACS NT Server Configuration (Continued)*

Use This Display	To Do This
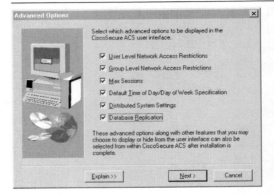	In the Advanced Options screen, define the advanced options that will appear in the Cisco Secure NT user interface. Check the following advanced options: <ul><li>User Level Network</li><li>Access Restrictions</li><li>Group Level Network Access Restrictions</li><li>Max Sessions</li><li>Default Time of Day/Day of Week Specification</li><li>Distributed System Settings</li><li>Database Replication</li><li>Click Next.</li></ul>
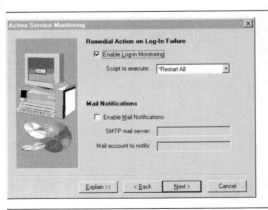	In the Active Service Monitoring screen, do the following: <ul><li>Check Enable Log-in Monitoring.</li><li>Select Script to execute: *Restart All.</li><li>Click Next.</li></ul>

Table 2-4   *Cisco Secure ACS NT Server Configuration (Continued)*

Use This Display	To Do This
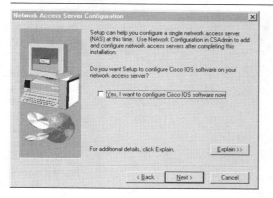	In the Network Access Server Configuration screen, click Next. Because you have already configured the home gateway, you need not use this automated configuration feature. Remember, Cisco Secure NT calls the home gateway the NAS. The installation is now complete.
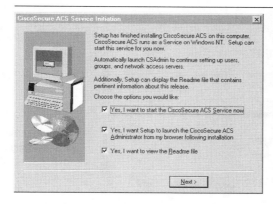	In the Cisco Secure ACS Service Initiation screen, you are asked whether you want to start Cisco Secure NT service immediately and whether you want Setup to launch the Cisco Secure NT Administrator from the installed browser immediately. To do so, do the following: • Check Yes, I want to start CiscoSecure ACS Service now. • Check Yes, I want Setup to launch the CiscoSecure ACS Administrator from my browser following installation. • Click Next.

continues

Table 2-4 *Cisco Secure ACS NT Server Configuration (Continued)*

Use This Display	To Do This
	In the Cisco Secure ACS Welcome screen, click Network Configuration. The address 127.0.0.1 is a loopback address. If you run the browser from the same system that Cisco Secure NT is installed on, this IP address appears in the HTTP browser field. However, if you want to run the browser on a system that differs from the one on which Cisco Secure NT has been installed, the actual IP address of the device appears in the box.
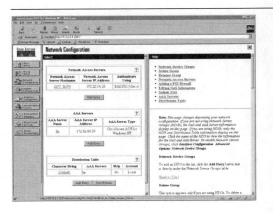	For Cisco Secure NT to authenticate a user, you must strip the domain name from the incoming username so that the username matches the form that Cisco Secure NT uses in its username/password database. In the Network Configuration screen, do the following: • Click Add Entry below the Distribution Table.

Table 2-4   *Cisco Secure ACS NT Server Configuration (Continued)*

Use This Display	To Do This
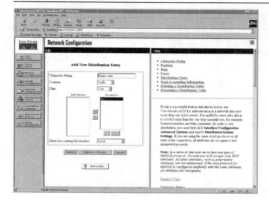	In the Add New Distribution Entry pane of the Network Configuration window, create a distribution entry: • Type **@hgw.com** in the Character string box. • Select Suffix in the Position box. • Select Yes in the Strip box. • Select ENT_HGW in the Forward to: box and click the right arrow to move it to the Forward To column. • Click Submit + Restart.
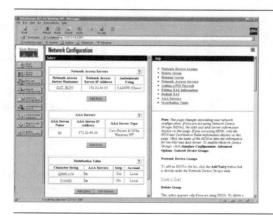	After you click Submit + Restart, a summary of the information you have configured appears. • Click User Setup.

continues

Table 2-4   *Cisco Secure ACS NT Server Configuration (Continued)*

Use This Display	To Do This
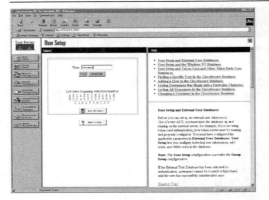	In the User Setup window, to create a user, do the following: • Type **jeremy** in the User box. • Click Add/Edit.
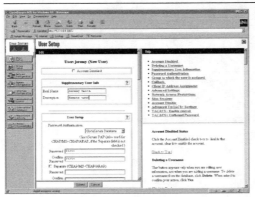	In the User Setup screen, add the following supplementary user information: • Type **Jeremy Smith** in the Real Name box. • Type **Remote user** in the Description box. • Select CiscoSecure Database in the Password Authentication box. • Type **subaru** in the Password box. • Type **subaru** in the Confirm box. • Click Submit. You have now created a user named jeremy.

Verifying the Access VPDN

This section describes how to verify that the end-to-end connections function as shown in Figure 2-11:

Step 1   Check the NAS Final Running Configuration

Step 2   Check the Home Gateway Final Running Configuration

Step 3   Dial In to the NAS

Step 4   Ping the Home Gateway

Step 5   Display Active Call Statistics on the Home Gateway

Step 6   Ping the Client

Step 7   Verify That the Virtual Access Interface Is Up and That LCP Is Open

Step 8   Display Active L2F Tunnel Statistics

After you successfully test these connections, the final end-to-end solution is built. If you experience problems, see the section "Troubleshooting the Access VPDN."

Step 1: Check the NAS Final Running Configuration

In this step, enter the **show running-config** privileged EXEC command to make sure that the NAS accepted the commands you entered. Commands in the following configuration that were not discussed in the preceding text do not directly pertain to the access VPDN and are therefore beyond the scope of this book.

```
ISP_NAS# show running-config

Building configuration...

Current configuration:
!
version 11.3
service timestamps debug datetime msec
service timestamps log datetime msec
service password-encryption
!
hostname ISP_NAS
!
```

continues

(Continued)

```
aaa new-model
aaa authentication ppp default radius
aaa authorization network default radius
enable secret 5 $1$AXl/$27hOM6j51a5P76Enq.LCf0
!
username jane-admin password 7 0501090A6C5C4F1A0A1218000F
username ENT_HGW password 7 104D000A0618
username ISP_NAS password 7 13061E010803
vpdn enable
!
vpdn search-order domain dnis
async-bootp dns-server 171.68.10.70 171.68.10.140
isdn switch-type primary-5ess
!
controller T1 0
 framing esf
 clock source line primary
 linecode b8zs
 pri-group timeslots 1-24
!
controller T1 1
 framing esf
 clock source line secondary
 linecode b8zs
 pri-group timeslots 1-24
!
controller T1 2
 framing esf
 clock source internal
 linecode b8zs
 pri-group timeslots 1-24
!
controller T1 3
 framing esf
 clock source internal
 linecode b8zs
 pri-group timeslots 1-24
!
!
interface Ethernet0
 ip address 172.22.66.23 255.255.255.192
!
interface Serial0:23
 no ip address
 isdn switch-type primary-5ess
 isdn incoming-voice modem
 no cdp enable
!
interface Serial1:23
 no ip address
 isdn switch-type primary-5ess
 isdn incoming-voice modem
 no cdp enable
!
interface Serial2:23
 no ip address
 isdn switch-type primary-5ess
 isdn incoming-voice modem
 no cdp enable
!
interface Serial3:23
 no ip address
```

```
 isdn switch-type primary-5ess
 isdn incoming-voice modem
 no cdp enable
!
interface FastEthernet0
 no ip address
 shutdown
!
interface Group-Async1
 ip unnumbered Ethernet0
 encapsulation ppp
 async mode interactive
 no peer default ip address
 ppp authentication chap pap
 group-range 1 96
!
ip classless
ip route 0.0.0.0 0.0.0.0 172.22.66.1
!
radius-server host 172.22.66.16 auth-port 1645 acct-port 1646
radius-server key cisco
!
line con 0
 transport input none
line 1 96
 autoselect during-login
 autoselect ppp
 modem inout
line aux 0
line vty 0 4
!
end
```

Step 2: Check the Home Gateway Final Running Configuration

In this step, enter the **show running-config** privileged EXEC command to make
sure that the home gateway accepted the commands you entered. Commands in the
following configuration that were not discussed in the preceding text do not directly
pertain to the access VPDN and are therefore beyond the scope of this book.

```
ENT_HGW# show running-config

Building configuration...

Current configuration:
!
version 12.0
service timestamps debug datetime msec
service timestamps log uptime
service password-encryption
!
hostname ENT_HGW
!
aaa new-model
aaa authentication login default local
aaa authentication ppp default local radius
aaa authorization network default radius
```

continues

(Continued)

```
                    aaa accounting network default start-stop radius
                    enable secret 5 $1$44oH$gZlAZLwylZJSNKGDk.BKb0
                    !
                    username jane-admin password 7 00001C05
                    username ISP_NAS password 7 070C285F4D06
                    username ENT_HGW password 7 104D000A0618
                    ip subnet-zero
                    ip domain-name cisco.com
                    ip name-server 171.68.10.70
                    !
                    vpdn enable
                    !
                    vpdn-group 1
                     accept dialin
                       protocol l2f
                       virtual-template 1
                     terminate-from hostname ISP_NAS
                     local name ENT_HGW
                    !
                    async-bootp dns-server 172.23.1.10 172.23.2.10
                    async-bootp nbns-server 172.23.1.11 172.23.2.11
                    !
                    !
                    !
                    interface FastEthernet0/0
                     ip address 172.22.66.25 255.255.255.192
                     no ip directed-broadcast
                    !
                    .
                    .
                    .
                    interface Virtual-Template1
                     ip unnumbered FastEthernet0/0
                     peer default ip address pool default
                     ppp authentication chap
                    !
                    ip local pool default 172.30.2.1 172.30.2.96
                    ip classless
                    ip route 0.0.0.0 0.0.0.0 172.22.66.1
                    !
                    radius-server host 172.22.66.13 auth-port 1645 acct-port 1646
                    radius-server key cisco
                    !
                    line con 0
                     transport input none
                    line aux 0
                    line vty 0 4
                     password 7 045F0405
                    !
                    end
```

Step 3: Dial In to the NAS

In this step, from the client, dial in to the NAS by using the PRI telephone number assigned to the NAS T1 trunks. Sometimes this telephone number is called the hunt group number.

As the call comes into the NAS, a LINK-3-UPDOWN message automatically appears on the NAS terminal screen. In this example, the call comes in to the NAS on asynchronous interface 14. The asynchronous interface is up.

```
*Jan  1 21:22:18.410: %LINK-3-UPDOWN: Interface Async14, changed state
to up
```

NOTE	No **debug** commands are turned on to display this log message. Start troubleshooting the NAS if this message does not display within 30 seconds of the client initiating the call.

Step 4: Ping the Home Gateway

In this step, from the client, ping the home gateway. On the desktop of the client, perform the following steps:

Step 1   Click Start.

Step 2   Select Run.

Step 3   Enter **ping 172.22.66.25**.

Step 4   Click OK.

Step 5   Look at the terminal screen and verify that the home gateway is sending ping reply packets to the client.

Step 5: Display Active Call Statistics on the Home Gateway

In this step, from the home gateway, enter the **show caller** user EXEC command and **show caller user jeremy@hgw.com** user EXEC command to verify that the client received an IP address. This example shows that Jeremy is using interface virtual access 1 and IP address 172.30.2.1. The network administrator jane-admin is using console 0.

```
ENT_HGW# show caller

    Line          User             Service      Active
    con 0         jane-admin        TTY         00:00:25
    Vi1           jeremy@hgw.com    PPP   L2F   00:01:28

ENT_HGW# show caller user jeremy@hgw.com
```

continues

(Continued)

```
User: jeremy@hgw.com, line Vi1, service PPP L2F, active 00:01:35
  PPP: LCP Open, CHAP (<- AAA), IPCP
  IP: Local 172.22.66.25, remote 172.30.2.1
VPDN: NAS ISP_NAS, MID 1, MID open
      HGW  ENT_HGW, NAS CLID 36, HGW CLID 1, tunnel open
Counts: 105 packets input, 8979 bytes, 0 no buffer
        0 input errors, 0 CRC, 0 frame, 0 overrun
        18 packets output, 295 bytes, 0 underruns
        0 output errors, 0 collisions, 0 interface resets
```

NOTE   The **show caller** command was introduced in Cisco IOS Release 11.3(5)AA. If your Cisco IOS software does not include the **show caller** command, use the **show user** command instead.

Step 6: Ping the Client

In this step, from the home gateway, ping the client at IP address 172.30.2.1:

```
ENT_HGW# ping 172.30.2.1

Type escape sequence to abort.
Sending 5, 100-byte ICMP Echos to 172.30.2.1, timeout is 2 seconds:
!!!!!
Success rate is 100 percent (5/5), round-trip min/avg/max = 128/132/152
  ms
```

Step 7: Verify That the Virtual Access Interface Is Up and That LCP Is Open

In this step, from the home gateway, enter the **show interfaces virtual-access 1** privileged EXEC command to verify that the interface is up, LCP is open, and no errors are reported:

```
ENT_HGW# show interfaces virtual-access 1

Virtual-Access1 is up, line protocol is up
  Hardware is Virtual Access interface
  Interface is unnumbered. Using address of FastEthernet0/0
    (172.22.66.25)
  MTU 1500 bytes, BW 115 Kbit, DLY 100000 usec,
      reliabilility 255/255, txload 1/255, rxload 1/255
  Encapsulation PPP, loopback not set, keepalive set (10 sec)
  DTR is pulsed for 5 seconds on reset
  LCP Open
  Open: IPCP
  Last input 00:00:02, output never, output hang never
  Last clearing of "show interface" counters 3d00h
  Queueing strategy: fifo
```

```
Output queue 1/40, 0 drops; input queue 0/75, 0 drops
   5 minute input rate 0 bits/sec, 0 packets/sec
   5 minute output rate 0 bits/sec, 0 packets/sec
      114 packets input, 9563 bytes, 0 no buffer
      Received 0 broadcasts, 0 runts, 0 giants, 0 throttles
      0 input errors, 0 CRC, 0 frame, 0 overrun, 0 ignored, 0 abort
      27 packets output, 864 bytes, 0 underruns
      0 output errors, 0 collisions, 0 interface resets
      0 output buffer failures, 0 output buffers swapped out
      0 carrier transitions
```

Step 8: Display Active L2F Tunnel Statistics

In this step, from the home gateway, display active tunnel statistics by entering the **show vpdn** privileged EXEC command and **show vpdn tunnel all** privileged EXEC command:

```
ENT_HGW# show vpdn

% No active L2TP tunnels

L2F Tunnel and Session

NAS CLID HGW CLID NAS Name        HGW Name        State
36       1         ISP_NAS        ENT_HGW         open
                   172.22.66.23   172.22.66.25

CLID   MID     Username                 Intf   State
36     1       jeremy@hgw.com           Vi1    open

ENT_HGW# show vpdn tunnel all

% No active L2TP tunnels

L2F Tunnel
NAS name: ISP_NAS
NAS CLID: 36
NAS IP address 172.22.66.23
Gateway name: ENT_HGW
Gateway CLID: 1
Gateway IP address 172.22.66.25
State: open
Packets out: 52
Bytes out: 1799
Packets in: 100
Bytes in: 7143
```

Troubleshooting the Access VPDN

This section provides the ISP and enterprise customer with a methodology for troubleshooting the access VPDN as described in Figure 2-12. Step 1 shows debug output from a successful call. If your debug output does not match the successful output, follow the remaining steps to begin troubleshooting the network. The shaded lines of debug output indicate important information.

Step 1 Compare Your Debug Output to the Successful Debug Output

Step 2 Troubleshoot L2F Negotiation

Step 3 Troubleshoot PPP Negotiation

Step 4 Troubleshoot AAA Negotiation

If you are accessing the NAS and home gateway through a Telnet connection, you need to enable the **terminal monitor** user EXEC command. This command ensures that your EXEC session is receiving the logging and debug output from the devices.

When you finish troubleshooting, use the **undebug all** privileged EXEC command to turn off all **debug** commands. Isolating debug output helps you efficiently build a network.

Figure 2-12 *Troubleshooting Flow Diagram for Access VPDN with Remote AAA*

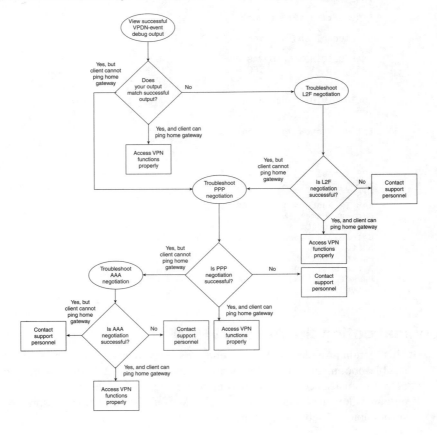

Step 1: Compare Your Debug Output to the Successful Debug Output

In this step, enable the **debug vpdn-event** privileged EXEC command on both the NAS and the home gateway and dial in to the NAS. The following debug output shows successful VPDN negotiation on the NAS and home gateway:

```
ISP_NAS#
Jan  7 00:19:35.900: %LINK-3-UPDOWN: Interface Async9, changed state to
  up
Jan  7 00:19:39.532: sVPDN: Got DNIS string As9
Jan  7 00:19:39.532: As9 VPDN: Looking for tunnel -- hgw.com --
Jan  7 00:19:39.540: As9 VPDN: Get tunnel info for hgw.com with NAS
  ISP_NAS,
IP172.22.66.25
Jan  7 00:19:39.540: As9 VPDN: Forward to address 172.22.66.25
Jan  7 00:19:39.540: As9 VPDN: Forwarding...
Jan  7 00:19:39.540: As9 VPDN: Bind interface direction=1
Jan  7 00:19:39.540: As9 VPDN: jeremy@hgw.com is forwarded
Jan  7 00:19:40.540: %LINEPROTO-5-UPDOWN: Line protocol on Interface
  Async9,
changed state to up

ENT_HGW#
Jan  7 00:19:39.967: VPDN: Chap authentication succeeded for ISP_NAS
Jan  7 00:19:39.967: Vi1 VPDN: Virtual interface created for
  jeremy@hgw.com
Jan  7 00:19:39.967: Vi1 VPDN: Set to Async interface
Jan  7 00:19:39.971: Vi1 VPDN: Clone from Vtemplate 1 filterPPP=0
  blocking
6w5d: %LINK-3-UPDOWN: Interface Virtual-Access1, changed state to up
Jan  7 00:19:40.051: Vi1 VPDN: Bind interface direction=2
Jan  7 00:19:40.051: Vi1 VPDN: PPP LCP accepted rcv CONFACK
Jan  7 00:19:40.051: Vi1 VPDN: PPP LCP accepted sent CONFACK
6w5d: %LINEPROTO-5-UPDOWN: Line protocol on Interface Virtual-Access1,
changed state to up
```

If you see this debug output but cannot ping the home gateway, go on to the section "Step 3: Troubleshoot PPP Negotiation."

If you do not see this debug output, go on to the section "Step 2: Troubleshoot L2F Negotiation."

Step 2: Troubleshoot L2F Negotiation

This step describes several common misconfigurations that prevent successful L2F negotiation.

- Misconfigured NAS Tunnel Secret
- Misconfigured Home Gateway Tunnel Secret
- Misconfigured Tunnel Name

Misconfigured NAS Tunnel Secret

The NAS and the home gateway must both have the same usernames with the same password to authenticate the L2F tunnel. These usernames are called the tunnel secret. In this solution, these usernames are ISP_NAS and ENT_HGW. The password is "cisco" for both usernames on both systems.

If one of the tunnel secrets on the NAS is incorrect, you will see the following debug output when you dial in to the NAS and the **debug vpdn l2x-errors** privileged EXEC command is enabled on the NAS and home gateway:

```
ISP_NAS#
Jan  1 00:26:49.899: %LINK-3-UPDOWN: Interface Async3, changed state to
  up
Jan  1 00:26:54.643: %LINEPROTO-5-UPDOWN: Line protocol on Interface
  Async3, changed state to up
Jan  1 00:27:00.559: L2F: Resending L2F_OPEN, time #1
Jan  1 00:27:05.559: L2F: Resending L2F_ECHO, time #1
Jan  1 00:27:05.559: L2F: Resending L2F_OPEN, time #2
Jan  1 00:27:10.559: L2F: Resending L2F_ECHO, time #2
Jan  1 00:27:10.559: L2F: Resending L2F_OPEN, time #3
Jan  1 00:27:15.559: L2F: Resending L2F_ECHO, time #3
Jan  1 00:27:15.559: L2F: Resending L2F_OPEN, time #4
Jan  1 00:27:20.559: L2F: Resending L2F_ECHO, time #4
Jan  1 00:27:20.559: L2F: Resending L2F_OPEN, time #5
Jan  1 00:27:25.559: L2F: Resending L2F_ECHO, time #5
Jan  1 00:27:25.559: L2F: Resend packet (type 2) around too long,
time to kill off the tunnel
ISP_NAS#

ENT_HGW#
Jan  1 00:26:53.645: L2F: Packet has bogus2 key C8353FAB B6369121
5w6d: %VPDN-6-AUTHENFAIL: L2F HGW , authentication failure for  tunnel
ISP_NAS; Invalid key
5w6d: %VPDN-5-UNREACH: L2F NAS 172.22.66.23 is unreachable
Jan  1 00:27:00.557: L2F: Gateway received tunnel OPEN while in state
  closed
ENT_HGW#
```

The phrase "time to kill off the tunnel" in the NAS debug output indicates that the tunnel was not opened. The phrase "Packet has bogus2 key" in the home gateway debug output indicates that the NAS has an incorrect tunnel secret.

To avoid this problem, make sure that you configure both the NAS and home gateway for the same two tunnel secret usernames with the same password.

Misconfigured Home Gateway Tunnel Secret

If one of the tunnel secret usernames on the home gateway is incorrect, you will see the following debug output when you dial in to the NAS and the **debug vpdn l2x-errors** privileged EXEC command is enabled on the NAS and home gateway.

```
ISP_NAS#
Jan  1 00:45:27.123: %LINK-3-UPDOWN: Interface Async7, changed state
  to up
Jan  1 00:45:30.939: L2F: Packet has bogus1 key B6C656EE 5FAC6B3
Jan  1 00:45:30.939: %VPDN-6-AUTHENFAIL: L2F NAS ISP_NAS,
  authentication failure
  for  tunnel ENT_HGW; Invalid key
Jan  1 00:45:31.935: %LINEPROTO-5-UPDOWN: Line protocol on Interface
  Async7, changed state to up
Jan  1 00:45:35.559: L2F: Resending L2F_OPEN, time #1
Jan  1 00:45:35.559: L2F: Packet has bogus1 key B6C656EE 5FAC6B3

ENT_HGW#
Jan  1 00:45:30.939: L2F: Tunnel authentication succeeded for ISP_NAS
Jan  1 00:45:35.559: L2F: Gateway received tunnel OPEN while in state
  open
Jan  1 00:45:40.559: L2F: Gateway received tunnel OPEN while in state
  open
Jan  1 00:45:45.559: L2F: Gateway received tunnel OPEN while in state
  open
Jan  1 00:45:50.559: L2F: Gateway received tunnel OPEN while in state
  open
```

Notice how this output is similar to the debug output you see when the NAS has a misconfigured tunnel secret username. This time you see the phrase "Packet has bogus1 key" on the NAS rather than the home gateway. This message tells you that the home gateway has an incorrect tunnel secret username.

To avoid this problem, make sure that you configure both the NAS and home gateway for the same two tunnel secret usernames with the same password.

Misconfigured Tunnel Name

If the NAS and home gateway do not have matching tunnel names, they cannot establish an L2F tunnel. On the home gateway, these tunnel names are configured under the **vpdn-group 1** global configuration command by using the **local name** VPDN group command. On the NAS, these names are configured on the Cisco Secure UNIX server.

The home gateway must be configured to accept tunnels from the name the NAS sends it. This is done by configuring a VPDN group using the following commands:

```
vpdn-group 1
 accept dialin
  protocol l2f
  virtual-template 1
 terminate-from hostname ISP_NAS
 local name ENT_HGW
```

On the Cisco Secure UNIX server, the tunnel names are configured by adding profiles to the NAS_Group group with the names ISP_NAS and ENT_HGW.

The home gateway is configured to accept tunnels from a NAS identifying itself as ISP_NAS. The name the home gateway returns to the NAS is configured by using the **local name ENT_HGW** VPDN group configuration command where ENT_HGW is the name.

In the following debug output, the NAS attempted to open a tunnel by using the name isp. Because the home gateway did not know this name, it did not open the tunnel. To see the following debug output, enable the **debug vpdn l2x-events** and **debug vpdn l2x-errors** privileged EXEC commands on the home gateway:

```
ENT_HGW#
Jan  1 01:28:54.207: L2F: L2F_CONF received
Jan  1 01:28:54.207: L2X: Never heard of isp
Jan  1 01:28:54.207: L2F: Couldn't find tunnel named isp
```

To avoid this problem, make sure that the tunnel names match on the home gateway and on the Cisco Secure UNIX server.

If you fixed the problem in your configuration, return to the section "Verifying Basic Dial Access."

If your call still cannot successfully complete L2F negotiation, contact your support personnel.

Step 3: Troubleshoot PPP Negotiation

In this step, enable the **debug ppp negotiation** privileged EXEC command on the home gateway and dial in to the NAS. You should not need to enable this command on the NAS because you already verified dialup connectivity to the NAS in the section "Configuring the NAS for Basic Dial Access."

The following debug output shows successful PPP negotiation on the home gateway:

```
1d02h: %LINK-3-UPDOWN: Interface Virtual-Access1, changed state to up
*Feb  4 14:14:40.505: Vi1 PPP: Treating connection as a dedicated line
*Feb  4 14:14:40.505: Vi1 PPP: Phase is ESTABLISHING, Active Open
```

```
*Feb  4 14:14:40.505: Vi1 PPP: Treating connection as a dedicated line
*Feb  4 14:14:40.505: Vi1 PPP: Phase is AUTHENTICATING, by this end
*Feb  4 14:14:40.509: Vi1 PPP: Phase is UP
```

If your call successfully completed PPP negotiation but you still cannot ping the home gateway, go to the section "Step 4: Troubleshoot AAA Negotiation."

If your call cannot successfully complete PPP negotiation, contact your support personnel.

Step 4: Troubleshoot AAA Negotiation

The following sections show debug output of successful AAA negotiation and then explains the following common misconfigurations that prevent successful AAA negotiation.

- Incorrect User Password
- Error Contacting RADIUS Server
- Misconfigured AAA Authentication

Successful AAA Negotiation

Enable the **debug aaa authentication** and **debug aaa authorization** privileged EXEC commands on the home gateway and dial in to the NAS.

The following debug output shows successful AAA negotiation on the home gateway. This output has been edited to exclude repetitive lines.

```
ENT_HGW#
Jan  7 19:29:44.132: AAA/AUTHEN: create_user (0x612D550C)
  user='ENT_HGW' ruser='
' port='' rem_addr='' authen_type=CHAP service=PPP priv=1
Jan  7 19:29:44.132: AAA/AUTHEN/START (384300079): port=''
  list='default' action
=SENDAUTH service=PPP
Jan  7 19:29:44.132: AAA/AUTHEN/START (384300079): found list default
Jan  7 19:29:44.132: AAA/AUTHEN/START (384300079): Method=LOCAL
Jan  7 19:29:44.132: AAA/AUTHEN (384300079): status = PASS
Jan  7 19:29:44.132: AAA/AUTHEN: create_user (0x612D550C)
  user='ISP_NAS' ruser='
' port='' rem_addr='' authen_type=CHAP service=PPP priv=1
Jan  7 19:29:44.132: AAA/AUTHEN/START (2545876944): port=''
  list='default' actio
n=SENDAUTH service=PPP
Jan  7 19:29:44.132: AAA/AUTHEN/START (2545876944): found list default
```

continues

(Continued)

```
Jan  7 19:29:44.132: AAA/AUTHEN/START (2545876944): Method=LOCAL
Jan  7 19:29:44.132: AAA/AUTHEN (2545876944): status = PASS
Jan  7 19:29:44.228: AAA/AUTHEN: create_user (0x612F1F78)
 user='jeremy@hgw.com'
ruser='' port='Virtual-Access1' rem_addr='408/5550945'
 authen_type=CHAP service=
PPP priv=1
Jan  7 19:29:44.228: AAA/AUTHEN/START (101773535): port='Virtual
 Access1'
list='' action=LOGIN service=PPP
Jan  7 19:29:44.228: AAA/AUTHEN/START (101773535): using "default"
 list
Jan  7 19:29:44.228: AAA/AUTHEN/START (101773535): Method=LOCAL
Jan  7 19:29:44.228: AAA/AUTHEN (101773535): status = ERROR
Jan  7 19:29:44.228: AAA/AUTHEN/START (101773535): Method=RADIUS
Jan  7 19:29:44.692: AAA/AUTHEN (101773535): status = PASS
Jan  7 19:29:44.692: Vi1 AAA/AUTHOR/LCP: Authorize LCP
Jan  7 19:29:44.692: AAA/AUTHOR/LCP Vi1 (3630870259): Port='Virtual
 Access1'
list='' service=NET
Jan  7 19:29:44.692: AAA/AUTHOR/LCP: Vi1 (3630870259)
 user='jeremy@hgw.com'
Jan  7 19:29:44.692: AAA/AUTHOR/LCP: Vi1 (3630870259) send AV
 service=ppp
Jan  7 19:29:44.692: AAA/AUTHOR/LCP: Vi1 (3630870259) send AV
 protocol=lcp
Jan  7 19:29:44.692: AAA/AUTHOR/LCP (3630870259) found list "default"
Jan  7 19:29:44.692: AAA/AUTHOR/LCP: Vi1 (3630870259) Method=RADIUS
Jan  7 19:29:44.692: AAA/AUTHOR (3630870259): Post authorization
 status =
PASS_REPL
Jan  7 19:29:44.696: Vi1 AAA/AUTHOR/FSM: We can start IPCP
6w5d: %LINEPROTO-5-UPDOWN: Line protocol on Interface Virtual-Access1,
changed state to up
Jan  7 19:29:47.792: Vi1 AAA/AUTHOR/IPCP: Start.  Her address 0.0.0.0,
we want 172.30.2.1
```

If this debug output appears but you still cannot ping the home gateway, contact your support personnel and troubleshoot your network backbone.

If you did not see this debug output, you need to troubleshoot AAA negotiation.

Incorrect User Password

If the user password is incorrect (or it is incorrectly configured), the tunnel will be established but the home gateway will not authenticate the user. If the user password is incorrect, the following debug output appears on the NAS and home gateway when you dial in to the NAS and the **debug vpdn l2x-errors** and **debug vpdn l2x-events** privileged EXEC commands are enabled:

```
ISP_NAS#
Jan  1 01:00:01.555: %LINK-3-UPDOWN: Interface Async12, changed state
   to up
Jan  1 01:00:05.299:  L2F: Tunnel state closed
Jan  1 01:00:05.299:  L2F: MID   state closed
Jan  1 01:00:05.299: L2F: Open UDP socket to 172.22.66.25
Jan  1 01:00:05.299:  L2F: Tunnel state opening
Jan  1 01:00:05.299: As12 L2F: MID jeremy@hgw.com state
   waiting_for_tunnel
Jan  1 01:00:05.303: L2F: L2F_CONF received
Jan  1 01:00:05.303: L2F: Removing resend packet (L2F_CONF)
Jan  1 01:00:05.303: ENT_HGW L2F: Tunnel state open
Jan  1 01:00:05.307: L2F: L2F_OPEN received
Jan  1 01:00:05.307: L2F: Removing resend packet (L2F_OPEN)
Jan  1 01:00:05.307: L2F: Building nas2gw_mid0
Jan  1 01:00:05.307: L2F: L2F_CLIENT_INFO: CLID/DNIS 4089548021/
   5550945
Jan  1 01:00:05.307: L2F: L2F_CLIENT_INFO: NAS-Port Async12
Jan  1 01:00:05.307: L2F: L2F_CLIENT_INFO: Client-Bandwidth-Kbps 115
Jan  1 01:00:05.307: L2F: L2F_CLIENT_INFO: NAS-Rate L2F/26400/28800
Jan  1 01:00:05.307: As12 L2F: MID jeremy@hgw.com state opening
Jan  1 01:00:05.307: L2F: Tunnel authentication succeeded for ENT_HGW
Jan  1 01:00:05.391: L2F: L2F_OPEN received
Jan  1 01:00:05.391: L2F: Got a MID management packet
Jan  1 01:00:05.391: L2F: Removing resend packet (L2F_OPEN)
Jan  1 01:00:05.391: As12 L2F: MID jeremy@hgw.com state open
Jan  1 01:00:05.391: As12 L2F: MID synced NAS/HG Clid=47/12 Mid=1
Jan  1 01:00:05.523: L2F: L2F_CLOSE received
Jan  1 01:00:05.523: %VPDN-6-AUTHENERR: L2F HGW ENT_HGW cannot locate
a AAA server for As12 user jeremy@hgw.com; Authentication failure

ENT_HGW#
Jan  1 01:00:05.302: L2F: L2F_CONF received
Jan  1 01:00:05.302: L2F: Creating new tunnel for ISP_NAS
Jan  1 01:00:05.302:  L2F: Tunnel state closed
Jan  1 01:00:05.302: L2F: Got a tunnel named ISP_NAS, responding
Jan  1 01:00:05.302: L2F: Open UDP socket to 172.22.66.23
Jan  1 01:00:05.302: ISP_NAS L2F: Tunnel state opening
Jan  1 01:00:05.306: L2F: L2F_OPEN received
Jan  1 01:00:05.306: L2F: Removing resend packet (L2F_CONF)
Jan  1 01:00:05.306: ISP_NAS L2F: Tunnel state open
Jan  1 01:00:05.306: L2F: Tunnel authentication succeeded for ISP_NAS
Jan  1 01:00:05.310: L2F: L2F_OPEN received
Jan  1 01:00:05.310: L2F: L2F_CLIENT_INFO: CLID/DNIS 4089548021/
   5550945
Jan  1 01:00:05.310: L2F: L2F_CLIENT_INFO: NAS-Port Async12
Jan  1 01:00:05.310: L2F: L2F_CLIENT_INFO: Client-Bandwidth-Kbps 115
Jan  1 01:00:05.310: L2F: L2F_CLIENT_INFO: NAS-Rate L2F/26400/28800
```

continues

(Continued)

```
Jan  1 01:00:05.310: L2F: Got a MID management packet
Jan  1 01:00:05.310:  L2F: MID  state closed
Jan  1 01:00:05.310: L2F: Start create mid intf process for
  jeremy@hgw.com
5w6d: %LINK-3-UPDOWN: Interface Virtual-Access1, changed state to up
Jan  1 01:00:05.390: Vi1 L2X: Discarding packet because of no mid
  session
Jan  1 01:00:05.390: Vi1 L2F: Transfer NAS-Rate L2F/26400/28800 to LCP
Jan  1 01:00:05.390: Vi1 L2F: Finish create mid intf for
  jeremy@hgw.com
Jan  1 01:00:05.390: Vi1 L2F: MID jeremy@hgw.com state open
5w6d: %VPDN-6-AUTHENERR: L2F HGW ENT_HGW cannot locate a AAA server
  for Vi1
user jeremy@hgw.com; Authentication failure
```

Error Contacting RADIUS Server

If the **aaa authorization** global configuration command on the home gateway is
configured with the **default radius none** keywords, the home gateway may allow
unauthorized access to your network.

This command is an instruction to first use RADIUS for authorization. The home
gateway first contacts the RADIUS server (because of the **radius** keyword). If
an error occurs when the home gateway contacts the RADIUS server, the home
gateway does not authorize the user (because of the **none** keyword).

To display the following debug output, enable the **debug aaa authorization**
privileged EXEC command on the home gateway and dial in to the NAS:

```
ENT_HGW#
*Feb  5 17:27:36.166: Vi1 AAA/AUTHOR/LCP: Authorize LCP
*Feb  5 17:27:36.166: AAA/AUTHOR/LCP Vi1 (3192359105): Port='Virtual
  Access1' list='' service=NET
*Feb  5 17:27:36.166: AAA/AUTHOR/LCP: Vi1 (3192359105)
  user='jeremy@hgw.com'
*Feb  5 17:27:36.166: AAA/AUTHOR/LCP: Vi1 (3192359105) send AV
  service=ppp
*Feb  5 17:27:36.166: AAA/AUTHOR/LCP: Vi1 (3192359105) send AV
  protocol=lcp
*Feb  5 17:27:36.166: AAA/AUTHOR/LCP (3192359105) found list "default"
*Feb  5 17:27:36.166: AAA/AUTHOR/LCP: Vi1 (3192359105) Method=RADIUS
*Feb  5 17:27:36.166: AAA/AUTHOR (3192359105): Post authorization
  status = ERROR
*Feb  5 17:27:36.166: AAA/AUTHOR/LCP: Vi1 (3192359105) Method=NONE
*Feb  5 17:27:36.166: AAA/AUTHOR (3192359105): Post authorization
  status = PASS_ADD
*Feb  5 17:27:36.166: Vi1 CHAP: O SUCCESS id 1 len 4
```

CAUTION	Using the **none** keyword can allow unauthorized access to your network. Because of the risk of such errors occurring, we strongly suggest that you do not use the **none** keyword in your **aaa** commands.

Misconfigured AAA Authentication

If you reverse the order of the **local** and **radius** keywords in the **aaa authentication ppp** global configuration command on the home gateway, the L2F tunnel cannot be established. The command should be configured as **aaa authentication ppp default local radius**.

If you configure the command as **aaa authentication ppp default radius local**, the home gateway first tries to authenticate the L2F tunnel using RADIUS. The RADIUS server sends the following message to the home gateway. To display this message, enable the **debug radius** EXEC command.

```
ENT_HGW#
Jan  1 01:34:47.827: RADIUS: SENDPASS not supported (action=4)
```

The RADIUS protocol does not support inbound challenges, which means that RADIUS is designed to authenticate user information, but it is not designed to be authenticated by others. When the home gateway requests the tunnel secret from the RADIUS server, it responds with the "SENDPASS not supported" message.

To avoid this problem, use the **aaa authentication ppp default local radius** command on the home gateway.

If your call still cannot successfully complete AAA negotiation, contact your support personnel.

CHAPTER 3

Access VPDN Dial-In Using L2TP Solution

An access virtual private dial network (VPDN) is a shared network infrastructure that enables users belonging to different organizations to access their different LANs by using remote dial connections. Access VPDNs maintain the same security and management policies as a private network. They are a cost-effective way to establish long-distance point-to-point connections between remote users and a private network.

NOTE   Access VPDNs should not be confused with dedicated virtual private networks (VPNs)—also called intranet VPNs or extranet VPNs. Dedicated VPNs connect remote offices to private networks using permanent, dedicated connections. Access VPDNs provide remote access to private networks using analog, ISDN, mobile IP, and cable technologies.

This chapter describes the basics of designing, implementing, and verifying an access VPDN dial-in network that uses L2TP as the tunneling protocol. In this solution, a large ISP partners with a medium-sized service provider and an enterprise customer to implement the network.

This chapter does not discuss advanced topics associated with access VPDNs such as remote AAA, accounting, load balancing and backup, user segmentation, L2TP dial-out, multihop VPDN, and network management.

This chapter contains the following sections:

- Business Objectives
- Possible Solutions
- Proposed Solution: NAS-Initiated VPDN Using L2TP
- Implementation
- Device Characteristics and Configuration Files
- Verifying the Access VPDN Network

Business Objectives

This section describes the business objectives of the three partners in this solution: a large ISP, a medium-sized service provider, and an enterprise customer.

ISP

ISPs need to offer value-added services to their customers to differentiate themselves in increasingly competitive markets. ISPs want to expand beyond traditional Internet access service and offer IT outsourcing to enterprises, but they do not want to take on the added responsibilities of maintaining user databases of enterprises. Access VPDNs enable ISPs to offer IT outsourcing in which enterprises maintain their own user databases.

Medium-Sized Service Provider

Medium-sized service providers want to be able to offer roaming service that enables their customers to log in from remote locations. To provide this service using their own network, service providers need to either maintain servers in remote locations or support long-distance phone numbers or 800 numbers. However, these options can be very expensive. Therefore, service providers can instead partner with large ISPs to lease use of their extended network infrastructures. This practice is called wholesale dial service. Wholesale dial enables medium-sized service providers to quickly, easily, and relatively inexpensively expand the range of their networks and stay competitive with large ISPs.

Enterprise Customer

Enterprises need to enable their employees to access their private networks from remote locations. Traditionally, meeting this need requires the purchase of expensive network access servers (NASs), monthly charges for WAN circuit connections, the hiring of network administrators to maintain the NASs, and expensive long-distance and 800 number phone bills. Access VPDNs offer a simpler and less expensive alternative.

Original Network Topology

This section describes the service provider and enterprise networks before they implement the access VPDN network. Their networks are shown in Figure 3-1.

Figure 3-1   *Original Network Topology*

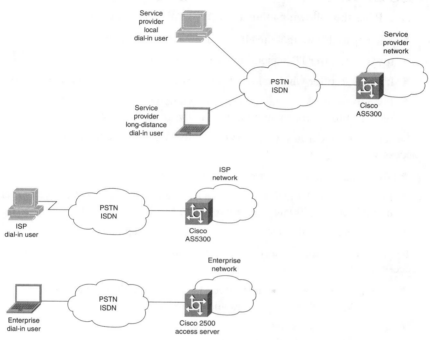

NOTE	The devices in the lighter shade of gray in Figure 3-1 are not involved in the implementation of the access VPDN network.

The three networks function independently of each other. The ISP, service provider, and enterprise each maintains its own access server.

The ISP has traffic only from its own dial-in users.

To provide worldwide roaming dialup service, the service provider must maintain an 800 number that generates expensive long-distance phone calls. When customers need to access the network from overseas, they must deal with expensive and often problematic international phone service.

The enterprise customer must maintain its own access server in order to allow employees and partners to remotely access the enterprise network. The enterprise must maintain its own IT infrastructure and networking expertise, including leasing its own IP address subnet and WAN circuits. These IT responsibilities distract from its core business responsibilities. When employees need to access the network from remote locations, the enterprise must pay for expensive long-distance phone calls.

Business Drivers

The ISP has the following motivations for establishing the access VPDN:

- It needs to differentiate itself in the competitive ISP market.
- It wants to offer IT outsourcing service to enterprise customers.
- It wants to offer wholesale dial services to medium-sized service providers.
- It wants to focus on maintaining its own network while limiting added responsibilities for maintaining the networks of its customers.

The service provider has the following motivations for establishing the access VPDN:

- To remain competitive, it must offer worldwide roaming dialup service.
- Leasing access VPDN service from a large ISP is more cost-effective than maintaining an 800 number for roaming service.
- It does not have the resources to maintain geographically dispersed PoPs.

The enterprise customer has the following motivations for establishing the access VPDN:

- As the enterprise grows, it is forced to purchase additional access servers and lease additional phone lines to allow its employees remote access.
- As the IT infrastructure of the enterprise increases, the enterprise must hire additional network administrators.
- The increasing complexity of the IT infrastructure of the enterprise causes increased network delays and failures.
- As the territory of the enterprise expands, costs of long-distance and 800 number phone bills from employees accessing the enterprise network increase.

Possible Solutions

This section describes the fundamental design choices that define an access VPDN solution. VPDNs are designed based on one of two architectural options: client-initiated or network access server (NAS)-initiated VPDNs. A NAS is an access server, maintained by the ISP, to which users dial in and that forwards the call to the network. The options are described as follows:

- **Client-initiated VPDNs**—Users establish an encrypted IP tunnel across the ISP shared network to the customer network. The customer manages the client software that initiates the tunnel. The main advantage of client-initiated VPDNs is that they secure the connection between the client and the ISP. However, client-initiated VPDNs are not as scalable as NAS-initiated VPDNs.

- **NAS-initiated VPDNs**—Users dial in to the ISP NAS, which establishes an encrypted tunnel to the customer private network. NAS-initiated VPDNs are more robust than client-initiated VPDNs, allow users to connect to multiple networks by using multiple tunnels, and do not require the client to maintain the tunnel-creating software. NAS-initiated VPDNs do not encrypt the connection between the client and the ISP, which is not a concern for most customers because the PSTN is much more secure than the Internet.

VPDNs can use any of the following three Layer 2 tunneling protocols:

- **Layer 2 Forwarding (L2F)**—L2F is a Cisco Systems proprietary tunneling protocol. Its main advantage is that it is a stable tunneling protocol supported by many vendors and client software applications. It is the most stable of the Layer 2 tunneling protocols. The trade-off for this stability is the fact that L2F does not scale as well as L2TP, nor does it support the advanced features L2TP does.

- **Point-to-Point Tunneling Protocol (PPTP)**—PPTP is a Microsoft proprietary tunneling protocol. It is bundled into many Microsoft Windows operating systems, which makes it an easily deployable solution for many enterprises.

- **Layer 2 Tunneling Protocol**—L2TP is the Internet Engineering Task Force (IETF) standard Layer 2 tunneling protocol that was designed to merge the best features of L2F and PPTP. L2TP offers the best performance and scalability of the three, and recent releases of Cisco IOS software have greatly improved the stability of L2TP tunnels.

In the current Cisco implementation of access VPDNs, client-initiated VPDNs use PPTP, and NAS-initiated VPDNs can use either L2F or L2TP.

Proposed Solution: NAS-Initiated VPDN Using L2TP

This solution describes how a large ISP plans, designs, and implements a NAS-initiated access VPDN that uses L2TP as the tunneling protocol. In this solution, the ISP works with two customers—a medium-sized service provider and an enterprise customer—to create two main types of VPDN service: wholesale dial for service providers and service for enterprise customers.

Wholesale Dial VPDN for Service Providers

The L2TP network is primarily designed to provide wholesale dial service to medium-sized service providers. In a wholesale dial scenario, the large ISP maintains geographically dispersed PoPs. The ISP then offers VPDN service to medium-sized service providers that do not have the resources to maintain multiple PoPs, but want to offer geographically extended dial services (called roaming services) to their customers. The customers of the service providers dial in to the ISP local PoP, and the ISP then creates a VPDN tunnel to the home networks of the service providers.

VPDN Service for Enterprise Customers

The ISP L2TP network also is designed to provide VPDN service to enterprise customers who want to outsource their IT responsibilities. Enterprise customers want to establish secure, comprehensive dial service for their employees and partners. Some enterprises also want dial-out service to upload information from their central network to remote sites.

The rest of this chapter refers to the three companies—the ISP, service provider, and enterprise—as the partners. This chapter refers to the service provider and the enterprise as the customers of the ISP.

Strategy

Figure 3-2 illustrates the business scenario represented in this solution.

Figure 3-2   *VPDN Business Scenario*

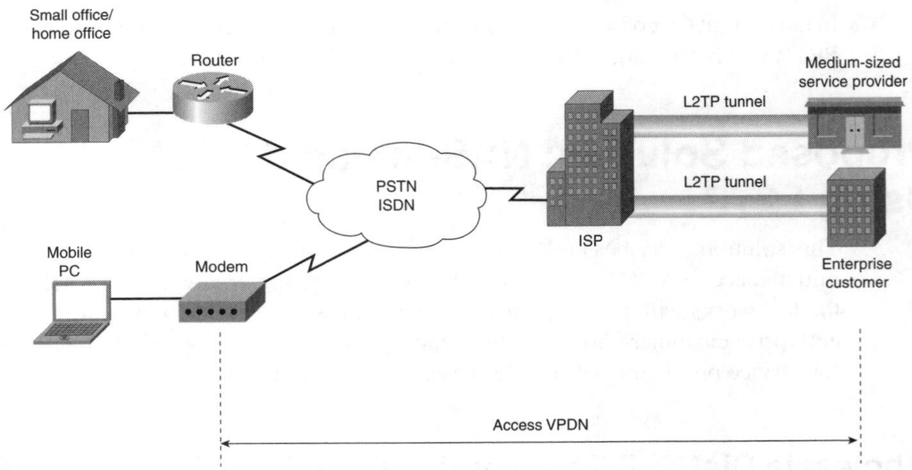

The goal of the ISP is to design an access VPDN network that meets the requirements of as many customers as possible. To design this network, the ISP meets with two different types of customers: a medium-sized service provider interested in wholesale dial VPDN service and an enterprise customer interested in access VPDN service. The ISP, service provider, and enterprise decide to partner to create the access VPDN network.

To ensure a smooth transition from their previous networks to the new networks, they begin with a basic VPDN network: a single L2TP access concentrator (LAC) that creates VPDN tunnels with two L2TP network servers (LNSs). All tunnel endpoint information and usernames and passwords are stored locally on the devices.

The ISP wants to make the VPDN network as flexible as possible. Although the initial implementation will be a basic VPDN network, it is designed to easily increase in scale and complexity. The service provider wants only the ISP to forward its user calls without relinquishing any further control of its network. The enterprise customer wants to outsource as much IT responsibility as possible. The enterprise will use the equipment, IP address space, and networking expertise of the ISP. The enterprise then will be solely responsible for maintaining its usernames and passwords.

Network Topology

This section describes networks of the partners after they implement the access VPDN network. Their networks are shown in Figure 3-3.

Figure 3-3   *Postimplementation Network Topology*

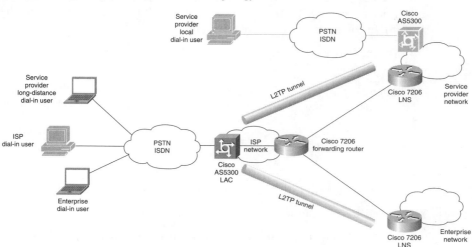

NOTE   The devices in the lighter shade of gray in Figure 3-3 are not involved in the access VPDN network.

Service provider customers and enterprise employees and partners who need to access the networks outside of the local calling area can dial in to the ISP access servers. The ISP then forwards the calls over the Internet to the proper network, which eliminates long-distance and 800 number costs. The ISP maintains the access servers, modems, phone lines, core and edge routers, circuits between its devices, and internetworking expertise. The service provider and enterprise can then focus on their core business responsibilities.

How This Solution Works

The partners will implement the access VPDN network as follows:

1 The service provider and enterprise lease access VPDN dial-in service from the ISP.

2 The ISP works with the service provider and enterprise to determine the level of service they require. The service provider only needs calls from its remote users forwarded to its home network.

3 The enterprise requires more extensive VPDN service: It leases IP address space from the ISP, it leases the LNS from the ISP, and it contracts with the ISP to configure and maintain this equipment.

4 The partners work together to configure the devices to establish L2TP tunnels from the LAC to the customer LNSs.

5 After the partners verify that the access VPDN network works, the service provider and enterprise configure the usernames and passwords of their users on their LNSs.

Benefits

Access VPDNs benefit ISPs, service providers, and enterprise customers.

The benefits to ISPs and service providers are as follows:

• Offers end-to-end custom solutions that help differentiate the ISP in a competitive market

• Eliminates responsibility of managing the enterprise customer user database

• Allows expansion to broadband technologies (such as cable and wireless) as they become available

The benefits to enterprise customers are as follows:

- Allows enterprise customers to focus on their core business responsibilities
- Minimizes equipment costs
- Simplifies complexity of upgrading technology
- Eliminates need to maintain internetworking expertise
- Reduces long-distance and 800 number costs
- Increases flexibility and scalability of connecting and disconnecting branch offices, users, and external partners
- Prioritizes traffic to ensure bandwidth for critical applications

Ramifications

After the VPDN network is configured, the partners face the following implications.

ISP implications are as follows:

- **Scalability**—The Cisco AS5300 access server can support a maximum of 192 concurrent VPDN sessions. If the ISP needs to support more than 192 concurrent sessions, it will either need to switch to a different platform for its LAC (such as a Cisco AS5800 access server), or it will need to configure additional LACs to form a stack group bidding protocol (SGBP) stack group. All the LACs can then answer incoming calls using the same PRI numbers, which makes the change transparent to VPDN users.

- **Offload router**—When the ISP adds LACs, it can either allow all the LACs to answer calls and establish VPDN sessions, or it can dedicate offload routers to establish VPDN sessions that do not answer calls. Because the ISP is using the Cisco AS5300 access server, it need not designate offload routers. Cisco AS5300 access servers have enough CPU power to handle both answering calls and establishing VPDN sessions without impacting performance. If the ISP were using the Cisco AS5200 access server, it would consider using offload routers.

- **Remote authentication, authorization, and accounting (AAA)**—If the ISP wants to store VPDN tunnel information on a server separate from the LACs, it will need to configure a remote AAA server. AAA servers provide more advanced authorization and accounting functions than when AAA is performed locally on the router. The ISP will then need to decide which AAA protocol it will run—either RADIUS or TACACS.

- **Multilink support**—If the ISP customers require the ability to establish Multilink PPP (MLPPP) connections using VPDN, the ISP will need to reconfigure the LACs for multilink VPDN.

- **L2TP dial-out**—If the ISP customers require the ability to use VPDN to dial out from their networks to remote clients, the ISP will need to configure the dialers and VPDN groups on the LACs for L2TP dial-out.

- **Encryption**—If the ISP customers require secure VPDN service, the ISP will need to configure the LACs to encrypt the VPDN tunnels using IPSec.

Service provider implications are as follows:

- **Scalability and backup**—The Cisco 7206 router can support a maximum of 1000 concurrent VPDN sessions. If the service provider needs to support more than 1000 concurrent sessions, it will either need to switch to a different platform for its LNS, or it will need to configure additional LNSs and have the ISP reconfigure the LACs to properly direct calls to the LNSs. The LNSs can balance the calls equally between them, or the LNSs can be designated as being primary or backup only.

- **Remote AAA**—If the service provider wants to store its user information on a server separate from the LNSs, it will need to configure a remote AAA server. AAA servers provide more advanced authorization and accounting functions than when AAA is performed locally on the router. The service provider will then need to decide which AAA protocol it will run—either RADIUS or TACACS.

- **Multilink support**—If the service provider customers require the ability to establish MLPPP connections using VPDN, the service provider will need to reconfigure the LNSs for multilink VPDN.

- **Multihop VPDN**—If the service provider wants to provide multihop VPDN service, it will need to reconfigure its LNSs to function to establish VPDN tunnels to forward multihop calls to their proper destination.

Enterprise implications are as follows:

- **Scalability and backup**—See the description in the preceding service provider implications list.

- **Remote AAA**—See the description in the preceding service provider implications list.

- **Multilink support**—See the description in the preceding service provider implications list.

- **User segmentation**—If the enterprise wants to distinguish different levels of access, it will need to configure user segmentation. For example, the enterprise might want to give its employees access to the entire network, but only give limited access to its outside partners. The easiest way to configure user segmentation is through the remote AAA server.

- **Encryption**—To provide added security to VPDN sessions, the enterprise can work with the ISP to configure IPSec encryption on its VPDN tunnels.

Implementation

Implementing a VPDN network solution requires planning and preparation on the part of the local network administrators and partners in the network topology. The roles, responsibilities, information needs of the network partners involved in the implementation effort are described in the following sections:

- Prerequisites and Design Considerations
- Implementation Process Steps

The information covered in these sections applies to the postimplementation network topology shown in Figure 3-3.

Prerequisites and Design Considerations

Among the prerequisites for implementing the design are the information-gathering tasks described in the following sections:

- Identifying the VPDN Services Requirements
- Identifying the Network Requirements
- Identifying the IP Address Space
- Identifying Roles and Resources

Identifying the VPDN Services Requirements

To begin planning the L2TP network, the service provider and enterprise complete a VPDN services questionnaire. The ISP uses the information from this questionnaire to design the L2TP network. Table 3-1 lists the design questions and the customer responses.

Table 3-1   *VPDN Services Questionnaire*

Design Questions	Design Options	Enterprise Customer	Service Provider
How many simultaneous sessions must be supported?	—	150 sessions	500 sessions
Which access media are used for the dial services?	Analog lines and modems or ISDN BRI lines	Analog lines and modems	Analog lines and modems
Will you maintain your own LNS or will you lease an LNS from the ISP?	Use own LNS or Lease LNS from ISP	Lease LNS from ISP	Maintain own LNS
Will you maintain your own IP address space, or will you lease IP addresses from the ISP?	Use own addresses or Lease ISP addresses	Lease ISP addresses	Use own addresses
Will you use DNIS or domain name to determine the tunnel endpoint?	DNIS or Domain name	Domain name	Domain name
Will you use local AAA or a remote AAA server?	Local AAA or Remote AAA server	Local AAA	Local AAA
Will you use CHAP or PAP for tunnel authentication?	CHAP or PAP	CHAP	CHAP

Identifying the Network Requirements

Based on the design choices in Table 3-1, the ISP determines that the partners will require the equipment and services described in Table 3-2.

Table 3-2 *Customer Network Requirements*

ISP Requirements	Enterprise Requirements	Service Provider Requirements
One Cisco AS5300 access server	One Cisco 7206 router	One Cisco 7206 router
4 PRI lines	Analog lines and modem	Analog lines and modem
—	Lease LNS from ISP	Maintain own LNS
—	Lease IP addresses from the ISP	Use own IP addresses
—	Domain name–based tunneling	Domain name–based tunneling
—	CHAP tunnel authentication	CHAP tunnel authentication

Identifying the IP Address Space

Before the partners configure the networks, the ISP prepares Table 3-3 to document all the involved networks and subnets. This table should be posted in the network operations centers (NOCs) of each partner for easy reference.

Table 3-3 *IP Address Networks and Subnets*

Network Element	Assigned Subnet	Description
ISP network	172.22.0.0/16	The ISP Class B network
ISP equipment	172.22.0.0/17	This subnet of the ISP network is reserved for the service provider devices (LNSs, RADIUS servers, and so on).
ISP-operated devices	172.22.16.0/20	This subnet of the ISP equipment subnet is reserved for devices the ISP manages (as opposed to devices the ISP leases to customers).
ISP-leased devices	172.22.64.0/20	This subnet of the ISP equipment subnet is reserved for devices the ISP leases to its customers (as opposed to devices the ISP operates itself).

continues

Table 3-3   *IP Address Networks and Subnets (Continued)*

Network Element	Assigned Subnet	Description
ISP remote nodes	172.22.128.0/17	This subnet of the ISP network is reserved for IP address pools that are assigned to incoming dial-in sessions.
Service provider networks	192.168.48.0/24 192.168.49.0/24	The two service provider Class C networks
Service provider equipment	192.168.48.0/25	This subnet of the service provider network is reserved for the service provider devices.
Service provider remote nodes	192.168.49.0/25	This subnet of the service provider network is reserved for the IP address pools that are assigned to incoming L2TP sessions.

Identifying Roles and Resources

Table 3-4 describes the partner roles and resources for the VPDN network.

Table 3-4   *Roles and Resources*

Partner	Role	Resources
ISP	Configure ISP-LAC-1 and ISP-RTR-1 Supervise configuration and operation of the VPDN network	A Cisco AS5300 access server to serve as ISP-LAC-1 A Cisco 7206 router to serve as ISP-RTR-1
Service provider	Configure SER-LNS-1	A Cisco 7206 router to serve as SER-LNS-1
Enterprise	Configure ENT-LNS-1	A Cisco 7206 router to serve as ENT-LNS-1

Implementation Process Steps

To implement the access VPDN network, the partners perform the following tasks:

1 The partners design the network topology and create a device characteristics table.

2 The ISP configures the LAC and forwarding router.

3 The service provider and enterprise configure their LNSs.

4 The partners verify that they can establish L2TP tunnels to both LNSs.

Details of each of these implementation steps are provided in the following section.

Device Characteristics and Configuration Files

Table 3-5 describes the hardware, software, and interface IP addresses of the devices used in the access VPDN.

Table 3-5   *Device Characteristics*

Host Name	ISP-LAC-1	ISP-RTR-1	ENT-LNS-1	SER-LNS-1
Device description	ISP LAC	Forwarding router	Enterprise LNS	Service provider LNS
Chassis type	Cisco AS5300 NAS	Cisco 7206 router	Cisco 7206 router	Cisco 7206 router
Admin username and password	jane-admin pass2me	jane-admin pass2me	jane-admin pass2me	jane-admin pass2me
VPDN usernames and passwords	ser-test-1 ser-pass-1 ent-test-1 ent-pass-1	—	ent-test-1 ent-pass-1	ser-test-1 ser-pas-1
Local name	ISP-LAC-1	—	—	—
L2TP tunnel password	tunnel4me	—	tunnel4me	tunnel4me

continues

Table 3-5 *Device Characteristics (Continued)*

Host Name	ISP-LAC-1	ISP-RTR-1	ENT-LNS-1	SER-LNS-1
Interfaces and IP addresses	Ethernet 0 172.22.16.1/20	Ethernet 0 172.22.16.9/20	Ethernet 0 172.22.64.1/20	Ethernet 0 192.168.48.1/24
Primary/ secondary DNS servers	172.22.16.70 172.22.16.140	172.22.16.70 172.22.16.140	172.22.16.70 172.22.16.140	192.168.48.70 192.168.48.140
Primary/ Secondary NBNS Servers	172.22.16.71 172.22.16.141	—	172.22.16.71 172.22.16.141	172.22.16.71 172.22.16.141
Domain names	—	—	enterprise.com	service.com
Address pool	172.22.128.1 172.22.128. 254	—	172.22.129.1 172.22.129.254	192.168.49.1 192.168.49.126
Tunnel endpoints	Enterprise: 172.22.64.1 Service provider: 192.168.48.1	—	172.22.16.1	172.22.16.1

Detailed information for configuring the access VPDN using L2TP solution is presented in the following sections:

- Configuring ISP Devices
- Configuring Service Provider Devices
- Configuring Enterprise Devices

Configuring ISP Devices

This section describes the configuration of the ISP LAC and forwarding router in the following sections:

- ISP LAC Description
- Configuring ISP-LAC-1
- ISP Forwarding Router Description
- Configuring ISP-RTR-1

ISP LAC Description

ISP-LAC-1 is a Cisco AS5300 access server maintained by the ISP. In the access VPDN network, its function is to receive dial-in calls, negotiate L2TP tunnels with the LNSs, and forward the calls on to ISP-RTR-1, which then forwards the calls to the appropriate LNS.

See Table 3-5 earlier in this chapter for the list of ISP LAC characteristics.

Configuring ISP-LAC-1

To configure ISP-LAC-1 to initiate L2TP tunnels using local AAA, perform the following tasks:

1 Configure basic settings.

2 Commission the T1 controllers.

3 Configure the serial channels.

4 Configure the modems and asynchronous lines.

5 Configure the group-asynchronous interface.

6 Configure the VPDN groups.

NOTE   The configuration files in this chapter and in the rest of this book are presented unabridged. Extensive explanatory comments are included in the configurations. These comments are prefaced by an exclamation point (!), and refer to the following command line.

If you would like more detailed information, or if you would like to see configurations broken up into smaller sections, refer to the configurations in Chapter 2, "Access VPDN Dial-In Using L2F Solution." Although Chapter 2 describes an L2F network, the configurations and explanations are relevant to all VPDNs.

The configuration in Example 3-1 sets up the LAC to establish L2TP tunnels with the LNSs and to forward calls to the forwarding router.

Example 3-1 *ISP-LAC-1 Configuration*

```
!
!Identifies the version of Cisco IOS software running on the LAC
version 12.1
```

continues

Example 3-1 *ISP-LAC-1 Configuration (Continued)*

```
!Includes millisecond time stamps on log and debug entries that are
!useful for troubleshooting and optimizing the network
service timestamps debug datetime msec localtime show-timezone
service timestamps log datetime msec localtime show-timezone
!Specifies that passwords will not be encrypted in configuration
!output. This is useful when first configuring a network, but is a
!security risk when the network is operational.
no service password-encryption
!
!Configures the host name for the LAC.
hostname ISP-LAC-1
!
!Retains 100000 bytes of debug output in the internal log buffer
logging buffered 100000 debugging
!
!Configures AAA on the LAC. Specifies that the LAC will authenticate and
!authorize VPDN tunnels locally using the local user database.
aaa new-model
aaa authentication ppp default local
aaa authorization network default local
!Configures the enable password
enable password cisco
!
!Configures the network administrator username and password. Because
!the ISP configures an L2TP tunnel password in the VPDN groups, it does
!not need to configure VPDN tunnel secrets as usernames.
username jane-admin password 0 cisco
!
!
resource-pool disable
!
!
!
!
!
!Configures the timezone and Daylight Savings Time adjustment.
clock timezone PST -8
clock summer-time PDT recurring
!Instructs the LAC to use its internal hardware clock to set the
!software clock when the router reloads.
clock calendar-valid
!Allows for the configuration of the first subnet in each classful
!network.
ip subnet-zero
!
```

Example 3-1 *ISP-LAC-1 Configuration (Continued)*

```
!Turns on VPDN.
vpdn enable
!Instructs the LAC to first attempt to tunnel VPDN calls based on the
!user domain name, and to then attempt to tunnel based on the DNIS
!number if the user does not have a domain name.
vpdn search-order domain dnis
!
!This is the VPDN group for the service provider.
vpdn-group 1
!Configures a request dial-in VPDN subgroup.
 request-dialin
!Configures L2TP as the tunnel protocol.
  protocol l2tp
!Specifies that users with the domain name service.com will be tunneled
!by this VPDN group.
   domain service.com
!Specifies the IP address of the service provider LNS. The priority
!keyword is only necessary if the service provider had multiple LNSs.
!To equally share the load of calls between all the LNSs, each IP
!address would be given the same priority number.To specify an LNS as
!a backup, it would be given a higher priority number.
 initiate-to ip 192.168.48.1 priority 1
!Configures the local name that the ISP will use to identify itself for
!L2TP tunnel authentication with the service provider LNS. If the ISP
!expands to a stacked-LAC environment, it will need to use the same
!local name on all of the LACs.
 local name ISP-LAC-1
!Configures the L2TP tunnel password that is used to authenticate L2TP
!tunnels with SER-LNS-1. Both tunnel endpoints must have the same L2TP
!tunnel password configured.
 l2tp tunnel password 7 tunnel4me
!
!This is the VPDN group for the service provider.
vpdn-group 2
!Configures a request dial-in VPDN subgroup.
 request-dialin
!Configures L2TP as the tunnel protocol.
  protocol l2tp
!Specifies that users with the domain name enterprise.com will be
!tunneled by this VPDN group.
   domain enterprise.com
```

continues

Example 3-1 *ISP-LAC-1 Configuration (Continued)*

```
!Specifies the IP address of the enterprise LNS. The priority keyword
!is only necessary if the enterprise had multiple LNSs. To equally
!share the load of calls between all the LNSs, each IP address would
!be given the same priority number. To specify an LNS as a backup, it
!would be given a higher priority number.
 initiate-to ip 172.22.64.1 priority 1
!Configures the local name that the ISP will use to identify itself
!for L2TP tunnel authentication with the enterprise LNS. If the ISP
!expands to a stacked-LAC environment, it will need to use the same
!local name on all of the LACs.
 local name ISP-LAC-1
!Configures the L2TP tunnel password that is used to authenticate L2TP
!tunnels with ENT-LNS-1. Both tunnel endpoints must have the same
!L2TP tunnel password configured.
l2tp tunnel password 7 tunnel4me
!
!Configures the IP addresses of DNS servers that translate host names
!to IP addresses.
async-bootp dns-server 171.68.10.70 171.68.10.140
!Configures the telco switch type. When the switch type is configured
!in global configuration mode, it is automatically propagated into
!the individual serial interfaces.
isdn switch-type primary-5ess
cns event-service server
mta receive maximum-recipients 0
!
!
!
!
controller T1 0
!Configures the T1 framing type as super frame (ESF).
 framing esf
!Configures the LAC to gets its primary clocking from T1 controller 0.
 clock source line primary
!Configures the T1 line code type as B8ZS.
 linecode b8zs
!Assigns all 24 T1 timeslots as ISDN PRI channels and creates a D
!channel serial interface (Serial interface 0:23). Individual
!B-channel serial interfaces are also created (Serial interfaces 0:0
!through 0:22), but they are not shown in the configuration.
 pri-group timeslots 1-24
```

Example 3-1 *ISP-LAC-1 Configuration (Continued)*

```
!
!The same configuration on controller T1 0 is applied to the three
!remaining controllers. The only exception is that the they are
!configured to be secondary clocking resources.
controller T1 1
 framing esf
 clock source line secondary 1
 linecode b8zs
 pri-group timeslots 1-24
!
controller T1 2
 framing esf
 clock source line secondary 2
 linecode b8zs
 pri-group timeslots 1-24
!
controller T1 3
 framing esf
 clock source line secondary 3
 linecode b8zs
 pri-group timeslots 1-24
!
!
!
!
!
interface Ethernet0
 no ip address
 shutdown
!
!Serial interface 0:23 is the D channel that corresponds to controller
!T1 0. The behavior of the B-channel serial interfaces (0:0 through
!0:22) is controlled by the configuration of Serial interface 0:23.
interface Serial0:23
!Specifies that the interface does not require an IP address.
 no ip address
 encapsulation ppp
 ip mroute-cache
 dialer-group 1
!This command is automatically configured on all of the serial
!interfaces by the isdn switch-type global configuration mode command.
 isdn switch-type primary-5ess
!Specifies that analog modem voice calls coming in through the B
!channels to be connected to the integrated modems.
 isdn incoming-voice modem
 fair-queue 64 256 0
```

continues

Example 3-1 *ISP-LAC-1 Configuration (Continued)*

```
 ppp authentication chap pap
 ppp multilink
 !
 !The same configuration on Serial interface 0:23 is applied to the other
 !three D channels (Serial interfaces 1:23, 2:23, and 3:23).
 interface Serial1:23
  no ip address
  encapsulation ppp
  ip mroute-cache
  dialer-group 1
  isdn switch-type primary-5ess
  isdn incoming-voice modem
  fair-queue 64 256 0
  ppp authentication chap pap
  ppp multilink
 !
 interface Serial2:23
  no ip address
  encapsulation ppp
  ip mroute-cache
  dialer-group 1
  isdn switch-type primary-5ess
  isdn incoming-voice modem
  fair-queue 64 256 0
  ppp authentication chap pap
  ppp multilink
 !
 interface Serial3:23
  no ip address
  encapsulation ppp
  ip mroute-cache
  dialer-group 1
  isdn switch-type primary-5ess
  isdn incoming-voice modem
  fair-queue 64 256 0
  ppp authentication chap pap
  ppp multilink
 !
 !Configures the Fast Ethernet interface that is used to forward VPDN
 !traffic to ISP-RTR-1, which then forwards VPDN traffic on to the LNSs.
 interface FastEthernet0
 description to ISP-RTR-1 for forwarding of VPDN traffic
  ip address 172.22.16.1 255.255.240.0
  duplex full
  speed 100
 !
 !Configures the group-asynchronous interface that controls the
 !configuration of all asynchronous interfaces on the LAC.
```

Example 3-1   *ISP-LAC-1 Configuration (Continued)*

```
interface Group-Async1
!Specifies that the asynchronous interfaces will use the IP address
!of FastEthernet0.
 ip unnumbered FastEthernet0
!Enables PPP.
 encapsulation ppp
!Configures interactive mode on the asynchronous interfaces.
  Interactive mode
!allows for dial-in clients to either receive a router prompt or
!establish a PPP session, as opposed to dedicated mode, which only
!allows dial-in clients to establish PPP sessions.
 async mode interactive
!Specifies the range of asynchronous interfaces that are included in
!the group.
 group-range 1 60
!
ip default-gateway 172.22.16.9
ip classless
no ip http server
!
!
!
!
line con 0
 transport input none
!Specifies the range of modems.
line 1 60
!The following two autoselect commands relate to the interactive mode
!on the asynchronous interfaces. Displays the username:password prompt
!as the modems connect. autoselect during-login Enables PPP dial-in
!clients to bypass the EXEC prompt and automatically start PPP.
 autoselect ppp
!Enables support for both incoming and outgoing modem calls.
 modem InOut
!Specifies which protocols can be used for outgoing connections from
!these lines.
 transport output pad telnet rlogin udptn v120 lapb-ta
line aux 0
line vty 0 4
 password cisco
!
!The Network Time Protocol (NTP) clock-period is automatically updated
!by the NTP server.
```

continues

Example 3-1   *ISP-LAC-1 Configuration (Continued)*

```
ntp clock-period 17179843
!Configures NTP to periodically update the LAC hardware calendar.
ntp update-calendar
!Specifies the IP address of the NTP server. In this network,
!ISP-RTR-1 is the NTP server for all of the devices in the network.
!This ensures that all of the devices will be synchronized.
ntp server 172.22.16.9
end
```

ISP Forwarding Router Description

ISP-RTR-1 is a Cisco 7206 router maintained by the ISP. In the access VPDN network, its function is to forward VPDN traffic from ISP-LAC-1 to SER-LNS-1 and ENT-LNS-1. Two serial interfaces are dedicated to forwarding VPDN traffic, and static routes are configured to the service provider and enterprise networks.

See Table 3-5 earlier in this chapter for a list of ISP forwarding router characteristics.

Configuring ISP-RTR-1

To configure ISP-RTR-1 to forward L2TP sessions, perform the following steps:

1 Configure basic settings.

2 Configure the serial interfaces.

3 Configure static routes.

The configuration in Example 3-2 sets up ISP-RTR-1 to forward VPDN traffic to the service provider and enterprise networks.

Example 3-2   *ISP-RTR-1 Configuration*

```
!
!Identifies the version of Cisco IOS software running on the LAC
version 12.1
!Includes millisecond time stamps on log and debug entries that are
  useful for
!troubleshooting and optimizing the network
service timestamps debug datetime msec localtime show-timezone
service timestamps log datetime msec localtime show-timezone
!Specifies that passwords will not be encrypted in configuration
!output. This is useful when first configuring a network, but is a
!security risk when the network is operational.
no service password-encryption
```

Example 3-2 *ISP-RTR-1 Configuration (Continued)*

```
!
!Configures the host name of the forwarding router.
hostname ISP-RTR-1
!
!Retains 100000 bytes of debug output in the internal log buffer.
logging buffered 100000 debugging
!Configures local login authentication.
aaa new-model
aaa authentication login default local
!Configures the enable password
enable password cisco
!
!Configures the network administrator username and password.
username jane-admin password 0 cisco
!
!
!
!Configures the timezone and Daylight Savings Time adjustment.
clock timezone PST -8
clock summer-time PDT recurring
!Instructs the LAC to use its internal hardware clock to set the
!software clock when the router reloads.
clock calendar-valid
!Allows for the configuration of the first subnet in each classful
!network.
ip subnet-zero
no ip domain-lookup
!
!Configures the IP addresses of DNS servers that translate host names
!to IP addresses.
async-bootp dns-server 171.68.10.70 171.68.10.140
!
!
cns event-service server
!
!
!
!
!
!Configures the IP address for interface Fast Ethernet 0/0, which is
!used to forward all VPDN traffic.
interface FastEthernet0/0
 ip address 172.22.16.9 255.255.240.0
 full-duplex
!
!This interface is dedicated to forwarding VPDN traffic to the service
!provider network.
```

continues

Example 3-2 *ISP-RTR-1 Configuration (Continued)*

```
interface Serial2/0
 description to SER-LNS-1
 ip unnumbered FastEthernet0/0
 clockrate 2015232
!
!This interface is dedicated to forwarding VPDN traffic to the
!enterprise network.
interface Serial2/1
 description to ENT-LNS-1
 ip unnumbered FastEthernet0/0
 clockrate 2015232
!
interface Serial2/2
 no ip address
 shutdown
!
interface Serial2/3
 no ip address
 shutdown
!
ip classless
!This static route is to the enterprise device subnet.
ip route 172.22.64.0 255.255.240.0 Serial2/1
!This static route is to the enterprise IP address pool subnet.
ip route 172.22.129.0 255.255.255.0 Serial2/1
!This static route is to the service provider device subnet.
ip route 192.168.48.0 255.255.255.0 Serial2/0
!This static route is to the service provider IP address pool subnet.
ip route 192.168.49.0 255.255.255.0 Serial2/0
no ip http server
!
!
line con 0
 exec-timeout 0 0
 transport input none
line aux 0
line vty 0 4
!
!Configures ISP-RTR-1 to be the NTP master for the network.
!This means that ISP-RTR-1 synchronizes the calendars of all of the
!devices on the network.
ntp master
!Configures NTP to periodically update the LAC hardware calendar.
ntp update-calendar
end
```

Configuring Service Provider Devices

This section describes the configuration of the service provider LNS in the following sections:

- Service Provider LNS Description
- Configuring SER-LNS-1

Service Provider LNS Description

SER-LNS-1 is a Cisco 7206 router owned and maintained by the service provider. In the access VPDN network, its function is to terminate VPDN tunnels from ISP-LAC-1 and negotiate VPDN sessions with long-distance dial-in users of the service provider.

See Table 3-5 earlier in this chapter for the list of SER-LNS-1 characteristics.

Configuring SER-LNS-1

To configure SER-LNS-1 to terminate L2TP tunnels using local AAA, perform the following tasks:

1 Configure basic settings.

2 Configure AAA settings.

3 Configure the VPDN group.

4 Configure the virtual template.

5 Specify the IP address pool.

The configuration in Example 3-3 sets up SER-LNS-1 to authenticate and authorize VPDN tunnels and users locally using the local user database.

Example 3-3   *SER-LNS-1 Configuration*

```
!Identifies the version of Cisco IOS software running on the LAC
version 12.1
!Includes millisecond time stamps on log and debug entries that are
!useful for troubleshooting and optimizing the network.
service timestamps debug datetime msec localtime show-timezone
service timestamps log datetime msec localtime show-timezone
!Specifies that passwords will not be encrypted in configuration
!output. This is useful when first configuring a network, but is
!a security risk when the network is operational.
```

continues

Example 3-3 *SER-LNS-1 Configuration (Continued)*

```
no service password-encryption
!
!Configures the host name of the router.
hostname SER-LNS-1
!
!Retains 100000 bytes of debug output in the internal log buffer
logging buffered 100000 debugging
!
!Configures AAA on the LNS. Specifies that the LNS will authenticate and
!authorize VPDN tunnels and users locally using the local user
!database.
aaa new-model
aaa authentication login default local
aaa authentication ppp default local
aaa authorization network default local
!Configures the enable password
enable password cisco
!
!Configures username and password for the network administrator.
username jane-admin password 7 pass2me
!Configures the username and password for the VPDN test user.
username ser-test-1@service.com password 7 ser-pass-1
!
!
!
!Configures the timezone and Daylight Savings Time adjustment.
clock timezone PST -8
clock summer-time PDT recurring
!Instructs the LNS to use its internal hardware clock to set the
!software clock when the router reloads.
clock calendar-valid
!Allows for the configuration of the first subnet in each classful
!network.
ip subnet-zero
ip name-server 171.68.10.70
!
!Turns on VPDN.
vpdn enable
!
!Creates the VPDN group for the LNS.
vpdn-group 1
!Creates an accept dial-in VPDN subgroup.
 accept-dialin
!Specifies L2TP as the tunneling protocol.
  protocol l2tp
!Instructs the LNS to clone virtual access interfaces for VPDN sessions
!from virtual template 1.
```

Example 3-3   *SER-LNS-1 Configuration (Continued)*

```
 virtual-template 1
!Specifies that this VPDN group will negotiate L2TP tunnels with LACs
!that identify themselves with the local name ISP-LAC-1.
 terminate-from hostname ISP-LAC-1
!Configures the L2TP tunnel password that is used to authenticate L2TP
!tunnels with ISP-LAC-1. Both tunnel endpoints must have the same
!L2TP tunnel password configured.
 l2tp tunnel password 7 tunnel4me
!Instructs the LNS to use the IP address of Fast Ethernet interface
!0/0 for all traffic for this VPDN group. This command should be used
!when the LNS has more than one IP address configured on it.
 source-ip 192.168.48.1
!
!Configures the IP addresses of DNS servers that translate host names to
!IP addresses.
async-bootp dns-server 172.23.1.10 172.23.2.10
!Configures the IP addresses of WINS servers that provide dynamic
!NetBIOS names that Windows devices use to communicate without
!IP addresses.
async-bootp nbns-server 172.23.1.11 172.23.2.11
!
!
cns event-service server
!
!
!
!
!
!Configures the IP address of FastEthernet 0/0, through which all VPDN
!traffic passes.
interface FastEthernet0/0
 ip address 192.168.48.1 255.255.255.0
 media-type MII
 full-duplex
!
interface Serial2/0
 ip unnumbered FastEthernet0/0
!
interface Serial2/1
 no ip address
 shutdown
!
```

continues

Example 3-3 *SER-LNS-1 Configuration (Continued)*

```
interface Serial2/2
 no ip address
 shutdown
!
interface Serial2/3
 no ip address
 shutdown
!
!Creates virtual template 1, which is used to clone virtual access
!interfaces for incoming VPDN sessions.
interface Virtual-Template1
!Specifies that the virtual access interfaces will use the IP address of
!Fast Ethernet interface 0/0.
 ip unnumbered FastEthernet0/0
!Instructs the LNS to assign an IP address to VPDN sessions from the
!default pool.
 peer default ip address pool default
!Enables CHAP authentication using the local username database.
 ppp authentication chap
!Enables PPP.
 encapsulation ppp
!
!Creates a pool of IP addresses that are assigned to incoming VPDN
!sessions.
ip local pool default 192.168.49.1 192.168.49.126
ip classless
ip route 0.0.0.0 0.0.0.0 Serial2/0
no ip http server
!
!
!
line con 0
 transport input none
line aux 0
line vty 0 4
 password 7 cisco
!The NTP clock-period is automatically updated by the NTP server.
ntp clock-period 17179843
!Configures NTP to periodically update the LAC hardware calendar.
ntp update-calendar
!Specifies the IP address of the NTP server. In this network,
!ISP-RTR-1 is the NTP server for all of the devices in the network.
!This ensures that all of the devices will be synchronized.
ntp server 172.22.16.9
end
```

Configuring Enterprise Devices

This section describes the configuration of the enterprise LNS in the following sections:

- Enterprise LNS Description
- Configuring ENT-LNS-1

Enterprise LNS Description

ENT-LNS-1 is a Cisco 7206 router that the enterprise leases from the ISP. In the access VPDN network, its function is to terminate VPDN tunnels from ISP-LAC-1 and negotiate VPDN sessions with employees and partners of the enterprise that want to remotely access the enterprise network.

See Table 3-5 earlier in this chapter for the list of ENT-LNS-1 characteristics.

Configuring ENT-LNS-1

To configure ENT-LNS-1 to terminate L2TP tunnels using local AAA, perform the following tasks:

1 Configure basic settings.

2 Configure AAA.

3 Configure the VPDN group.

4 Configure the virtual template.

5 Specify the IP address pool.

The configuration in Example 3-4 sets up ENT-LNS-1 to authenticate and authorize VPDN tunnels and users locally using the local user database.

Example 3-4 *ENT-LNS-1 Configuration*

```
!Identifies the version of Cisco IOS software running on the LAC.
version 12.1
!Includes millisecond time stamps on log and debug entries that are
!useful for troubleshooting and optimizing the network.
service timestamps debug datetime msec localtime show-timezone
service timestamps log datetime msec localtime show-timezone
```

continues

Example 3-4 *ENT-LNS-1 Configuration (Continued)*

```
!Specifies that passwords will not be encrypted in configuration
!output. This is useful when first configuring a network, but is a
!security risk when the network is operational.
no service password-encryption
!
!Configures the host name of the router.
hostname ENT-LNS-1
!
!Retains 100000 bytes of debug output in the internal log buffer.
logging buffered 100000 debugging
!
!Configures AAA on the LNS. Specifies that the LNS will authenticate and
!authorize VPDN tunnels and users locally using the local user
!database.
aaa new-model
aaa authentication login default local
aaa authentication ppp default local
aaa authorization network default local
!Configures the enable password.
enable password cisco
!
!Configures username and password for the network administrator.
username jane-admin password 7 pass2me
!Configures the username and password for the VPDN test user.
username ent-pass-1@enterprise.com password 7 ent-pass-1
!
!
!
!
!Configures the timezone and Daylight Savings Time adjustment.
clock timezone PST -8
clock summer-time PDT recurring
!Instructs the LNS to use its internal hardware clock to set the
!software clock when the router reloads.
clock calendar-valid
!Allows for the configuration of the first subnet in each classful
!network.
ip subnet-zero
ip name-server 171.68.10.70
!
!Turns on VPDN.
vpdn enable
!
!Creates the VPDN group for the LNS.
vpdn-group 1
!Creates an accept dial-in VPDN subgroup.
 accept-dialin
!Specifies L2TP as the tunneling protocol.
```

Example 3-4   *ENT-LNS-1 Configuration (Continued)*

```
    protocol l2tp
!Instructs the LNS to clone virtual access interfaces for VPDN sessions
!from virtual template 1.
    virtual-template 1
!Specifies that this VPDN group will negotiate L2TP tunnels with LACs
!that identify themselves with the local name ISP-LAC-1.
    terminate-from hostname ISP-LAC-1
!Configures the L2TP tunnel password that is used to authenticate L2TP
!tunnels with ISP-LAC-1. Both tunnel endpoints must have the same
!L2TP tunnel password configured.
    l2tp tunnel password 7 tunnel4me
!Instructs the LNS to use the IP address of Fast Ethernet interface
!0/0 for all traffic for this VPDN group. This command should be
!used when the LNS has more than one IP address configured on it.
    source-ip 172.22.64.1
!
!Configures the IP addresses of DNS servers that translate host names
!to IP addresses.
async-bootp dns-server 172.23.1.10 172.23.2.10
!Configures the IP addresses of WINS servers that provide dynamic
!NetBIOS names that Windows devices use to communicate without
!IP addresses.
async-bootp nbns-server 172.23.1.11 172.23.2.11
!
!
cns event-service server
!
!
!
!
!
!Configures the IP address of FastEthernet 0/0, through which all VPDN
!traffic passes.
interface FastEthernet0/0
 ip address 172.22.64.1 255.255.240.0
 shutdown
 media-type MII
 full-duplex
!
interface Serial2/0
 ip unnumbered FastEthernet0/0
 no fair-queue
!
```

continues

Example 3-4 *ENT-LNS-1 Configuration (Continued)*

```
interface Serial2/1
 no ip address
 shutdown
!
interface Serial2/2
 no ip address
 shutdown
!
interface Serial2/3
 no ip address
 shutdown
!
interface FastEthernet3/0
 no ip address
 shutdown
 half-duplex
!
!Creates virtual template 1, which is used to clone virtual access
!interfaces for incoming VPDN sessions.
interface Virtual-Template1
!Specifies that the virtual access interfaces will use the IP address
!of Fast Ethernet interface 0/0.
 ip unnumbered FastEthernet0/0
!Instructs the LNS to assign an IP address to VPDN sessions from the
!default pool.
 peer default ip address pool default
!Enables CHAP authentication using the local username database.
 ppp authentication chap
!Enables PPP.
 encapsulation ppp
!
!Creates a pool of IP addresses that are assigned to incoming VPDN
!sessions.
ip local pool default 172.22.128.1 172.22.128.254
ip classless
ip route 0.0.0.0 0.0.0.0 Serial2/0
no ip http server
!
!
!
line con 0
 transport input none
line aux 0
line vty 0 4
 password 7 cisco
!
!The NTP clock-period is automatically updated by the NTP server.
ntp clock-period 17179843
```

Example 3-4 *ENT-LNS-1 Configuration (Continued)*

```
!Configures NTP to periodically update the LAC hardware calendar.
ntp update-calendar
!Specifies the IP address of the NTP server. In this network,
!ISP-RTR-1 is the NTP server for all of the devices in the network.
!This ensures that all of the devices will be synchronized.
ntp server 172.22.16.9
end
```

Verifying That the Access VPDN Network Functions Properly

When the partners have configured the network, they verify that it functions properly by performing the tasks described in the following sections:

- Dialing In to ISP-LAC-1
- Pinging the LNS from the Client
- Displaying VPDN Information on the LAC and LNS

The following sections show verification information for a session to the service provider network using the username "ser-test-1." When the partners have verified VPDN connectivity with the service provider network, they repeat the following steps to verify VPDN connectivity with the enterprise network.

Before you begin, you should have the following applications open:

- Dialup utility on the dial-in client
- MS-DOS prompt on the dial-in client
- Telnet or console connection to ISP-LAC-1
- Telnet or console connection to SER-LNS-1

Dialing In to ISP-LAC-1

From the client, dial in to ISP-LAC-1 using a dialup utility. You will need to specify the following information in the dialup utility:

- username: ser-test-1@service.com
- password: ser-pass-1
- PRI telephone number (the PRI number assigned to the LAC)

When ISP-LAC-1 receives the call, the following message appears on the console screen of ISP-LAC-1:

```
*May 16 21:35:52.595: %LINK-3-UPDOWN: Interface Async8, changed state
   to up
```

NOTE   No **debug** commands are turned on to display this log message. If you are using Telnet to access the NAS rather than the NAS's console port, you will need to enable the **terminal monitor** user EXEC command to display these log messages. Start troubleshooting the NAS if this message does not display within 30 seconds of the client initiating the call.

This message indicates that an asynchronous interface has been assigned to the call and brought up, and that the modem has reached steady state.

Pinging the LNS from the Client

From the MS-DOS prompt on the client, enter the **ping user 192.168.48.1** EXEC command, (192.168.48.1 is the IP address of SER-LNS-1) and verify that the client can successfully ping SER-LNS-1. The messages in Example 3-5 show a successful ping.

Example 3-5   *Pinging the LNS from the Client*

```
Pinging 192.168.48.1 with 32 bytes of data:

Reply from 192.168.48.1: bytes=32 time=5ms TTL=244
Reply from 192.168.48.1: bytes=32 time=4ms TTL=244
Reply from 192.168.48.1: bytes=32 time=4ms TTL=244
Reply from 192.168.48.1: bytes=32 time=5ms TTL=244

Ping statistics for 192.168.48.1:
    Packets: Sent = 4, Received = 4, Lost = 0 (0% loss),
Approximate round trip times in milli-seconds:
Minimum = 4ms, Maximum =  5ms, Average =  4ms
```

Displaying VPDN Information on the LAC and LNS

On ISP-LAC-1, enter the **show vpdn** EXEC command to display information about the L2TP tunnel and session. As you can see in Example 3-6, the first line displays a summary of the active L2TP tunnels and sessions on ISP-LAC-1. The second two lines display information about the L2TP tunnel between ISP-LAC-1 and SER-LNS-1. The next two lines display information about the L2TP session for ser-test-1.

Example 3-6 show vpdn *Command Output*

```
ISP-LAC-1# show vpdn

L2TP Tunnel and Session Information Total tunnels 1 sessions 1

LocID RemID Remote Name   State  Remote Address  Port  Sessions
8173  15991 SER-LNS-1     est    192.168.48.1    1701  1

LocID RemID TunID Intf   Username       State  Last Chg Fastswitch
6     4     8173  As8    ser-test-1@se  est    00:07:55 enabled

% No active L2F tunnels
```

On SER-LNS-1, enter the **show caller** user EXEC command to display
information about active sessions. The output in Example 3-7 shows ser-test-
1@service.com connected through virtual access interface 1 (listed as Vi1) for
both PPP and L2TP service.

Example 3-7 show caller *Command Output*

```
SER-LNS-1# show caller

                                      Active   Idle
    Line         User          Service  Time     Time
    con 0        jane-admin        TTY   00:12:49 00:00:00
    Vi1          ser-test-1@service.com \
                                   PPP   L2TP  00:02:46 00:00:04
```

On SER-LNS-1, enter the **show caller user ser-test-1@service.com** privileged
EXEC command to display detailed information about the L2TP session, as
displayed in Example 3-8. The IP address of SER-LNS-1 is listed as the local IP
address, and the IP address assigned to ser-test-1@service.com from the local IP
address pool is listed as the remote IP address.

Example 3-8 show caller user *Command Output*

```
SER-LNS-1# show caller user ser-test-1@service.com

  User: ser-test-1@service.com, line Vi1, service PPP L2TP
        Active time 00:02:56, Idle time 00:00:04
  Timeouts:          Absolute  Idle
      Limits:           -        -
      Disconnect in:    -        -
  PPP: LCP Open, CHAP (<- AAA), IPCP
  IP: Local 192.168.48.1, remote 192.168.49.1
  VPDN: NAS ISP-LAC-1, MID 4, MID close-wait
        HGW  , NAS CLID 0, HGW CLID 0, tunnel open
  Counts: 97 packets input, 7732 bytes, 0 no buffer
          0 input errors, 0 CRC, 0 frame, 0 overrun
          85 packets output, 4510 bytes, 0 underruns
          0 output errors, 0 collisions, 0 interface resets
```

On the Telnet or console connection to SER-LNS-1, enter the **show interfaces virtual-access 1** privileged EXEC command to display detailed information (shown in Example 3-9) about the virtual access interface for ser-test-1@service.com.

Example 3-9 **show interface virtual-access** *Command Output*

```
SER-LNS-1# show interfaces virtual-access 1

Virtual-Access1 is up, line protocol is up
  Hardware is Virtual Access interface
  Interface is unnumbered. Using address of FastEthernet0/0
    (192.168.48.1)
  MTU 1500 bytes, BW 49 Kbit, DLY 100000 usec,
    reliability 255/255, txload 1/255, rxload 1/255
  Encapsulation PPP, loopback not set
  Keepalive set (10 sec)
  DTR is pulsed for 5 seconds on reset
  LCP Open
  Open: IPCP
  Last input 00:00:03, output never, output hang never
  Last clearing of "show interface" counters 3d16h
  Queueing strategy: fifo
  Output queue 0/40, 0 drops; input queue 0/75, 0 drops
  5 minute input rate 0 bits/sec, 0 packets/sec
  5 minute output rate 0 bits/sec, 0 packets/sec
     80 packets input, 6304 bytes, 0 no buffer
     Received 0 broadcasts, 0 runts, 0 giants, 0 throttles
     0 input errors, 0 CRC, 0 frame, 0 overrun, 0 ignored, 0 abort
     68 packets output, 3671 bytes, 0 underruns
     0 output errors, 0 collisions, 0 interface resets
     0 output buffer failures, 0 output buffers swapped out
     0 carrier transitions
```

On SER-LNS-1, enter the **show vpdn session all** user EXEC command to display detailed information about the L2TP session for ser-test-1@service.com (shown in Example 3-10).

Example 3-10 show vpdn session all *Command Output*

```
SER-LNS-1# show vpdn session all

L2TP Session Information Total tunnels 1 sessions 1

Call id 4 is up on tunnel id 15991
Remote tunnel name is ISP-LAC-1
  Internet Address is 172.22.16.1
  Session username is ser-test-1@service.com, state is established
    Time since change 00:02:33, interface Vi1
    Remote call id is 6
    Fastswitching is enabled
    74 packets sent, 85 received, 2443 bytes sent, 7654 received
      Sequencing is on
      Ss 74, Sr 85, Remote Ns 84, Remote Nr 74
```

Example 3-10 show vpdn session all *Command Output (Continued)*

```
        0 out of order packets received

% No active L2F tunnels
```

On SER-LNS-1, enter the **show vpdn tunnel all** user EXEC command to display
detailed information about the L2TP tunnel (shown in Example 3-11).

Example 3-11 show vpdn tunnel all *Command Output*

```
SER-LNS-1# show vpdn tunnel all

L2TP Tunnel Information Total tunnels 1 sessions 1

Tunnel id 15991 is up, remote id is 8173, 1 active sessions
  Tunnel state is established, time since change 00:02:44
  Remote tunnel name is ISP-LAC-1
    Internet Address 172.22.16.1, port 1701
  Local tunnel name is SER-LNS-1
    Internet Address 192.168.48.1, port 1701
  78 packets sent, 89 received, 2471 bytes sent, 8009 received
  Control Ns 2, Nr 4
  Local RWS 3000 (default), Remote RWS 800
  Retransmission time 1, max 1 seconds
  Unsent queuesize 0, max 0
  Resend queuesize 0, max 1
  Total resends 0, ZLB ACKs sent 2
  Current nosession queue check 0 of 5
  Retransmit time distribution: 0 0 0 0 0 0 0 0
  Sessions disconnected due to lack of resources 0
```

On SER-LNS-1, enter the **show ip local pool** privileged EXEC command to display
information about the local IP address pool. The following output shows the range of
IP addresses in the pool and that one of the IP addresses is in use:

```
SER-LNS-1# show ip local pool
Pool                      Begin           End             Free  In use
  default                 192.168.49.1    192.168.49.126  125        1
```

On SER-LNS-1, enter the **ping 192.168.49.1** user EXEC command to verify that
SER-LNS-1 can ping the client:

```
SER-LNS-1# ping 192.168.49.1

Type escape sequence to abort.
Sending 5, 100-byte ICMP Echos to 192.168.49.1, timeout is 2 seconds:
!!!!!
Success rate is 100 percent (5/5), round-trip min/avg/max = 96/111/128
  ms
SER-LNS-1#
```

If SER-LNS-1 can successfully ping the client, the access VPDN is functioning
properly between the ISP network and the service provider network. Now repeat
this verification procedure for the enterprise network.

CHAPTER 4

Access VPDN Dial-In Using IPSec over L2TP Solution

This chapter describes how an Internet service provider (ISP) partners with one of its enterprise customers to add Internet Protocol Security (IPSec) encryption to an existing virtual private dial-up network (VPDN).

VPDNs are networks that extend dial access to users over a shared infrastructure. They use Layer 2 tunneling protocols (L2F, L2TP, or PPTP) to tunnel user calls over the Internet (or other shared IP networks operated by ISPs that are not part of the Internet). They are a cost-effective way to establish long-distance point-to-point connections between remote users and a private network.

However, the Internet is subject to many security threats including loss of privacy, loss of data integrity, identity spoofing, and denial of service. The Layer 2 tunneling protocols do not offer protection from these threats. The goal of IPSec is to minimize all of these threats in the existing network infrastructure itself, without requiring expensive host and application modifications.

NOTE	Although the network used to document this solution is a fully functioning, end-to-end network and the complete configurations for the devices are included, this chapter focuses on the IPSec configurations. It does not discuss in detail such features as basic IP connectivity and VPDN configuration.

This chapter contains the following sections:

- Business Objectives
- Possible Solutions
- Proposed Solution: IPSec Tunnel Between the Peer and LNS
- Implementation

Business Objectives

The ISP has established a VPDN to offer remote access service to its customers. It now wants to expand this VPDN service to include encryption. The goal of the ISP is to implement this encryption service as quickly, easily, and inexpensively as possible without disrupting the existing network or purchasing new equipment.

The enterprise company has leased VPDN service from the ISP to connect its remote office to its headquarters office. This VPDN service is sufficient for nonsensitive traffic, but now the enterprise wants to be able to securely send sensitive traffic between the remote office and the headquarters. The enterprise determines that only the connection between the remote office and headquarters needs encryption—mobile users who dial in from laptop PCs need not establish encrypted sessions.

Original Network Topology

The enterprise and ISP have already configured a VPDN. Figure 4-1 shows the original VPDN topology without IPSec.

Figure 4-1   *Original Network Topology*

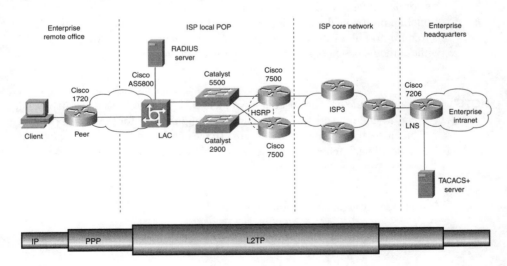

Figure 4-1 shows the entire end-to-end network topology; however, only the devices described in Table 4-1 are critical to the VPDN functionality.

Table 4-1   *VPDN Devices*

Device Name	Device Chassis	Location	Maintained By	Function
Peer	Cisco 1720 router	Enterprise remote office	Enterprise	Remote users are connected to the peer. The peer initiates VPDN calls from the remote office to the enterprise headquarters.
LAC	Cisco AS5800 access server	Local ISP point of presence (PoP)	ISP	The L2TP access concentrator (LAC) receives calls from the peer and then negotiates L2TP tunnels and sessions with the L2TP network server (LNS) to forward the calls to the LNS.
LNS	Cisco 7206 router	Enterprise headquarters	Enterprise	The LNS negotiates L2TP tunnels and sessions with he LAC.
LNS TACACS+ server	UNIX server	Enterprise headquarters	Enterprise	Usernames, passwords, and accounting records for the LNS are stored on the LNS AAA server. When the LNS receives a request to establish an L2TP session from the LAC, it forwards the user information to the LNS AAA server for authentication and authorization.

In this network, users at the enterprise remote office are connected to the peer. The access VPDN functions as follows:

1 The peer establishes a PPP session with the local L2TP access concentrator (LAC) of the ISP.

2 The LAC retrieves L2TP tunneling information from the LAC AAA server, and then establishes an L2TP tunnel and session with the L2TP network server (LNS) at the enterprise headquarters.

3 The LNS forwards the username and password to the LNS AAA server for authentication and authorization.

4 After the user has been authenticated and authorized, the user has access to the headquarters network.

Business Drivers

The preexisting VPDN uses L2TP to tunnel PPP traffic over the Internet. Because L2TP does not encrypt traffic, both the control and data packets of the L2TP protocol are vulnerable to the following types of attacks:

- Discovery of user identities by snooping data packets.
- Modification packets (both control and data).
- Hijacking of the L2TP tunnel or the PPP connection inside the tunnel.
- Denial-of-service attacks that terminate PPP connections or L2TP tunnels.
- Disruption of the PPP Encryption Control Protocol (ECP) negotiation in order to weaken or remove confidentiality protection.
- Disruption of the PPP Link Control Protocol (LCP) authentication negotiation so as to weaken the PPP authentication process or gain access to user passwords.

IPSec addresses these threats in the following ways:

- Providing authentication, integrity, and replay protection of control packets.
- Providing integrity and replay protection of data packets.
- Protecting control packet confidentiality.
- Providing the option of a scalable approach to key management.

L2TP tunnels use PPP authentication (either PAP or CHAP) to provide mutual authentication between the LAC and the LNS at tunnel origination. PAP offers authentication only. CHAP also encrypts the password, but does not encrypt the data payload. Therefore, CHAP and PAP authenticate the client to the LNS, but they do not protect control and data traffic on a per-packet basis, nor do they provide per-packet authentication, integrity, or replay protection.

IPSec is the best method to ensure per-packet authentication, integrity, and replay protection.

Possible Solutions

The following are three possible IPSec over L2TP solutions:

- IPSec tunnel between the LAC and LNS
- IPSec tunnel between the peer and LNS
- IPSec tunnel between the client and LNS

Possible Solution 1: IPSec Tunnel Between the LAC and LNS

The client initiates a PPP session (either by itself or by using a peer) to the LAC. The LAC negotiates an L2TP tunnel with the LNS and forwards the client PPP session to the LNS. The LAC and LNS then negotiate an IPSec tunnel to encrypt the client PPP session. The session is encrypted between the LAC and LNS, which is the segment of the network most susceptible to attack, but it is not encrypted between the client and the LAC.

Possible Solution 2: IPSec Tunnel Between the Peer and LNS

The client connects to the peer, and the peer initiates a PPP session to the LAC. The LAC negotiates an L2TP tunnel with the LNS and forwards the client PPP session to the LNS. The peer and LNS then negotiate an IPSec tunnel to encrypt the client PPP session. In this solution, the only segment of the network that is not encrypted is the connection between the client and the peer. Because the client and peer are typically in the same office, however, this solution usually is not a security risk.

Possible Solution 3: IPSec Tunnel Between the Client and LNS

The client initiates a PPP session (either by itself or by using a peer) to the LAC. The LAC negotiates an L2TP tunnel with the LNS and forwards the client PPP session to the LNS. The client and LNS then negotiate an IPSec tunnel to encrypt the client PPP session. In this solution, the entire network is encrypted. This solution proves useful when a peer is shared by different parties. It also proves useful for mobile users who do not have access to a peer but still need a secure remote connection. The disadvantages of this solution are that it requires that every client be configured for IPSec (instead of just the single peer) and that IPSec negotiation may take longer on clients than on the peer.

Figure 4-2 shows these three possible solutions.

Figure 4-2 *IPSec over L2TP Possible Solutions*

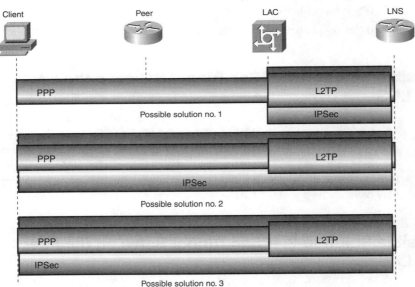

Proposed Solution: IPSec Tunnel Between the Peer and LNS

The enterprise company decides to implement solution 2, IPSec tunnel between the peer and LNS, because it is the simplest solution that provides the encryption it needs: The enterprise requires that the entire session be encrypted—not just the link between the LAC and LNS. The enterprise maintains its own peer at the remote office, so it need not encrypt the connections between clients and the peer. The enterprise does not need encryption for its mobile users, so it need not configure client-initiated IPSec.

Overview

Adding IPSec to an existing VPDN is a relatively simple process. Usually, no new equipment is required; the existing VPDN devices can be reconfigured to perform IPSec. The two situations in which the partners would need to purchase new equipment are as follows:

- If the existing equipment does not have enough CPU power to perform IPSec negotiation in addition to its existing responsibilities

- If the enterprise wants to support home modem users who require the purchase of peer routers (such as Cisco 800 or 1720 series routers) to perform IPSec negotiation

Network Topology

Figure 4-3 shows the end-to-end IPSec VPDN.

Figure 4-3 *Postimplementation Network Topology*

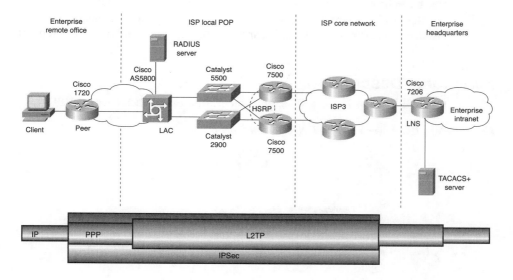

In the new IPSec network, the peer, LAC, and LNS establish L2TP tunnels and sessions exactly as they did in the original network. When the L2TP tunnel and session are established, the peer initiates IPSec negotiation with the LNS. (The LAC is not involved in IPSec.) Once the peer and LNS complete IPSec negotiation, the connection is secured from the peer in the remote office to the LNS at the headquarters office.

Benefits

The following are some of the benefits of this solution:

- Because IPSec is standards-based, the network will be able to interoperate with other non-Cisco IPSec-compliant devices.

- If the enterprise already has the necessary equipment, IPSec is fast, easy, and inexpensive to deploy on existing VPDNs. (If necessary, upgrading to proper Cisco IOS releases and any associated memory upgrades would incur additional costs.)

- Deploying IPSec on the Integrated Services Digital Network (ISDN) router rather than on individual PCs eliminates the need to reconfigure every PC in the office.

- IPSec is a flexible security solution. Multiple encryption types are supported.

IPSec can be reconfigured for more complex, large-scale service that uses such features as digital certificates, dynamic crypto maps, dynamic tunnel endpoint discovery, wildcard preshared keys, and multiple certificate authority roots support.

Functional Description

Figure 4-4 shows how an IPSec-encrypted call is established over the VPDN.

Figure 4-4   *IPSec over VPDN Call Negotiation Process*

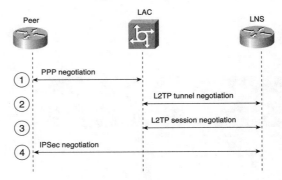

The following list describes the sequence of events shown in Figure 4-4:

1 A user in the enterprise remote office initiates a call to the headquarters office from a PC connected to the peer. The peer places a call over the Public Switched Telephone Network (PSTN) and ISDN to forward the user PPP session to the LAC.

2 When the LAC receives the PPP session, it negotiates an L2TP tunnel with the LNS at the enterprise headquarters.

3 After the LAC and LNS establish an L2TP tunnel, the LAC forwards the user information to the LNS. The LNS authenticates the user and establishes an L2TP session for the user.

4 Once the L2TP tunnel and session are established, the remote user has connectivity to the enterprise headquarters. The peer then initiates IPSec negotiation directly with the LNS. (The LAC is not involved in IPSec.)

For detailed information about IPSec negotiation, see the "Encryption Technologies" section of Chapter 1, "Access VPDN Technologies Overview."

Implementation

The following sections describe how the IPSec network is implemented:

- Prerequisites
- Design Considerations
- Ramifications
- Device Characteristics
- Configuration Files

Prerequisites

Before IPSec is configured, the ISP and enterprise need to establish VPDN connectivity between the enterprise remote office and the headquarters using the ISP LAC to establish L2TP tunnels with the enterprise LNS.

IPSec uses IP protocols 50 and 51, and Internet Key Exchange (IKE) traffic passes on protocol 17, port 500 (UDP 500). Before configuring IPSec, ensure that these protocols and ports are permitted by access lists.

Before configuring IPSec, you should configure only known IP addresses in your access lists and not use the **any** keyword.

Design Considerations

When designing an IPSec network, you must make a number of decisions. Most involve choosing between increased performance and increased security. The following sections provide details on these decisions:

- Authentication Only, or Authentication and Encryption
- Encryption Algorithm
- Hash Algorithm
- Authentication Method
- Diffie-Hellman Group Identifier Options
- Security Association Lifetimes

Authentication Only, or Authentication and Encryption

IPSec can be configured to perform authentication only, or both authentication and encryption.

Decision: The enterprise decides that its data needs to be both authenticated and encrypted.

Encryption Algorithm

IPSec offers the choice of two encryption algorithms: 56-bit DES-CBC or 168-bit DES. 168-bit DES is the more secure of the two encryption algorithms, but it requires more time and processing power than 56-bit DES-CBC. Also, there are international restrictions on 168-bit encryption.

Decision: The enterprise decides that 56-bit DES-CBC encryption is sufficient for its needs.

Hash Algorithm

IPSec offers the choice of two hash algorithms: SHA-1 and MD5. MD5 is slightly faster. There has been a demonstrated successful (but extremely difficult) attack against MD5; however, the HMAC variant used by IKE prevents this attack.

Decision: The enterprise decides to use the SHA-1 hash algorithm.

Authentication Method

IPSec offers three authentication methods, as follows:

- **Rivest, Shamir, and Adelman (RSA) signatures**—The most secure and the most scalable authentication method. However, the signatures require the use of a certification authority, which makes RSA signatures the most difficult option to configure.

- **RSA encrypted nonces**—Nonces are random numbers that are used in encryption and authentication. They do not require that the peers possess the public keys of each other, nor do they require the use of a certification authority. They are easier to configure in a small network, but do not scale well for large-scale networks.

- **Preshared keys**—The simplest authentication method, preshared keys do not scale well for large-scale networks and are not as secure as RSA signatures.

Decision: The enterprise decides to make its initial IPSec configuration as simple as possible, so it decides to use preshared keys.

Diffie-Hellman Group Identifier Options

The Diffie-Hellman identifier is used for deriving key materials between peers. IPSec offers the choice of 768-bit or 1024-bit Diffie-Hellman groups. The 1024-bit Diffie-Hellman group is more secure, but requires more CPU time to execute.

Decision: The enterprise decides that the 768-bit Diffie-Hellman group is sufficient for its needs.

Security Association Lifetimes

The lifetimes of IKE security associations can be configured to any desired value. The default value is 86,400 seconds, or one day. When the first IKE negotiation begins, SAs are negotiated. Each peer retains the SAs until the SA lifetime expires. Any subsequent IKE negotiations can reuse these SAs, which speeds future negotiations. Therefore, longer lifetimes can increase performance, but they also increase SAs exposure to attack. The longer an SA is used, the more encrypted traffic can be gathered by an attacker and used in an attack.

Decision: The enterprise decides to use the default value of 86,400-second SA lifetimes.

Ramifications

The following are possible ramifications of implementing this solution:

- **Scaling limitations**—Although using preshared authentication keys is the simplest way to implement IPSec, it is not a practical solution for large-scale networks. Therefore, if the ISP wants to expand its IPSec service, it should reconfigure IPSec to use digital certificates obtained from a certificate authority.

- **Limitations of initiating IPSec at the ISDN router**—When IPSec is initiated at the ISDN router, the connection between the PC and the ISDN router is not encrypted. Usually, this unencrypted link is not a security concern because the PC and ISDN router are both located in the same office. In some circumstances, however, multiple parties may share the ISDN router. In this case, the connection between the PC and ISDN router could be subject to attack.

  Also, initiating IPSec at the ISDN router limits security for mobile users. The connection between the mobile PC and the ISDN router will not be encrypted. This connection is over the PSTN and ISDN, which is less susceptible to attack than is the Internet. Therefore it is not a critical security concern, but it is a concern for highly sensitive data.

Device Characteristics

Figure 4-5 shows added details of the devices critical to performing IPSec over VPDN.

Figure 4-5 *Details of Network Topology*

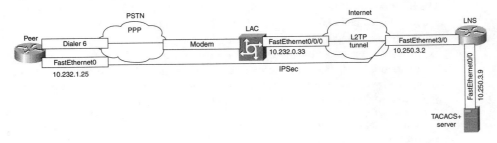

Table 4-2 describes the devices shown in Figure 4-5.

Table 4-2   *Device Characteristics*

	ISDN Router	LAC	LNS
Host Name	isdn4	NAS5-58-RS	ISP3AC5
Chassis Type	Cisco 1720 router	Cisco AS5800 access server	Cisco 7206 VXR router
Physical Interfaces	2 serial 1 BRI 1 Fast Ethernet 6 dialers	5 Fast Ethernet 6 Ethernet 6 serial 3 dialers	4 Fast Ethernet 5 Ethernet
Software Loaded	Cisco IOS Release 12.1(4)T	Cisco IOS Release 12.1(4)T	Cisco IOS Release 12.1(3)
IP Addresses, Subnet Masks, and IP Address Ranges	Fast Ethernet 0: 10.232.1.25 255.255.255.248	Fast Ethernet 0/0/0: 10.232.0.33 255.255.255.248 (primary) Fast Ethernet 0/5/0: 10.232.0.41 255.255.255.248 (secondary)	Fast Ethernet 0/0: 10.250.3.9 255.255.255.248 (to RADIUS server) Fast Ethernet 3/0: 10.250.3.2 255.255.255.248 (to ISP3DA4, used for VPDN traffic) IP local pool ISP3POOL: 10.239.192.1 10.239.199.254

Configuration Files

The following sections contain the parts of the device configurations needed to enable IPSec on an L2TP network:

- Configuring the Peer for IPSec over VPDN
- Configuring the LAC for IPSec over VPDN
- Configuring the LNS for IPSec over VPDN
- Configuring the LNS TACACS+ Server for VPDN

Configuring the Peer for IPSec over VPDN

The commands in Example 4-1 are necessary to enable a peer to dial in to the LAC and negotiate IPSec with the LNS.

Example 4-1 *Configuring the Peer for IPSec over VPDN*

```
!Identifies the version of Cisco IOS software running on the LAC.
version 12.1
!Includes millisecond timestamps on log and debug entries that are
!useful for troubleshooting and optimizing the network.
service timestamps debug datetime msec localtime show-timezone
service timestamps log datetime msec localtime show-timezone
!Specifies that passwords will not be encrypted in configuration
!output. This is useful when first configuring a network, but is a
!security risk when the network is operational.
no service password-encryption
!
!Configures the hostname of the router.
hostname isdn4
!
logging buffered 4096 debugging
enable secret 5 $1$r4OC$rE0tf7GTYYZFc80M5SRJL0
!
username nas2-52 password 0 lab
!
!
memory-size iomem 15
!Configures the timezone and Daylight Savings Time adjustment.
clock timezone PDT -8
clock summer-time PDT recurring
!Allows for the configuration of the first subnet in each classfull
!network.
ip subnet-zero
!
isdn switch-type basic-5ess
isdn voice-call-failure 0
!
!
!Creates IKE policy 1, which would be given highest priority if there
!were additional IKE policies.
crypto isakmp policy 1
!Specifies that IKE will use pre-shared keys for authentication.
 authentication pre-share
!By default, this IKE policy will use the 56-bit DES-CBC encryption
!algorithm, the SHA-1 hash algorithm, the 768-bit Diffie-Hellman group,
!and 86400 second SA lifetimes.
!
```

Example 4-1 *Configuring the Peer for IPSec over VPDN (Continued)*

```
!Specifies the pre-shared key as cisco123 for negotiation with the
!LNS at IP address 10.250.3.2. This pre-shared key must also be
!specified on the LNS for the peer IP address.
crypto isakmp key cisco123 address 10.250.3.2
!By default, the peer's ISAKMP identity is set as its IP address,
!10.232.1.25.
!
!Creates the transform set called e2e. It includes an AH transform,
!an ESP encryption transform, and an ESP authentication transform.
!The transform set on the LNS must include all three of these transforms
!for successful negotiation.
crypto ipsec transform-set e2e ah-md5-hmac esp-des esp-md5-hmac
!
!
!Creates the crypto map called vpdn-isg, gives it a sequence number
!(priority) of 10, and specifies that IKE will be used to establish
!IPSec security associations.
crypto map vpdn-isg 10 ipsec-isakmp
!Specifies the IP address of the LNS.
 set peer 10.250.3.2
!Instructs the crypto map to use the e2e transform set.
 set transform-set e2e
!Specifies that extended access list 101 will be used to determine
!which traffic is to be protected by IPSec.
 match address 101
!
cns event-service server
!
!
interface BRI0
 description "Lucent BRI # 60153"
 no ip address
 encapsulation ppp
 no ip route-cache
 no ip mroute-cache
 dialer pool-member 1
 isdn switch-type basic-5ess
 isdn incoming-voice modem
 no fair-queue
 no cdp enable
!Specifies that traffic using BRI 0 is to be encrypted by crypto map
!vpdn-isg.
 crypto map vpdn-isg
!
!FastEthernet 0 is the interface that is used for VPDN and IPSec
!traffic.
```

continues

Example 4-1 *Configuring the Peer for IPSec over VPDN (Continued)*

```
interface FastEthernet0
 ip address 10.232.1.25 255.255.255.248
 speed auto
 half-duplex
 no cdp enable
!
!Dialer 6 is used to establish the initial PPP connection to the LAC.
interface Dialer6
 description "vpdn dialup to ISP3AC5 10.250.3.0 via NAS5-58-RS"
 ip unnumbered FastEthernet0
 encapsulation ppp
 no ip route-cache
 no ip mroute-cache
 dialer pool 1
!Specifies the remote name of the LAC.
 dialer remote-name isp3ac5-hgw
!Specifies the PRI number of the LAC.
 dialer string 50127
 dialer-group 1
 no cdp enable
 ppp authentication chap pap callin
 ppp chap hostname isdn4@isp3-2.com
 ppp chap password 7 09404F0B
!Specifies that traffic using dialer 6 is to encrypted by crypto map
!vpdn-isg.
 crypto map vpdn-isg
 !
ip classless

ip route 10.250.3.2 255.255.255.255 Dialer6
ip route 0.0.0.0 0.0.0.0 Dialer6
no ip http server
 !
!Specifies that traffic from 10.232.1.24 (the peer) to 10.250.3.0
!(the LNS) is to be permitted.
!Because this access list is reference in crypto map vpdn-isg,
!traffic meeting the requirements of this access list will be
!encrypted by crypto map vpdn-isg.
access-list 101 permit ip 10.232.1.24 0.0.0.7 10.250.3.0 0.0.0.7
dialer-list 1 protocol ip permit
 !
end
```

Configuring the LAC for IPSec over VPDN

The commands in Example 4-2 are necessary to enable the LAC to receive calls from the peer and forward them to the LNS using L2TP. The LAC is not involved in IPSec negotiation.

Example 4-2 *Configuring the LAC for IPSec over VPDN*

```
!Identifies the version of Cisco IOS software running on the LAC
  version 12.1
!Includes millisecond timestamps on log and debug entries that are
!useful for troubleshooting and optimizing the network
service timestamps debug datetime msec localtime show-timezone
service timestamps log datetime msec localtime show-timezone
!Specifies that passwords will not be encrypted in configuration
!output. This is useful when first configuring a network, but is a
!security risk when the network is operational.
no service password-encryption
!
!Configures the hostname for the LAC.
hostname NAS5-58-RS
!
boot system flash c5800-p456i-mz.121-4.0.1.T
!Configures AAA and specifies that the LAC will authenticate
!VPDN tunnels with RADIUS.
aaa new-model
aaa authentication ppp default if-needed local group radius
!
!Configures the usernames and passwords that are used for
!VPDN tunnel negotiation.
!These usernames and passwords are called tunnel secrets.
username isp3ac5-hgw password 0 lab
username isdn-nas5-isp3 password 0 lab
!
!
!Configures the timezone and Daylight Savings Time adjustment.
clock timezone PDT -8
clock summer-time PDT recurring
dial-tdm-clock  priority 1 trunk-slot 0 port 0
!
!
!Allows for the configuration of the first subnet in each classfull
!network.
ip subnet-zero
ip cef
no ip domain-lookup
!
!Turns on VPDN.
vpdn enable
no vpdn logging
!Instructs the LAC to tunnel VPDN calls based on the user domain name.
vpdn search-order domain
!
!This is the VPDN group for the enterprise.
vpdn-group 1
!Configures a request dial-in VPDN subgroup.
```

continues

Example 4-2 *Configuring the LAC for IPSec over VPDN (Continued)*

```
 request-dialin
!Configures L2TP as the tunnel protocol.
  protocol l2tp
!Specifies that users with the domain name isp3-2.com will be
!tunneled by this VPDN group.
 domain isp3-2.com
!Specifies the IP address of the enterprise LNS.
 !
 initiate-to ip 10.250.3.2
!Configures the local name that the ISP will use to identify itself for
!L2TP tunnel authentication with the service provider LNS. If the
!ISP expands to a stacked-LAC environment, it will need to use the
!same local name on all of the LACs.
 local name isdn-nas5-isp3
 !
!Configures the telco switch type. When the switch type is configured
!in global configuration mode, it is automatically propagated into
!the individual serial interfaces.
isdn switch-type primary-5ess
 !
 !
 !
controller T1 1/0/4
!Configures the T1 framing type as super frame (ESF).
 framing esf
!Configures the LAC to gets its primary clocking from T1 controller 0.
 clock source line primary
!Configures the T1 line code type as B8ZS.
 linecode b8zs
!Assigns all 24 T1 timeslots as ISDN PRI channels and creates a
!D-channel serial interface (Serial interface 0:23). Individual
!B-channel serial interfaces are also created (Serial interfaces
!0:0 through 0:22), but they are not shown in the configuration.
 pri-group timeslots 1-24
!Includes the PRI number that corresponds to this controller in the
!configuration for easy reference.
 description LucentPRInumber = 50127
 !
 !
interface FastEthernet0/0/0
 description "This is the IP id for this router"
 ip address 10.232.0.33 255.255.255.248
 full-duplex
 !
interface FastEthernet0/5/0
```

Example 4-2   *Configuring the LAC for IPSec over VPDN (Continued)*

```
  description "This is the secondary interface for router"
  ip address 10.232.0.41 255.255.255.248
  full-duplex
 !
 !
 !
 !Serial interface 1/0/4:23 is the D channel that corresponds to
 !controller T1 1/0/4. The behavior of the B-channel serial interfaces
 !(1/0/4:0 through 1/0/4:22) is controlled by the configuration of
 !Serial interface 1/0/4:23.
 interface Serial1/0/4:23
 !Includes the PRI number that corresponds to this interface in the
 !configuration for easy reference.
  description LucentPRInumber = 50127
 !Specifies that the interface does not require an IP address.
  no ip address
  encapsulation ppp
  ip mroute-cache
  dialer rotary-group 1
  dialer-group 1
 !This command is automatically configured on all of the serial
 !interfaces by the isdn switch-type global configuration mode command.
  isdn switch-type primary-5ess
 !
 !
 interface Dialer1
  ip unnumbered FastEthernet0/0/0
  encapsulation ppp
  dialer in-band
  dialer map ip 10.232.1.25 name isdn4
  dialer-group 1
  peer default ip address pool NAS5POOL
  ppp authentication chap pap ms-chap
 !
 !
 ip classless


 no ip http server
 !
 dialer-list 1 protocol ip permit
 !
 !
 !
 !Specifies the IP address of the RADIUS server, and the ports that
 !are to be sued for authorization and accounting.
 radius-server host 10.232.0.122 auth-port 1645 acct-port 1646
```

continues

Example 4-2 *Configuring the LAC for IPSec over VPDN (Continued)*

```
!Configures the password for the RADIUS server.
radius-server key pass4me
!
!
!
end
```

Configuring the LNS for IPSec over VPDN

The commands in Example 4-3 are necessary to enable the LNS to establish L2TP tunnels and sessions with the LAC and to negotiate IPSec with the peer.

Example 4-3 *Configuring the LNS for IPSec over VPDN*

```
!Identifies the version of Cisco IOS software running on the LAC.
version 12.1
!Includes millisecond timestamps on log and debug entries that are
!useful for troubleshooting and optimizing the network.
service timestamps debug datetime msec localtime show-timezone
service timestamps log datetime msec localtime show-timezone
!Specifies that passwords will not be encrypted in configuration
!output. This is useful when first configuring a network, but is a
!security risk when the network is operational.
no service password-encryption
service udp-small-servers
service tcp-small-servers
!
!Configures the hostname of the router.
hostname ISP3AC5
!
boot system disk0:c7200-jo3s56i-mz.121-3.3
!
!Configures AAA and specifies that the LAC will authenticate
!VPDN tunnels with TACACS+.
aaa new-model
aaa authentication ppp default local group tacacs+
!
!
!
!Configures the usernames and passwords that are used for
!VPDN tunnel negotiation.
!These usernames and passwords are called tunnel secrets.
username isdn-nas5-isp3 password 0 lab
username isp3ac5-hgw password 0 lab
!
!
!Configures the timezone and Daylight Savings Time adjustment.
```

Example 4-3   *Configuring the LNS for IPSec over VPDN (Continued)*

```
clock timezone PST -8
clock summer-time PST recurring
!Allows for the configuration of the first subnet in each classfull
!network.
ip subnet-zero
no ip finger
no ip domain-lookup
!
!Turns on VPDN.
vpdn enable
no vpdn logging
!
!
!This is the VPDN group that negotiates with the ISP LAC.
vpdn-group 2
!Configures an accept-dialin VPDN subgroup.
 accept-dialin
!Specifies that this VPDN group will negotiate either L2F or L2TP
!tunnels.
   protocol any
!Instructs the LNS to clone virtual access interfaces for
!VPDN sessions from virtual template 3.
   virtual-template 3
!Specifies that this VPDN group will negotiate L2TP tunnels with LACs
!that identify themselves with the local name isdn-nas5-isp3.
 terminate-from hostname isdn-nas5-isp3
 local name isp3ac5-hgw
!
!Creates IKE policy 1, which would be given highest priority if there
!were additional IKE policies.
crypto isakmp policy 1
!Specifies that IKE will use pre-shared keys for authentication.
!authentication pre-share By default, this IKE policy will use the
!56-bit DES-CBC encryption algorithm, the SHA-1 hash algorithm, the
!768-bit Diffie-Hellman group, and 86400 second SA lifetimes.
!
!Specifies the pre-shared key as cisco123 for negotiation with the
!peer at IP address 10.232.1.25. This pre-shared key must also be
!specified on the peer for the LNS IP address. By default, the LNS's
!ISAKMP identity is set as its IP address, 10.250.3.2.
crypto isakmp key cisco123 address 10.232.1.25
!The next two pre-shared keys are for IPSec tunnels to other peers
!(not shown in this network) at the IP addresses 10.232.1.33.57,
!and 10.232.1.57.
```

continues

Example 4-3 *Configuring the LNS for IPSec over VPDN (Continued)*

```
crypto isakmp key cisco123 address 10.232.1.33
crypto isakmp key cisco123 address 10.232.1.57
!
!
!Creates the transform set called e2e. It includes an AH transform,
!an ESP encryption transform, and an ESP authentication transform.
!The transform set on the LNS must include all three of these
!transforms for successful negotiation.
crypto ipsec transform-set e2e ah-md5-hmac esp-des esp-md5-hmac
!
!Creates the crypto map called vpdn-isg, gives it a sequence number
!(priority) of 10, and specifies that IKE will be used to establish
!IPSec security associations.
crypto map vpdn-isg 10 ipsec-isakmp
!Specifies the IP address of the peer.
 set peer 10.232.1.25
!Instructs the crypto map to use the e2e transform set.
 set transform-set e2e
!Specifies that extended access list 102 will be used to determine which
!traffic is to be protected by IPSec.
 match address 102
!The next two crypto maps are for the IPSec tunnels to other peers not
!shown in this network.
crypto map vpdn-isg 20 ipsec-isakmp
 set peer 10.232.1.33
 set transform-set e2e
 match address 103
crypto map vpdn-isg 30 ipsec-isakmp
 set peer 10.232.1.57
 set transform-set e2e
 match address 104
!
cns event-service server
!
!
interface FastEthernet0/0
 description "network to the TACACS+ server - stss-ss20"
 ip address 10.250.3.9 255.255.255.248
 full-duplex
!
!
interface FastEthernet3/0
 description To ISP3DA4, Fa5/1
 ip address 10.250.3.2 255.255.255.248
 no ip route-cache
 no ip mroute-cache
 half-duplex
!
```

Example 4-3 *Configuring the LNS for IPSec over VPDN (Continued)*

```
!
!
!Creates virtual template 3, which is used to clone virtual access
!interfaces for incoming VPDN sessions.
interface Virtual-Template3
!Specifies that the virtual access interfaces will use the IP address of
!Fast Ethernet interface 3/0.
 ip unnumbered FastEthernet3/0
 no ip route-cache
 no keepalive
!Enables CHAP and PAP authentication.
 ppp authentication chap
!Specifies that traffic using virtual-access interfaces cloned from
!virtual template 3 is to be encrypted by crypto map vpdn-isg.
 crypto map vpdn-isg
 !
!Creates a pool of IP addresses that are assigned to incoming VPDN
!sessions.
ip local pool ISP3POOL 10.239.192.1 10.239.199.254
ip kerberos source-interface any
no ip classless
no ip http server
 !
!Specifies that traffic from 10.250.3.0 (the LNS) to 10.232.1.24 (the
!peer) is to be permitted. Because this access list is reference in
!crypto map vpdn-isg, traffic meeting the requirements of this access
!list will be encrypted by crypto map vpdn-isg.
access-list 102 permit ip 10.250.3.0 0.0.0.7 10.232.1.24 0.0.0.7
!The next two access lists are for the IPSec tunnels to other peers not
!shown in this network.
access-list 103 permit ip 10.250.3.0 0.0.0.7 10.232.1.32 0.0.0.7
access-list 104 permit ip 10.250.3.0 0.0.0.7 10.232.1.56 0.0.0.7
 !
!Specifies the IP address of the TACACS+ server.
tacacs-server host 223.255.254.254
!Configures the password for the TACACS+ server.
tacacs-server key cisco12345
 !
 !
 !
 !
end
```

Configuring the LNS TACACS+ Server for VPDN

The user profile in Example 4-4 is necessary to enable the LNS TACACS+ server to verify a user that dials in with the username isdn4@isp3-2com and the password lab.

Example 4-4 *Configuring the LNS TACACS+ Server for VPDN*

```
user = isdn4@isp3-2com{
        password = chap "lab"
        service=ppp {
        protocol=lcp {
        }
        protocol=ip {
        }
```

New Access VPDN Services: L2TP Dial-Out

The L2TP dial-out feature enables Layer 2 Tunneling Program (L2TP) network servers (LNSs) to tunnel dial-out VPDN calls using L2TP as the tunneling protocol.

This appendix includes the following sections:

- L2TP Dial-Out Overview
- L2TP Dial-Out Benefits
- L2TP Dial-Out Restrictions
- L2TP Supported Platforms
- L2TP Dial-Out Supported Standards, MIBs, and RFCs
- L2TP Dial-Out Configuration Tasks
- L2TP Dial-Out Verification
- L2TP Dial-Out Configuration Examples

L2TP Dial-Out Overview

The L2TP dial-out feature enables LNSs to tunnel dial-out VPDN calls using L2TP as the tunneling protocol. This feature enables a centralized network to efficiently and inexpensively establish a virtual point-to-point connection with any number of remote offices.

Using the L2TP dial-out feature, Cisco Systems routers can carry both dial-in and dial-out calls in the same L2TP tunnels. Previously, only dial-in VPDN calls were supported. L2TP dial-out involves two devices:

- An LNS
- An L2TP access concentrator (LAC)

When the LNS wants to perform L2TP dial-out, it negotiates an L2TP tunnel with the LAC. The LAC then places a PPP call to the client(s) the LNS wants to dial out to.

For more information on the operation of the L2TP dial-out feature, see Chapter 1 "Access VPDN Technologies Overview."

L2TP Dial-Out Benefits

The benefits of L2TP dial-out are as follows:

- Dial flexibility
- Centralized billing
- Callback support

L2TP Dial-Out Restrictions

L2TP dial-out restrictions are as follows:

- Large-scale dial-out is not supported.
- Border Area Protocol (BAP) and Dialer Watch are not supported.
- All configurations must be local on the router. For example, L2TP dial-out does not support remote AAA.

L2TP-Supported Platforms

L2TP-supported platforms are as follows:

- Cisco 1600 series
- Cisco 1720 VPN access router
- Cisco 2500 series
- Cisco 2600
- Cisco 3600 series
- Cisco 4000-M series (Cisco 4000-M, 4500-M, 4700-M)
- Cisco 7000 series

- Cisco 7100 series
- Cisco 7200 series
- Cisco 7500 series
- Cisco AS5200
- Cisco AS5300
- Cisco AS5800

L2TP Dial-Out-Supported Standards, MIBs, and RFCs

There are no L2TP dial-out-supported standards.

The MIBs are as follows:

- CISCO-VPDN-MGMT-MIB.my
- CISCO-VPDN-MGMT-MIB-V1SMI.my

For descriptions of supported MIBs by platform and Cisco IOS releases, and to download MIB modules, go to the Cisco MIB Web site:

www.cisco.com/public/sw-center/netmgmt/cmtk/mibs.shtml

L2TP is described in RFC 2661, "L2TP."

L2TP Dial-Out Configuration Tasks

The following L2TP dial-out configuration tasks are covered in this section.

- Configuring an LNS to request L2TP dial-out
- Configuring a LAC to accept L2TP dial-out
- Configuring the dialer on the LNS
- Configuring the dialer on the LAC

Configuring an LNS to Request L2TP Dial-Out

To configure an LNS to request dial-out tunneled PPP connections to a LAC, use the commands in Table A-1 beginning in global configuration mode.

Table A-1   *Configuring an LNS to Request L2TP Dial-Out*

Step	Command	Purpose
Step 1	**vpdn group** *name* dupree(config)#**vpdn group 1**	Creates a VPDN group with the specified name.
Step 2	**request dialout** dupree(config-vpdn)#**request dialout**	Enables the LAC to send L2TP dial-out requests.
Step 3	**protocol** {**l2f** | **l2tp** | **pppoe** | **pptp** | **any**} dupree(config-vpdn-req-out)#**protocol l2tp**	Specifies L2TP as the tunneling protocol. L2TP is the only protocol that supports dial-out.
Step 4	**pool-member** *pool-number* dupree(config-vpdn-req-out)#**pool-member 2** or **rotary-group** *group-number* dupree(config-vpdn-req-out)#**rotary-group 2**	Specifies the dialer profile pool that will be used to dial out. or Specifies the dialer rotary group that will be used to dial out. You can configure only one dialer profile pool or dialer rotary group. Attempting to configure a second dialer resource will remove the first from the configuration.
Step 5	**exit** dupree(config-vpdn-req-out)#**exit**	Exits from the configuration mode or submode.
Step 6	**initiate-to ip** *ip-address* [**limit** *limit-number*] [**priority** *priority-number*] dupree(config-vpdn-req-out)#**initiate-to ip 10.100.100.10 limit 200 priority 1**	Specifies the IP address that will be dialed out. Optionally, you can configure a maximum number of connections that this VPDN group will support and the priority of this VPDN group.
Step 7	**local name** *hostname* dupree(config-vpdn-req-out)#**local name tunnel3**	Specifies that the L2TP tunnel will identify itself with this host name.

Configuring a LAC to Accept L2TP Dial-Out

To configure a LAC to accept tunneled dial-out connections from an LNS, use the commands in Table A-2 beginning in global configuration mode.

Table A-2   *Configuring a LAC to Accept L2TP Dial-Out*

Step	Command	Purpose
Step 1	**vpdn group** *name* sugaree(config)#**vpdn group 1**	Creates VPDN group 1.
Step 2	**accept dialout** sugaree(config-vpdn)#**accept dialout**	Enables the LAC to accept L2TP dial-out requests.
Step 3	**protocol** {**l2f** | **l2tp** | **pppoe** | **pptp** | **any**} sugaree(config-vpdn-acc-out)#**protocol l2tp**	Specifies L2TP as the tunneling protocol. L2TP is the only protocol that supports dial-out.
Step 4	**dialer** *dialer-interface* sugaree(config-vpdn-acc-out)#**dialer 4**	Specifies the dialer that is used to dial out.
Step 5	**exit** sugaree(config-vpdn-acc-out)#**exit**	Exits from configuration mode or submode.
Step 6	**terminate-from hostname** *hostname* sugaree(config-vpdn)#**terminate-from hostname cerise**	Accepts L2TP tunnels that have this host name configured as a local name.

Configuring the Dialer on the LNS

To enable an LNS to request L2TP dial-out, use the commands in Table A-3 beginning in global configuration mode to configure the dialer of the LNS.

Table A-3   *Configuring the Dialer on the LNS*

Step	Command	Purpose
Step 1	**interface dialer** *name* dupree(config)#**interface dialer 1**	Defines a dialer rotary group.
Step 2	**ip address** *address mask* dupree(config-if)#**ip address 172.1.2.3 255.255.255.128**	Specifies an IP address for the group.
Step 3	**encapsulation ppp** dupree(config-if)#**encapsulation ppp**	Enables PPP encapsulation.
Step 4	**dialer remote-name** *peer-name* dupree(config-if)#**dialer remote-name reuben**	Specifies the name used to authenticate the remote router that is being dialed.

continues

Table A-3 *Configuring the Dialer on the LNS (Continued)*

Step	Command	Purpose
Step 5	**dialer string** *dialer-number* dupree(config-if)#**dialer string 8675309**	Specifies the number that is dialed.
Step 6	**dialer vpdn** dupree(config-if)#**dialer vpdn**	Enables L2TP dial-out.
Step 7	**dialer pool** *pool-number* dupree(config-if)#**dialer pool 5**	Specifies the dialer pool.
Step 8	**dialer-group** *group-number* dupree(config-if)#**dialer-group 5**	Assigns the dialer to the specified dialer group.
Step 9	**ppp authentication** {**chap** | **chap pap** | **pap chap** | **pap**} dupree(config-if)#**ppp authentication chap**	Specifies that CHAP authentication will be used.

Configuring the Dialer on the LAC

To enable a LAC to accept L2TP dial-out, use the commands in Table A-4 beginning in global configuration mode to configure the dialer of the LAC.

Table A-4 *Configuring the Dialer on the LAC*

Step	Command	Purpose
Step 1	**interface dialer** *number* sugaree(config)#**interface dialer 1**	Defines a dialer rotary group.
Step 2	**ip unnumbered** *interface-type number* sugaree(config-if)#**ip unnumbered ethernet0**	Configures the dialer to use the IP address of the specified interface.
Step 3	**encapsulation ppp** sugaree(config-if)#**encapsulation ppp**	Enables PPP encapsulation
Step 4	**dialer in-band** sugaree(config-if)#**dialer in-band**	Enables DDR on the dialer.
Step 5	**dialer aaa** sugaree(config-if)#**dialer aaa**	Enables the dialer to use the AAA server to locate profiles for dialing information.

Table A-4   *Configuring the Dialer on the LAC (Continued)*

Step	Command	Purpose
Step 6	**dialer-group** *group-number* sugaree(config-if)#**dialer-group 2**	Assigns the dialer to the specified hdialer group.
Step 7	**ppp authentication {chap	chap pap	pap chap	pap}** dupree(config-if)#**ppp authentication chap**	Specifies that CHAP authentication will be used.

L2TP Dial-Out Verification

Example A-1 displays sample output of the **show vpdn** user EXEC command for a dial-out session on a LAC.

Example A-1   *Sample* **show vpdn** *User EXEC Mode Command Output for a Dial-Out Session on a LAC*

```
LAC# show vpdn

L2TP Tunnel and Session Information (Total tunnels=1 sessions=1)

LocID RemID Remote Name   State  Remote Address  Port  Sessions
1     1     lns_l2x0      est    10.40.1.150     1701  1

LocID RemID TunID Intf    Username      State  Last Chg Fastswitch
1     1     1     Se0:22                est    00:00:02 enabled
```

Example A-2 displays sample output of the **show vpdn** user EXEC command for a dial-out session on an LNS.

Example A-2   *Sample* **show vpdn** *User EXEC Command Output for a Dial-Out Session on an LNS*

```
LNS# show vpdn

L2TP Tunnel and Session Information (Total tunnels=1 sessions=1)

LocID RemID Remote Name   State  Remote Address  Port  Sessions
1     1     lac_l2x0      est    10.30.1.130     1701  1

LocID RemID TunID Intf    Username      State  Last Chg Fastswitch
```

Example A-2 *Sample **show vpdn** User EXEC Command Output for a Dial-Out Session on an LNS*

```
LNS# show vpdn
1     1     1     Vi1                    est    00:00:42 enabled

% No active L2F tunnels
```

L2TP Dial-Out Configuration Examples

The following configuration examples are provided in this section:

- LNS configured for L2TP dial-out
- LAC configured for L2TP dial-out

LNS Configured for L2TP Dial-Out

In Example A-3, the LNS is configured to initiate L2TP tunnels to IP address 10.3.2.1. It identifies itself as cerise for tunnel identification purposes. The VPDN group belongs to dialer pool 1, which uses dialer 2 to initiate the L2TP dial-out session.

Example A-3 *LNS Configured for L2TP Dial-Out*

```
vpdn-group 1
 request dialout
  protocol l2tp
  pool-member 1
 initiate-to ip 10.3.2.1
 local name cerise
!
interface dialer 2
 ip address 172.1.2.3 255.255.128
 encapsulation ppp
 dialer remote-name reuben
 dialer string 5551234
 dialer vpdn
 dialer pool 1
 dialer-group 1
 ppp authentication chap
```

LAC Configured for L2TP Dial-Out

In Example A-4, a LAC is configured to receive L2TP tunnels from an LNS that identifies itself using the host name cerise. The LAC is configured for DDR, and the VPDN group uses dialer 2 to place the L2TP dial-out call.

Example A-4 *Lac Configured for L2TP Dial-Out*

```
VPDN-group 1
 accept dialout
  protocol l2tp
  dialer 2
 terminate-from hostname cerise
!
interface Dialer2
 ip unnumbered Ethernet0
 encapsulation ppp
 dialer in-band
 dialer aaa
 dialer-group 1
 ppp authentication chap
```

New Access VPDN Services: PPTP with MPPE

The Point-to-Point Tunneling Protocol (PPTP) with Microsoft Point-to-Point Encryption (MPPE) feature enables Cisco Systems access VPDNs to use PPTP as the tunneling protocol with MPPE encryption. This appendix includes the following sections:

- PPTP with MPPE Overview
- PPTP with MPPE Benefits
- PPTP with MPPE Restrictions
- PPTP with MPPE-Supported Platforms
- PPTP with MPPE-Supported Standards, MIBs, and RFCs
- PPTP with MPPE Prerequisite Tasks
- PPTP with MPPE Configuration Tasks
- PPTP with MPPE Connection Verification
- PPTP with MPPE Configuration Example

PPTP with MPPE Overview

PPTP is a network protocol that enables the secure transfer of data from a remote client to a private enterprise server by creating a VPN across TCP/IP-based data networks. PPTP supports on-demand, multiprotocol, virtual private networking over public networks, such as the Internet. The Cisco implementation of PPTP is for client-initiated access VPDNs.

MPPE is an encryption technology developed by Microsoft to encrypt point-to-point links. These PPP connections can be over a dial-up line or over a VPDN tunnel. MPPE works as a subfeature of Microsoft Point-to-Point Compression (MPPC).

For more information on PPTP and MPPE, see Chapter 1, "Access VPDN Technologies Overview."

PPTP with MPPE Benefits

This feature allows lower-cost, secure services and scalability, as described in the following sections.

Lower-Cost, Secure Services

Enterprises increasingly are looking to the Internet as a means of enabling new, lower-cost services for their users. The ubiquity of the Internet makes it very easy for remote and mobile users to connect anywhere on the planet; all that is required is an ISP to provide Internet access. At the same time, enterprises are hesitant to trust the Internet as a transport for private company data and are looking for means to use the Internet in a secure way.

The PPTP with MPPE feature provides a solution to this need. PPTP provides a mechanism to tunnel user data across the Internet to the edge of the enterprise network, which enables users to use any ISP account and any Internet-routable IP address to access the edge of the enterprise network. At the edge, the IP packet is detunneled and the IP address space of the enterprise is used for traversing the internal network. MPPE provides an encryption service that protects the data stream as it traverses the Internet. MPPE is available in two strengths: 40-bit encryption, which is widely available throughout the world; and 128-bit encryption, which may be subject to certain export controls when used outside the United States.

ISPs also can leverage PPTP with MPPE when deploying managed services for enterprise customers. In this model, the ISP deploys and manages the PPTP with MPPE tunnel server of the enterprise, or PPTP Network Server (PNS), and manages this service on behalf of the enterprise. The PNS may be located at the point of presence (PoP) of the ISP, or it may be located at the edge of the enterprise network, but it is managed by the ISP.

Scalability

A Cisco router running PPTP can support up to 2000 simultaneous PPTP tunnels without MPPE encryption. For PPTP tunnels with MPPE encryption, Cisco routers can currently support up to 500 simultaneous tunnels.

PPTP with MPPE Restrictions

The following are PPTP with MPPE restrictions:

- Only Cisco Express Forwarding (CEF) and process switching are supported. Regular Fast Switching is not supported.

- Only voluntary tunneling—not compulsory tunneling—is supported.
- PPTP does not support multilink.
- VPDN multihop is not supported.
- Because all PPTP signaling is over TCP, TCP configurations will affect PPTP performance in large-scale environments.
- MPPE is not supported with TACACS.
- MPPE is supported with RADIUS in Cisco IOS Releases 12.0(7)XE1 and later releases.

PPTP with MPPE-Supported Platforms

The following Cisco platforms support PPTP with MPPE:

- Cisco 1600 series
- Cisco 1720 VPN access router
- Cisco 2500 series
- Cisco 2600 series
- Cisco 3600 series
- Cisco 4000-M series (Cisco 4000-M, 4500-M, 4700-M)
- Cisco 7000 series
- Cisco 7100 series
- Cisco 7200 series
- Cisco 7500 series
- Cisco AS5200
- Cisco AS5300
- Cisco AS5800

The following Windows clients support PPTP with MPPE:

- Windows 95/98
- Windows NT 4.0
- Windows 2000

PPTP with MPPE-Supported Standards, MIBs, and RFCs

There are no supported standards or MIBs for PPTP with MPPE. For descriptions of supported MIBs by platform and Cisco IOS releases, and to download MIB modules, go to the Cisco MIB Web site on cisco.com:

www.cisco.com/public/sw-center/netmgmt/cmtk/mibs.shtml

PPTP with MPPE is described in RFC 2637, "PPTP."

For information about RFCs, go to the RFC editor Web site:

www.rfc-editor.org/

PPTP with MPPE Prerequisite Tasks

If you are performing mutual authentication with MS-CHAP and MPPE, both sides of the tunnel must use the same password.

NOTE   Microsoft Windows clients must use MS-CHAP authentication for MPPE to work.

To use MPPE with authentication, authorization, and accounting (AAA), you must use a RADIUS server that supports the Microsoft vendor-specific attribute for MPPE-KEYS.

Cisco Secure ACS NT supports MPPE beginning with release 2.6. Cisco Secure ACS UNIX does not support MPPE.

Before configuring PPTP, perform the tasks described in the following sections. Each task in the list is identified as either required or optional.

- Configuring AAA (optional)
- Configuring AAA on the RADIUS Server (optional)
- Creating the Virtual Template for Dial-In Sessions (required)
- Specifying the IP Address Pool and BOOTP Servers (optional)

Configuring AAA

To configure AAA on the PNS, use the commands in Table B-1 in global configuration mode.

Table B-1   *Configuring AAA*

Step	Command	Purpose
Step 1	**aaa authentication ppp default {group radius	local}** PNS(config)#**aaa authentication ppp default local**	Configures either local or RADIUS AAA authentication.
Step 2	**aaa authorization network default {group radius	local}** PNS(config)#**aaa authorization network default group radius**	Configures either local or RADIUS AAA authorization.
Step 3 (optional)	**aaa accounting network default start-stop radius** PNS(config)#**aaa accounting network default start-stop radius**	Enables AAA accounting that sends a stop accounting notice at the end of the requested user process.
Step 4	**radius-server host** *ip-address* **[auth-port** *number*] **[acct-port** *number*] PNS(config)#**radius-server host 10.3.2.1 auth-port 12 acct-port 16**	Specifies the IP address of the RADIUS server and optionally the ports to be used for authentication and accounting requests.
Step 5	**radius-server key** *key* PNS(config)#**radius-server key dare-to-go**	Sets the authentication key and encryption key for all RADIUS communication.

Configuring AAA on the RADIUS Server

To configure AAA on the RADIUS server, include the following attributes with the return list attributes:

```
Framed-Protocol = PPP
MS-CHAP-MPPE-Keys
Service-Type = Framed
```

Creating the Virtual Template for Dial-In Sessions

To configure the PNS to create virtual access interfaces from a virtual template for incoming PPTP calls, use the commands in Table B-2 beginning in global configuration mode.

Table B-2 *Creating the Virtual Template for Dial-In Sessions*

Step	Command	Purpose
Step 1	**interface virtual-template** *number* PNS(config)#**interface virtual-template 1**	Creates the virtual template that is used to clone virtual access interfaces.
Step 2	**ip unnumbered** *interface-type number* PNS(config-if)#**ip unnumbered Ethernet0**	Specifies the IP address of the interface the virtual access interfaces uses.
Step 3	**ppp authentication** {**chap** | **chap pap** | **pap chap** | **pap** | **ms-chap**} PNS(config-if)#**ppp authentication ms-chap**	Enables MS-CHAP authentication using the local username database. All windows clients using MPPE need to use MS-CHAP.
Step 4	**peer default ip address pool default** PNS(config-if)#**peer default ip address pool default**	Returns an IP address from the default pool to the client.
Step 5	**ip mroute-cache** PNS(config-if)#**ip mroute-cache**	Disables fast switching of IP multicast.
Step 6	**ppp encrypt mppe** {**auto** | **40** | **128**} [**passive** | **required**] [**stateful**] PNS(config-if)#**ppp encrypt mppe 40**	Enables MPPE encryption on the virtual template.

Specifying the IP Address Pool and BOOTP Servers

The IP address pool consists of the IP addresses that the PNS assigns to clients. You also can provide BOOTP servers. DNS servers, which are specified using the **async-bootp dns-server** global configuration command, translate host names to IP addresses. WINS servers, which are specified using the **async-bootp nbns-server** global configuration command, provide dynamic NetBIOS names that Windows devices use to communicate without IP addresses. To configure an IP address pool and BOOTP servers, use the commands in Table B-3 in global configuration mode.

Table B-3   *Specifying the IP Address Pool and BOOTP Servers*

Step	Command	Purpose
Step 1	**ip local pool** {**default** I *pool-name*} *low-ip-address* [*high-ip-address*] PNS(config)#**ip local pool default 10.1.1.0 10.1.4.255**	Configures the default local pool of IP addresses that will be used by clients.
Step 2 (optional)	**async-bootp dns-server** *ip-address1* [*additional-ip-address*] PNS(config)#**async-bootp dns-server 10.1.4.11**	Returns the configured addresses of domain name servers in response to BOOTP requests.
Step 3 (optional)	**async-bootp nbns-server** *ip-address1* [*additional-ip-address*] PNS(config)#**async-bootp nbns-server 10.1.1.4 10.1.4.11**	Returns the configured addresses of Windows NT servers in response to BOOTP requests.

PPTP with MPPE Configuration Tasks

The following configuration tasks for the PPTP with MPPE feature are covered in this section. Each task in the list is identified as either required or optional:

- Configuring a PNS to accept PPTP tunnels (required)
- Configuring MPPE on the ISA card (optional)
- Tuning PPTP (optional)

Configuring a PNS to Accept PPTP Tunnels

To configure a tunnel to accept tunneled PPP connections from a client, use the commands in Table B-4 beginning in global configuration mode.

Table B-4   *Configuring a PNS to Accept PPTP Tunnels*

Step	Command	Purpose
Step 1	**vpdn-group** *name* PNS(config)#**vpdn-group 1**	Creates VPDN group 1.
Step 2	**accept dialin** PNS(config-vpdn) #**accept dialin**	Enables the PNS to accept dial-in requests.
Step 3	**protocol {l2f	l2tp	pppoe	pptp	any}** PNS(config-vpdn-acc-in) #**protocol pptp**	Specifies the tunneling protocol. In this case, the protocol will be PPTP.
Step 4	**virtual-template** *template-number* PNS(config-vpdn-acc-in) #**virtual-template 1**	Specifies the number of the virtual template that will be used to clone the virtual access interface.
Step 5	**exit** PNS(config-vpdn-acc-in)#**exit**	Exits to a higher command mode.
Step 6 (optional)	**local name** *localname* PNS(config-vpdn)#**local name tunnel1**	Specifies that the PNS will identify itself with this local name. If no local name is specified, the PNS will identify itself with its host name.

Configuring MPPE on the ISA Card

To offload MPPE encryption from the PNS processor to the ISA card, use the commands in Table B-5 beginning in global configuration mode.

Table B-5   *Configuring MPPE on the ISA Card*

Step	Command	Purpose
Step 1	**controller isa** *slot/port* PNS(config)#**controller isa 8/2**	Enters controller configuration mode on the ISA card.
Step 2	**encryption mppe** PNS(config-controller) #**encryption mppe**	Enables MPPE encryption.

Tuning PPTP

To tune PPTP, use one or more of the commands in Table B-6 in VPDN configuration mode as needed.

Table B-6   *Tuning PPTP*

Command	Purpose
pptp flow-control receive-window *packets*	Specifies how many packets the client can send before it must wait for the acknowledgment from the PNS.
pptp flow-control static-rtt *milliseconds*	Specifies the timeout interval of the PNS between sending a packet to the client and receiving a response.
pptp tunnel echo *seconds*	Specifies the period of idle time on the tunnel that will trigger an echo message from the PNS to the client.

PPTP with MPPE Verification Connection

To verify that a PPTP network functions properly, perform the following steps:

Step 1   From the client, dial in to the ISP and establish a PPP session.

Step 2   From the client, dial in to the PNS.

Step 3   From the client desktop, ping the PNS by performing the following steps:

(a) Click Start.

(b) Select Run.

(c) Enter **ping** *tunnel-server-ip-address*.

(d) Click OK.

(e) Look at the terminal screen and verify that the PNS is sending ping reply packets to the client.

Step 4   From the PNS, enter the **show vpdn** user EXEC command and verify that the client has established a PPTP session:

```
PNS# show vpdn

% No active L2TP tunnels
```

```
% No active L2F tunnels

PPTP Tunnel and Session Information (Total tunnels=1
  sessions=1)

LocID RemID Remote Name      State     Remote Address  Port
   Sessions
13    13    10.1.2.41        estabd    10.1.2.41       1136  1


LocID RemID TunID Intf   Username      State   Last Chg
13    0     13    Vi3                  estabd  000030
```

Step 5   For more detailed information, enter the **show vpdn session
all** or **show vpdn session window** user EXEC command.

```
PNS# show vpdn session all

% No active L2TP tunnels

% No active L2F tunnels

PPTP Session Information (Total tunnels=1 sessions=1)

Call id 13 is up on tunnel id 13
Remote tunnel name is 10.1.2.41
  Internet Address is 10.1.2.41
  Session username is unknown, state is estabd
    Time since change 000106, interface Vi3
    Remote call id is 0
    10 packets sent, 10 received, 332 bytes sent, 448
      received
      Ss 11, Sr 10, Remote Nr 10, peer RWS 16
      0 out of order packets
      Flow alarm is clear.
```

The last line of output from the **show vpdn session
window** user EXEC command indicates the current status
of the flow control alarm (under the heading "Congestion")
and the number of flow control alarms that have gone off
during the session (under the heading "Alarms").

The flow control alarm goes off when the PNS detects
congestion (specifically, when it does not receive a response
from the client within the time interval specified by the **pptp**

flow-control static-rtt VPDN configuration command).
When a flow control alarm goes off, the PNS reduces
volatility and additional control traffic by establishing an
accompanying stateful MPPE session. For more information
on the operation of PPTP and MPPE, see Chapter 1.

```
PNS# show vpdn session window

% No active L2TP tunnels
0
% No active L2F tunnels

PPTP Session Information (Total tunnels=1 sessions=1)

LocID RemID TunID ZLB-tx  ZLB-rx  Congestion Alarms
  Peer-RWS
13    0     13    0       1       clear      0        16
```

Step 6 For information on the virtual access interface,
enter the **show ppp mppe virtual-access** *number*
user EXEC command:

```
PNS# show ppp mppe virtual-access3

Interface Virtual-Access3 (current connection)
  Hardware (ISA5/1, flow_id=13) encryption, 40 bit
    encryption, Stateless mode
  packets encrypted = 0       packets decrypted  = 1
  sent CCP resets   = 0       receive CCP resets = 0
  next tx coherency = 0       next rx coherency  = 0
  tx key changes    = 0       rx key changes     = 0
  rx pkt dropped    = 0       rx out of order pkt= 0
  rx missed packets = 0
```

To update the key change information, reissue the **show
ppp mppe virtual-access3** user EXEC command:

```
PNS# show ppp mppe virtual-access3

Interface Virtual-Access3 (current connection)
  Hardware (ISA5/1, flow_id=13) encryption, 40 bit
    encryption, Stateless mode
  packets encrypted = 0       packets decrypted  = 1
  sent CCP resets   = 0       receive CCP resets = 0
  next tx coherency = 0       next rx coherency  = 0
  tx key changes    = 0       rx key changes     = 1
  rx pkt dropped    = 0       rx out of order pkt= 0
  rx missed packets = 0
```

PPTP with MPPE Configuration Example

Example B-1 shows the **show running-config** privileged EXEC command output of a PNS configured to terminate PPTP tunnels. The PNS has an ISA card to perform MPPE encryption. The virtual template is configured for MS-CHAP tunnel authentication and 40-bit MPPE encryption. The PNS does not have a AAA configuration.

Example B-1 **show running-config** *Command Output from a PNS Configured to Terminate PPTP Tunnels*

```
Current configuration
!
version 12.0
service timestamps debug uptime
service timestamps log uptime
no service password-encryption
!
hostname PNS
!
no logging console guaranteed
enable password lab
!
username tester41 password 0 lab41
!
!
!
!
ip subnet-zero
no ip domain-lookup
!
vpdn enable
!
vpdn-group 1
! Default PPTP VPDN group
 accept-dialin
  protocol pptp
  virtual-template 1
 local name cisco_pns
!
!
!
memory check-interval 1
!
!
controller ISA 5/0
 encryption mppe
!
process-max-time 200
```

Example B-1 **show running-config** *Command Output from a PNS Configured*
to Terminate PPTP Tunnels (Continued)

```
!
interface FastEthernet0/0
 ip address 10.1.1.12 255.255.255.0
 no ip directed-broadcast
 duplex auto
 speed auto
!
interface FastEthernet0/1
 ip address 10.1.2.12 255.255.255.0
 no ip directed-broadcast
 duplex auto
 speed auto
!
interface Serial1/0
 no ip address
 no ip directed-broadcast
 shutdown
 framing c-bit
 cablelength 10
 dsu bandwidth 44210
!
interface Serial1/1
 no ip address
 no ip directed-broadcast
 shutdown
 framing c-bit
 cablelength 10
 dsu bandwidth 44210
!
interface FastEthernet4/0
 no ip address
 no ip directed-broadcast
 shutdown
 duplex half
!
interface Virtual-Template1
 ip unnumbered FastEthernet0/0
 no ip directed-broadcast
 ip mroute-cache
 no keepalive
 ppp encrypt mppe 40
 ppp authentication ms-chap
!
ip classless
ip route 172.29.1.129 255.255.255.255 1.1.1.1
ip route 172.29.63.9 255.255.255.255 1.1.1.1
no ip http server
```

continues

Example B-1 **show running-config** *Command Output from a PNS Configured to Terminate PPTP Tunnels (Continued)*

```
!
!
line con 0
 exec-timeout 0 0
 transport input none
line aux 0
line vty 0 4
 login
!
end
```

VPDN Command Summary

This appendix summarizes all the Cisco IOS commands used in the access VPDNs discussed in this book. For more detailed information on these commands, go to the Cisco IOS Software Configuration site on cisco.com: www.cisco.com/univercd/cc/td/doc/product/software/index.htm.

aaa accounting

To enable authentication, authorization, and accounting (AAA) accounting of requested services for billing or security purposes when you use RADIUS or TACACS+, use the **aaa accounting** global configuration command to disable AAA accounting, use the **no** form of this command. Table C-1 describes the syntax of the following commands:

```
aaa accounting {auth-proxy | system | network | exec | connection |
    commands level} {default | list-name} {start-stop | stop-only |
    wait-start | none} [broadcast] group groupname

no aaa accounting {auth-proxy | system | network | exec | connection |
    commands level} {default | list-name} [broadcast] group groupname
```

Table C-1   aaa accounting *Syntax Description*

Syntax	Description
auth-proxy	Provides information about all authenticated-proxy user events.
system	Performs accounting for all system-level events not associated with users, such as reloads.
network	Runs accounting for all network-related service requests, including SLIP[1], PPP[2], PPP NCPs[3], and ARAP[4].
exec	Runs accounting for EXEC shell session. This keyword might return user profile information such as what is generated by the **autocommand** command.

continues

Table C-1   **aaa accounting** *Syntax Description (Continued)*

Syntax	Description
connection	Provides information about all outbound connections made from the network access server, such as Telnet, LAT[5], TN3270, PAD[6], and rlogin.
commands *level*	Runs accounting for all commands at the specified privilege level. Valid privilege-level entries are integers from 0 through 15.
default	Uses the listed accounting methods that follow this argument as the default list of methods for accounting services.
list-name	Character string used to name the list of accounting methods.
start-stop	Sends a start accounting notice at the beginning of a process and a stop accounting notice at the end of a process. The start accounting record is sent in the background. The requested user process begins regardless of whether the start accounting notice was received by the accounting server.
stop-only	Sends a stop accounting notice at the end of the requested user process.
wait-start	Sends a start accounting notice at the beginning of a process and a stop accounting notice at the end of a process. The start accounting record is sent in the background. The requested user process does not begin until the server receives the start accounting notice.
none	Disables accounting services on this line or interface.
broadcast	(Optional) Enables sending accounting records to multiple AAA servers. Simultaneously sends accounting records to the first server in each group. If the first server is unavailable, fail over occurs using the backup servers defined within that group.
group *groupname*	At least one of the keywords described in the next two entries.
group radius	Uses the list of all RADIUS servers for authentication as defined by the **aaa group server radius** command.
group tacacs+	Uses the list of all TACACS+ servers for authentication as defined by the **aaa group server tacacs+** command.

[1]SLIP = Serial Line Internet Protocol

[2]PPP = Point-to-Point Protocol

[3]PPP NCPs = Point-to-Point Protocol Network Control Protocols

[4]ARAP = AppleTalk Remote Access Protocol

[5]LAT = local-area transport

[6]PAD = packet assembler/disassembler

aaa authentication ppp

To specify one or more AAA authentication methods for use on serial interfaces running PPP, use the **aaa authentication ppp** global configuration command to disable authentication, use the **no** form of this command. Table C-2 and Table C-3 describe the syntax of the following commands:

```
aaa authentication ppp {default | list-name} method1 [method2...]

no aaa authentication ppp {default | list-name} method1 [method2...]
```

Table C-2   **aaa authentication ppp** *Syntax Description*

Syntax	Description
default	Uses the listed authentication methods that follow this argument as the default list of methods when a user logs in.
list-name	Character string used to name the list of authentication methods tried when a user logs in.
method1 [*method2...*]	At least one of the keywords described in Table C-3.

Table C-3   **aaa authentication ppp** *Methods*

Keyword	Description
if-needed	Does not authenticate if user has already been authenticated on a tty line.
krb5	Uses Kerberos 5 for authentication (can be used only for PAP authentication).
local	Uses the local username database for authentication.
local-case	Uses case-sensitive local username authentication.
none	Uses no authentication.
group *group-name*	Uses a subset of RADIUS or TACACS+ servers for authentication as defined by the **aaa group server radius** or **aaa group server tacacs+** command.

aaa authorization

To set parameters that restrict user access to a network, use the **aaa authorization** global configuration command to disable authorization for a function, use the **no** form of this command. Table C-4 and Table C-5 describe the syntax of the following commands:

```
aaa authorization {network | exec | commands level | reverse-access |
    configuration} {default | list-name} method1 [method2...]
```

```
no aaa authorization {network | exec | commands level | reverse-access |
    configuration | default | list-name}
```

Table C-4   **aaa authorization** *Syntax Description*

Syntax	Description
network	Runs authorization for all network-related service requests, including SLIP[1], PPP[2], PPP NCPs[3], and ARAP[4].
exec	Runs authorization to determine whether the user is allowed to run an EXEC shell. This facility might return user profile information such as **autocommand** information.
commands	Runs authorization for all commands at the specified privilege level.
level	Specific command level that should be authorized. Valid entries are 0 through 15.
reverse-access	Runs authorization for reverse access connections, such as reverse Telnet.
configuration	Downloads the configuration from the AAA server.
default	Uses the listed authorization methods that follow this argument as the default list of methods for authorization.
list-name	Character string used to name the list of authorization methods.
method1 [*method2*...]	One of the keywords listed in Table C-5.

[1]Serial Line Protocol

[2]Point-to-Point Protocol

[3]Point-to-Point Protocol Network Control Programs

[4]AppleTalk Remote Access

Table C-5   **aaa authorization** *Methods*

Keyword	Description
group *group-name*	Uses a subset of RADIUS or TACACS+ servers for authentication as defined by the **aaa group server radius** or **aaa group server tacacs+** command.
if-authenticated	Allows the user to access the requested function if the user is authenticated.
krb5-instance	Uses the instance defined by the **kerberos instance map** command.
local	Uses the local database for authorization.
none	No authorization is performed.

aaa new-model

To enable the AAA access control model, issue the **aaa new-model** global configuration command to disable the AAA access control model, use the **no** form of this command.

```
aaa new-model
no aaa new-model
```

This command has no arguments or keywords.

accept dialin

To configure L2TP network servers (LNSs) to accept tunneled PPP connections from an L2TP access concentrator (LAC) and create an accept-dialin virtual private dial-up network (VPDN) subgroup, use the **accept dialin** VPDN group configuration command. To remove the accept-dialin subgroup from a VPDN group, use the **no** form of this command.

```
accept dialin
no accept dialin
```

This command has no arguments or keywords.

accept dialout

To accept requests to tunnel Layer 2 Tunneling Protocol (L2TP) dialout calls and create an accept-dialout VPDN subgroup, use the **accept dialout** VPDN group configuration command. To remove the accept-dialout subgroup from the VPDN group, use the **no** form of this command.

```
accept dialout
no accept dialout
```

This command has no arguments or keywords.

access-list

To configure the access list mechanism for filtering frames by protocol type or vendor code, use the **access-list** global configuration command. To remove the single specified entry from the access list, use the **no** form of this command. Table C-6 describes the syntax of the following commands:

```
access-list access-list-number {permit | deny} {type-code wild-mask |
    address mask}
no access-list access-list-number {permit | deny} {type-code wild-mask |
    address mask}
```

Table C-6   **access-list** *Syntax Description*

Syntax	Description
access-list-number	Integer that identifies the access list. If the *type-code wild-mask* arguments are included, this integer ranges from 200 to 299, indicating that filtering is by protocol type. If the *address* and *mask* arguments are included, this integer ranges from 700 to 799, indicating that filtering is by vendor code.
permit	Permits the frame.
deny	Denies the frame.
type-code	A 16-bit hexadecimal number written with a leading 0x (for example, 0x6000). Specify either a Link Service Access Point (LSAP) type code for 802-encapsulated packets or a SNAP type code for SNAP-encapsulated packets. (LSAP, sometimes called SAP, refers to the type codes found in the DSAP and SSAP fields of the 802 header.)
wild-mask	A 16-bit hexadecimal number whose 1 bits correspond to bits in the *type-code* argument. The *wild-mask* indicates which bits in the *type-code* argument should be ignored when making a comparison. (A mask for a DSAP/SSAP pair should always be 0x0101 because these two bits are used for purposes other than identifying the SAP code.)
address	A 48-bit Token Ring address written as a dotted triple of four-digit hexadecimal numbers. This field is used for filtering by vendor code.
mask	A 48-bit Token Ring address written as a dotted triple of four-digit hexadecimal numbers. The 1 bits in *mask* are the bits to be ignored in *address*. This field is used for filtering by vendor code.

For source address filtering, the mask always should have the high-order bit set. This is because the IEEE 802 standard uses this bit to indicate whether a RIF is present, not as part of the source address.

async mode interactive

To return a line that has been placed into Dedicated Asynchronous Network mode to Interactive mode, thereby enabling the **slip** and **ppp** EXEC commands, use the **async mode interactive** interface configuration command. To prevent users from implementing SLIP and PPP at the EXEC level, use the **no** form of this command.

```
async mode interactive
no async mode interactive
```

This command has no arguments or keywords.

async-bootp

To configure extended BOOTP requests for asynchronous interfaces as defined in RFC 1084, use the **async-bootp** global configuration command. To restore the default, use the **no** form of this command. Table C-7 and Table C-8 describe the syntax of the following commands:

```
async-bootp tag [:hostname] data
no async-bootp
```

Table C-7   **async-bootp** *Syntax Description*

Syntax	Description
tag	Item being requested; expressed as filename, integer, or IP dotted-decimal address. See Table C-8 for possible keywords.
:hostname	(Optional) This entry applies only to the host specified. The *:hostname* argument accepts both an IP address and a logical host name.
data	List of IP addresses entered in dotted-decimal notation or as logical host names, a number, or a quoted string.

Table C-8   *tag Keyword Options*

Keyword	Description
bootfile	Specifies use of a server boot file from which to download the boot program. Use the optional *:hostname* argument and the *data* argument to specify the filename.
subnet-mask *mask*	Dotted-decimal address specifying the network and local subnetwork mask (as defined by RFC 950).
time-offset *offset*	Signed 32-bit integer specifying the time offset of the local subnetwork in seconds from Universal Time Coordinated (UTC).
gateway *address*	Dotted-decimal address specifying the IP addresses of gateways for this subnetwork. A preferred gateway should be listed first.

continues

Table C-8 *tag Keyword Options (Continued)*

time-server *address*	Dotted-decimal address specifying the IP address of time servers (as defined by RFC 868).
IEN116-server *address*	Dotted-decimal address specifying the IP address of name servers (as defined by IEN 116).
nbns-server *address*	Dotted-decimal address specifying the IP address of Windows NT servers.
DNS-server *address*	Dotted-decimal address specifying the IP address of domain name servers (as defined by RFC 1034).
log-server *address*	Dotted-decimal address specifying the IP address of an MIT-LCS UDP log server.
quote-server *address*	Dotted-decimal address specifying the IP address of Quote of the Day servers (as defined in RFC 865).
lpr-server *address*	Dotted-decimal address specifying the IP address of Berkeley UNIX Version 4 BSD servers.
impress-server *address*	Dotted-decimal address specifying the IP address of Impress network image servers.
rlp-server *address*	Dotted-decimal address specifying the IP address of Resource Location Protocol (RLP) servers (as defined in RFC 887).
hostname *name*	The name of the client, which may or may not be domain qualified, depending upon the site.
bootfile-size *value*	A 2-octet value specifying the number of 512-octet (byte) blocks in the default boot file.

authen before-forward

To specify that the VPDN send the entire structured username to the AAA server the first time the router contacts the AAA server, use the **authen before-forward** VPDN group configuration command. To send just the domain name or Dialed Number Identification Service (DNIS), use the **no** form of this command.

```
authen before-forward

no authen before-forward
```

This command has no arguments or keywords.

autoselect

To configure a line to start an ARA, PPP, or SLIP session, use the **autoselect** line configuration command. To disable this function on a line, use the **no** form of this command. Table C-9 describes the syntax of the following commands:

```
autoselect {arap | ppp | slip | during-login}
no autoselect
```

Table C-9   **autoselect** *Syntax Description*

Syntax	Description
arap	ARA session.
ppp	PPP session.
slip	SLIP session.
during-login	Displays the username and/or password prompt without the user pressing the Return key. After the user logs in, the autoselect function begins.

clear vpdn tunnel

To shut down a specified tunnel and all sessions within the tunnel, use the **clear vpdn tunnel** privileged EXEC command. Table C-10 describes the syntax of the following commands:

```
clear vpdn tunnel [pptp | l2f | l2tp] network-access-server gateway-name
```

Table C-10   **clear vpdn tunnel** *Syntax Description*

pptp	(Optional) Clears the specified PPTP tunnel.
l2f	(Optional) Clears the specified Layer 2 Forwarding (L2F) tunnel.
l2tp	(Optional) Clears the specified L2TP tunnel.
network-access-server	Name of the network access server at the far end of the tunnel, probably the point of presence of the public data network or the ISP.
gateway-name	Host name of home gateway at the local end of the tunnel.

clock source

To configure the clock source of a DS1 link, enter the **clock source** interface configuration, controller configuration, or ATM interface configuration command.

To restore the default **line** setting, use the **no** form of this command. Table C-11 describes the syntax of the following commands:

```
clock source {line | internal | loop-timed}
no clock source
```

Table C-11   **clock source** *Syntax Description*

Syntax	Description
line	Specifies that the T1/E1 link uses the recovered clock from the line. This is the default.
internal	Specifies that the T1/E1 link uses the internal clock from the interface.
loop-timed	Specifies that the T1/E1 interface takes the clock from the Rx (line) and uses it for Tx.

[controller isa]

To enter the Controller Configuration mode on an ISA card, use the **controller isa** global configuration command. Table C-12 describes the syntax of the following command:

```
controller isa slot/1
```

Table C-12   **controller isa** *Syntax Description*

Syntax	Description
slot	Location of the ISA card in the dial shelf chassis.
1	The ISA card has only 1 port.

controller t1

To configure a T1 controller, use the **controller t1** global configuration command. To delete the defined controller, use the **no** form of this command. Table C-13 describes the syntax of the following commands:

```
controller t1 dial-shelf/slot/t3-port:t1-num
no controller t1 dial-shelf/slot/t3-port:t1-num
```

Table C-13   **controller t1** *Syntax Description*

Syntax	Description
dial-shelf	Dial shelf chassis in the Cisco AS5800 access server containing the CT3 interface card.
slot	Location of the CT3 interface card in the dial shelf chassis.
t3-port	T3 port number. The only valid value is 0.
:t1-num	T1 timeslot in the T3 line. The value can be from 1 to 28.

crypto ipsec transform-set

To define a transform set—an acceptable combination of security protocols and algorithms—use the **crypto ipsec transform-set** global configuration command. To delete a transform set, use the **no** form of the command. Table C-14 describes the syntax of the following commands:

```
crypto ipsec transform-set transform-set-name transform1
    [transform2 [transform3]]
no crypto ipsec transform-set transform-set-name
```

Table C-14   **crypto ipsec transform-set** *Syntax Description*

Syntax	Description
transform-set-name	Specify the name of the transform set to create (or modify).
transform1 *transform2* *transform3*	Specify up to three transforms. These transforms define the IPSec security protocols and algorithms.

crypto isakmp key

To configure a preshared authentication key, use the **crypto isakmp key** global configuration command. You must configure this key whenever you specify preshared keys in an Internet Key Exchange (IKE) policy. To delete a preshared authentication key, use the **no** form of this command. Table C-15 describes the syntax of the following commands:

```
crypto isakmp key keystring address peer-address [mask]
crypto isakmp key keystring hostname peer-hostname
no crypto isakmp key keystring address peer-address
no crypto isakmp key keystring hostname peer-hostname
```

Table C-15 **crypto isakmp key** *Syntax Description*

Syntax	Description
address	Use this keyword if the remote peer Internet Security Association Key Management Protocol identity was set with its IP address.
hostname	Use this keyword if the remote peer ISAKMP identity was set with its host name.
keystring	Specify the preshared key. Use any combination of alphanumeric characters up to 128 bytes. This preshared key must be identical at both peers.
peer-address	Specify the IP address of the remote peer.
peer-hostname	Specify the host name of the remote peer. This is the peer's host name concatenated with its domain name (for example, myhost.example.com).
mask	(Optional) Specify the subnet address of the remote peer. (The argument can be used only if the remote peer ISAKMP identity was set with its IP address.)

crypto isakmp policy

To define an IKE policy, use the **crypto isakmp policy** global configuration command. IKE policies define a set of parameters to be used during the IKE negotiation. To delete an IKE policy, use the **no** form of this command. Table C-16 describes the syntax of the following commands:

```
crypto isakmp policy priority
no crypto isakmp policy
```

Table C-16 **crypto isakmp policy** *Syntax Description*

Syntax	Description
priority	Uniquely identifies the IKE policy and assigns a priority to the policy. Use an integer from 1 to 10,000, with 1 being the highest priority and 10,000 the lowest.

crypto map (Global IPSec)

To create or modify a crypto map entry and enter the **crypto map** configuration mode, use the crypto map global configuration command. To delete a crypto map

entry or set, use the **no** form of this command. Table C-17 describes the syntax of
the following commands:

```
crypto map map-name seq-num ipsec-manual
crypto map map-name seq-num ipsec-isakmp [dynamic dynamic-map-name]
   [discover]
no crypto map map-name [seq-num]
```

NOTE   Issue the **crypto map** *map-name seq-num* command without a keyword to
modify an existing crypto map entry.

Table C-17   **crypto map** *(Global IPSec) Syntax Description*

Syntax	Description
map-name	The name that identifies the crypto map set. This is the name assigned when the crypto map was created.
seq-num	The number you assign to the crypto map entry. The number you assign to the *seq-num* argument should not be arbitrary. This number is used to rank multiple crypto map entries within a crypto map set. Within a crypto map set, a crypto map entry with a lower *seq-num* is evaluated before a map entry with a higher *seq-num*; that is, the map entry with the lower number has a higher priority.
	For example, imagine there is a crypto map set that contains three crypto map entries: mymap 10, mymap 20, and mymap 30.
	The crypto map set named mymap is applied to interface Serial 0. When traffic passes through the Serial 0 interface, the traffic is evaluated first for mymap 10. If the traffic matches a permit entry in the extended access list in mymap 10, the traffic will be processed according to the information defined in mymap 10 (including establishing IPSec security associations when necessary).
	If the traffic does not match the mymap 10 access list, the traffic will be evaluated for mymap 20, and then mymap 30, until the traffic matches a permit entry in a map entry. (If the traffic does not match a permit entry in any crypto map entry, it will be forwarded without any IPSec security.)

continues

Table C-17 **crypto map** *(Global IPSec) Syntax Description (Continued)*

Syntax	Description
ipsec-manual	Indicates that IKE will not be used to establish the IPSec security associations for protecting the traffic specified by this crypto map entry.
ipsec-isakmp	Indicates that IKE will be used to establish the IPSec security associations for protecting the traffic specified by this crypto map entry.
dynamic	(Optional) Specifies that this crypto map entry is to reference a preexisting dynamic crypto map. Dynamic crypto maps are policy templates used in processing negotiation requests from a peer IPSec device. If you use this keyword, none of the crypto map configuration commands will be available.
dynamic-map-name	(Optional) Specifies the name of the dynamic crypto map set that should be used as the policy template.
discover	(Optional) Enables peer discovery. By default, peer discovery is not enabled.

crypto map (Interface IPSec)

To apply a previously defined crypto map set to an interface, use the **crypto map** interface configuration command. To remove the crypto map set from the interface, use the **no** form of this command. Table C-18 describes the syntax of the following commands:

```
crypto map map-name
no crypto map [map-name]
```

Table C-18 **crypto map** *(Interface IPSec) Syntax Description*

Syntax	Description
map-name	Name that identifies the crypto map set. This is the name assigned when the crypto map was created.
	When the **no** form of the command is used, this argument is optional. Any value supplied for the argument is ignored.

debug aaa authentication

To display information on AAA/Terminal Access Controller Access Control System Plus (TACACS+) authentication, use the **debug aaa authentication** privileged EXEC command. To disable debugging command, use the **no** form of the command.

```
debug aaa authentication
no debug aaa authentication
```

This command has no arguments or keywords.

debug aaa authorization

To display information on AAA/TACACS+ authorization, use the **debug aaa authorization** privileged EXEC command. To disable debugging output, use the **no** form of the command.

```
debug aaa authorization
no debug aaa authorization
```

This command has no arguments or keywords.

debug ppp

Use the **debug ppp** privileged EXEC command to display information on traffic and exchanges in an internetwork implementing the PPP. The **no** form of this command disables debugging output. Table C-19 describes the syntax of the following commands:

```
debug ppp {packet | negotiation | error | authentication | compression |
    cbcp}

no debug ppp {packet | negotiation | error | authentication | compression
    | cbcp}
```

Table C-19   **debug ppp** *Syntax Description*

Syntax	Description
packet	Displays PPP packets being sent and received. (This command displays low-level packet dumps.)
negotiation	Displays PPP packets sent during PPP startup, where PPP options are negotiated.

continues

Table C-19   **debug ppp** *Syntax Description (Continued)*

Syntax	Description
error	Displays protocol errors and error statistics associated with PPP connection negotiation, and operation.
authentication	Displays authentication protocol messages, including Challenge Authentication Protocol (CHAP) packet exchanges and Password Authentication Protocol (PAP) exchanges.
compression	Displays information specific to the exchange of PPP connections using MPPC. This command is useful for obtaining incorrect packet sequence number information where MPPC compression is enabled.
cbcp	Displays protocol errors and statistics associated with PPP connection negotiations using MSCB.

debug ppp mppe

To display debug messages for Microsoft Point-to-Point Compression (MPPC) events, use the **debug ppp mppe** privileged EXEC command. Use the **no** form of this command to disable MPPC debugging.

```
debug ppp mppe
no debug ppp mppe
```

This command has no keywords or arguments.

debug vpdn

To display debug traces for the VPDNs, which provide PPP tunnels using the L2F protocol, use the **debug vpdn** privileged EXEC command. The **no** form of this command disables debugging output. Table C-20 describes the syntax of the following commands:

```
debug vpdn {errors | events | packets | 12x-errors | 12x-events |
    12x-packets}
no debug vpdn {errors | events | packets | 12x-errors | 12x-events |
    12x-packets}
```

Table C-20   **debug vpdn** *Syntax Description*

Syntax	Description
errors	Displays errors that prevent a tunnel from being established, or errors that cause an established tunnel to be closed.
events	Displays messages about events that are part of normal tunnel establishment or shutdown.
packets	Displays each protocol packet exchanged. This option may result in a large number of debug messages and should generally be used only on a debug chassis with a single active session.
l2x-errors	Displays L2F and L2TP protocol errors that prevent L2F and L2TP establishment or prevent its normal operation.
l2x-events	Displays messages about events that are part of normal tunnels establishment or shutdown for L2F and L2TP.
l2x-packets	Displays messages about L2F and L2TP protocol headers and status.

debug vpdn event

To display L2TP errors and events that are a part of normal tunnel establishment or shutdown for VPDNs, use the **debug vpdn event** privileged EXEC command to display. To disable debugging errors and events, use the **no** form of this command to disable debugging output. Table C-21 describes the syntax of the following commands:

```
debug vpdn event [protocol | flow-control]
no debug vpdn event [protocol | flow-control]
```

Table C-21   **debug vpdn event** *Syntax Description*

Syntax	Description
protocol	(Optional) Displays all errors for the tunneling protocols used by VPDNs, such as L2TP, L2F, PPTP, and events within these protocols.
flow control	(Optional) Displays L2TP flow-control errors.

dialer

To specify the dialer interface that an accept-dialout VPDN subgroup will use to dial out calls, use the **dialer** VPDN subgroup configuration command. To remove the dialer interface from the accept-dialout VPDN subgroup, use the **no** form of this command. Table C-22 describes the syntax of the following commands:

```
dialer dialer-interface
no dialer
```

Table C-22   **dialer** *Syntax Description*

Syntax	Description
dialer-interface	Number of the dialer interface.

dialer aaa

To allow a dialer to access the AAA server for dialing information, use the **dialer aaa** command in interface configuration mode. To disable this function, use the **no** form of this command. Table C-23 describes the syntax of the following commands:

```
dialer aaa suffix string password string
no dialer aaa password suffix string password string
```

Table C-23   **dialer aaa** *Syntax Description*

Syntax	Description
suffix *string*	Defines a suffix for authentication.
password *string*	Defines a nondefault password for authentication.

dialer in-band

To specify that dial-on-demand routing (DDR) is to be supported, use the **dialer in-band** interface configuration command. To disable DDR for the interface, use the **no** form of this command. Table C-24 describes the syntax of the following commands:

```
dialer in-band [no-parity | odd-parity]
no dialer in-band
```

Table C-24 **dialer in-band** *Syntax Description*

Syntax	Description
no-parity	(Optional) No parity is to be applied to the dialer string that is sent out to the modem on synchronous interfaces.
odd-parity	(Optional) Dialed number has odd parity (7-bit ASCII characters with the eighth bit as the parity bit) on synchronous interfaces.

dialer pool

To specify, for a dialer interface, which dialing pool to use to connect to a specific destination subnetwork, use the **dialer pool** interface configuration command. To remove the dialing pool assignment, use the **no** form of this command. Table C-25 describes the syntax of the following commands:

```
dialer pool number
no dialer pool number
```

Table C-25 **dialer pool** *Syntax Description*

Syntax	Description
number	Dialing pool number, in the range 1 through 255.

dialer remote-name

To specify the authentication name of the remote router on the destination subnetwork for a dialer interface, use the **dialer remote-name** interface configuration command. To remove the specified name, use the **no** form of this command. Table C-26 describes the syntax of the following commands:

```
dialer remote-name user-name
no dialer remote-name
```

Table C-26 **dialer remote-name** *Syntax Description*

Syntax	Description
user-name	Case-sensitive character string identifying the remote device; the maximum length is 255 characters.

dialer string

To specify the string (telephone number) to be called for interfaces calling a single site, use the **dialer string** interface configuration command. To delete the dialer string specified for the interface, use the **no** form of this command. Table C-27 describes the syntax of the following commands:

```
dialer string dial-string[:isdn-subaddress]
no dialer string
```

Table C-27   **dialer string** *Syntax Description*

Syntax	Description
dial-string	String of characters to be sent to a DCE device.
:isdn-subaddress	(Optional) ISDN subaddress.

dialer vpdn

To enable a dialer profile or DDR dialer to use Layer 2 Tunnel Protocol (L2TP) dialout, use the **dialer vpdn** interface configuration command. To disable L2TP dialout on a dialer profile or DDR dialer, use the **no** form of this command.

```
dialer vpdn
no dialer vpdn
```

This command has no arguments or keywords.

dialer-group

To control access by configuring an interface to belong to a specific dialing group, use the **dialer-group** interface configuration command. To remove an interface from the specified dialer access group, use the **no** form of this command. Table C-28 describes the syntax of the following commands:

```
dialer-group group-number
no dialer-group
```

Table C-28   **dialer-group** *Syntax Description*

Syntax	Description
group-number	Number of the dialer access group to which the specific interface belongs. This access group is defined with the **dialer-list** command. Acceptable values are nonzero, positive integers between 1 and 10.

dialer-list protocol

To define a DDR dialer list for dialing by protocol or by a combination of a protocol and a previously defined access list, use the **dialer-list protocol** global configuration command. To delete a dialer list, use the **no** form of this command. Table C-29 and Table C-30 describe the syntax of the following commands:

```
dialer-list dialer-group protocol protocol-name {permit | deny |
    list access-list-number | access-group}

no dialer-list dialer-group [protocol protocol-name [list
    access-list number | access-group]]
```

Table C-29   **dialer-list protocol** *Syntax Description*

Syntax	Description
dialer-group	Number of a dialer access group identified in any **dialer-group** interface configuration command.
protocol-name	One of the following protocol keywords: **appletalk**, **bridge**, **clns**, **clns_es**, **clns_is**, **decnet**, **decnet_router-L1**, **decnet_router-L2**, **decnet_node**, **ip**, **ipx**, **vines**, or **xns**.
permit	Permits access to an entire protocol.
deny	Denies access to an entire protocol.
list	Specifies that an access list will be used for defining a granularity finer than an entire protocol.
access-list-number	Access list numbers specified in any DECnet, Banyan VINES, IP, Novell IPX, or XNS standard or extended access lists, including Novell IPX extended service access point (SAP) access lists and bridging types. See Table C-30 for the supported access list types and numbers.
access-group	Filter list name used in the **clns filter-set** and **clns access-group** global configuration commands.

Table C-30   **dialer-list** *Command Supported Access List Types and Numbers*

Access List Type	Access List Number Range (Decimal)
AppleTalk	600–699
Banyan VINES (standard)	1–100
Banyan VINES (extended)	101–200
DECnet	300–399

continues

Table C-30 **dialer-list** *Command Supported Access List Types and Numbers (Continued)*

Access List Type	Access List Number Range (Decimal)
IP (standard)	1–99
IP (extended)	100–199
Novell IPX (standard)	800–899
Novell IPX (extended)	900–999
Transparent Bridging	200–299
XNS	500–599

dnis

To support additional DNIS groups for a specific VPDN tunnel, use the **dnis** VPDN group configuration command. To remove a DNIS from a VPDN group, enter the **no** form of this command. Table C-31 describes the syntax of the following commands:

```
dnis dnis-group-name
no dnis dnis-group-name
dnis dnis-number
no dnis dnis-number
```

NOTE   When Resource Pool Management (RPM) is enabled, this command uses the *dnis-group-name* keyword. When RPM is disabled, this command uses the *dnis-number* keyword.

Table C-31 **dnis** *Syntax Description*

Syntax	Description
dnis-group-name	DNIS group name used when RPM is enabled and the VPDN group is configured under the incoming customer profile.
dnis-number	DNIS group number used when RPM is disabled, or when a call is associated with a customer profile without any VPDN group configured for the customer profile.

domain

To request that PPP calls from a specific domain name be tunneled, or to support additional domain names for a specific VPDN group, use the **domain** request-dialin or VPDN group configuration command. To remove a domain from a VPDN group or subgroup, use the **no** form of this command. Table C-32 describes the syntax of the following commands:

```
domain domain-name
no domain [domain-name]
```

Table C-32   **domain** *Syntax Description*

Syntax	Description
domain-name	Case-sensitive name of the domain that will be tunneled.

[encapsulation ppp]

To set the encapsulation method used by the interface, use the **encapsulation** interface configuration command. Table C-33 describes the syntax of the following command:

```
encapsulation encapsulation-type
```

Table C-33   encapsulation *Syntax Description*

Syntax	Description
encapsulation-type	Encapsulation type; one of the following keywords:
	atm-dxi—Asynchronous Transfer Mode-Data Exchange Interface.
	bstun—Block Serial Tunnel.
	frame-relay—Frame Relay (for serial interface).
	hdlc—High-Level Data Link Control (HDLC) protocol for serial interface. This encapsulation method provides the synchronous framing and error detection functions of HDLC without windowing or retransmission. This is the default for synchronous serial interfaces.
	isl—Inter-Switch Link (ISL) (for virtual LANs).
	lapb—X.25 LAPB DTE operation (for serial interface).
	ppp—Point-to-Point Protocol (PPP) (for serial interface).
	sde—IEEE 802.10 Security Data Exchange.
	sdlc—IBM serial SNA.
	sdlc-primary—IBM serial SNA (for primary serial interface).
	sdlc-secondary—IBM serial SNA (for secondary serial interface).
	slip—Specifies SLIP encapsulation for an interface configured for Dedicated Asynchronous mode or DDR. This is the default for asynchronous interfaces.
	smds—Switched Multimegabit Data Services (SMDS) (for serial interface).

encryption mppe

To enable Microsoft Point-to-Point Encryption (MPPE) on an Industry-Standard Architecture (ISA) card, use the **encryption mppe** ISA controller configuration command. To disable MPPE, use the **no** form of this command.

```
encryption mppe
no encryption mppe
```

This command has no arguments or keywords.

force-local-chap

To force the LNS to reauthenticate the client, use the **force-local-chap** VPDN group configuration command. To disable reauthentication, use the **no** form of this command.

```
force-local-chap
no force-local-chap
```

This command has no arguments or keywords.

framing

To select the frame type for the T1 or E1 data line, use the **framing** controller configuration command. To turn off framing, use the **no** form of this command. Table C-34 describes the syntax of the following commands:

T1 line:

```
framing {sf | esf}
no framing
```

E1 line:

```
framing {crc4 | no-crc4} [australia]
no framing
```

Table C-34   **framing** *Syntax Description*

Syntax	Description
sf	Super Frame as the T1 frame type.
esf	Extended Super Frame as the T1 frame type.
crc4	CRC4 frame as the E1 frame type.
no-crc4	No CRC4 frame as the E1 frame type.
australia	(Optional) E1 frame type used in Australia.

group-range

To create a list of member asynchronous interfaces (associated with a group interface), use the **group-range** interface configuration command. To remove an interface from the member list, use the **no** form of this command. Table C-35 describes the syntax of the following commands:

```
group-range low-end-of-interfacerange high-end-of-interfacerange
no group-range interface
```

Table C-35 **group-range** *Syntax Description*

Syntax	Description
low-end-of-interfacerange	Beginning interface number to be made a member of the group interface.
high-end-of-interfacerange	Ending interface number to be made a member of the group interface.
interface	Interface number to be removed from the group interface.

hostname

To specify or modify the host name for the network server, use the **hostname** global configuration command. The host name is used in prompts and default configuration filenames. The **setup** command facility also prompts for a host name at startup. Table C-36 describes the syntax of the following command:

```
hostname name
```

Table C-36 **hostname** *Syntax Description*

Syntax	Description
name	New host name for the network server.

initiate-to

To specify the IP address that will be tunneled to, use the **initiate-to** VPDN group configuration command. To remove an IP address from the VPDN group, use the **no** form of this command. Table C-37 describes the syntax of the following commands:

```
initiate-to ip ip-address [limit limit-number] [priority priority
    number]

no initiate-to [ip ip-address]
```

Table C-37 **initiate-to** *Syntax Description*

Syntax	Description
ip *ip-address*	IP address of the router that will be tunneled to.
limit *limit-number*	(Optional) Maximum number of connections that can be made to this IP address.
priority *priority-number*	(Optional) Priority for this IP address. (1 is the highest.)

interface dialer

To define a dialer rotary group, use the **interface dialer** global configuration command. Table C-38 describes the syntax of the following command:

```
interface dialer number
```

Table C-38   **interface dialer** *Syntax Description*

Syntax	Description
number	Number of the dialer rotary group in the range 0 through 255.

interface group-async

To create a group interface that will serve as master, to which asynchronous interfaces can be associated as members, use the **interface group-async** global configuration command. To restore the default, use the **no** form of this command. Table C-39 describes the syntax of the following commands:

```
interface group-async unit-number
no interface group-async unit-number
```

Table C-39   **interface group-async** *Syntax Description*

Syntax	Description
unit-number	Number of the asynchronous group interface being created.

interface virtual-template

To create a virtual template interface that can be configured and applied dynamically in creating virtual access interfaces, use the **interface virtual-template** global configuration command. Table C-40 describes the syntax of the following command:

```
interface virtual-template number
```

Table C-40   **interface virtual-template** *Syntax Description*

Syntax	Description
number	Number used to identify the virtual template interface.

ip local pool

To configure a local pool of IP addresses to be used when a remote peer connects to a point-to-point interface, use the **ip local pool** global configuration command. To remove a range of addresses from a pool (longer form of the **no** command), or to delete an address pool (shorter form of the **no** command), use the **no** form of this command. Table C-41 describes the syntax of the following commands:

```
ip local pool {default | pool-name low-ip-address [high-ip-address]}

no ip local pool {default | pool-name low-ip-address [high-ip-address]}

no ip local pool {default | pool-name}
```

Table C-41 local pool *Syntax Description*

Syntax	Description
default	Defaults local address pool that is used if no other pool is named.
pool-name	Name of a specific local address pool.
low-ip-address	Lowest IP address in the pool.
high-ip-address	(Optional) Highest IP address in the pool. If this value is omitted, only the *low-ip-address* IP address argument is included in the local pool.

isdn incoming-voice

To route all incoming voice calls to the modem and determine how they will be treated, use the **isdn incoming-voice** interface configuration command. To disable the setting or return to the default, use the **no** form of this command. Table C-42 describes the syntax of the following commands:

```
isdn incoming-voice {voice | data [56 | 64] | modem [56 | 64]}

no isdn incoming-voice {voice | data [56 | 64] | modem [56 | 64]}
```

Table C-42 isdn incoming-voice *Syntax Description*

Syntax	Description
voice	Incoming voice calls bypass the modems and be handled as voice calls.
data	Incoming voice calls bypass the modems and be handled as digital data. If this keyword is selected, you can specify a B-channel bandwidth of either **56** kbps or **64** kbps. If no argument is entered, the default value is **64**.

Table C-42   **isdn incoming-voice** *Syntax Description (Continued)*

Syntax	Description
modem	Incoming voice calls are passed over to the digital modems, where they negotiate the appropriate modem connection with the far-end modem. If this keyword is selected, you can specify a B-channel bandwidth of either **56** kbps or **64** kbps. If no argument is entered, the default value is **64**.

isdn switch-type (BRI)

To specify the central office switch type on the ISDN interface, use the **isdn switch-type** global or interface configuration command. To remove an ISDN switch type, use the **no** form of this command. Table C-43 and Table C-44 describe the syntax of the following commands:

```
isdn switch-type switch-type
no isdn switch-type switch-type
```

Table C-43   **isdn switch-type** *(BRI) Syntax Description*

Syntax	Description
switch-type	ISDN service provider switch type. Table C-44 lists the supported switch types.

Table C-44   *ISDN Service Provider BRI Switch Types*

Keywords by Area	Switch Type
Voice/PBX Systems	
basic-qsig	PINX (PBX) switches with QSIG signaling per Q.931
Australia, Europe, UK	
basic-ts013	Australian BRI (TS013) switch
basic-1tr6	German 1TR6 ISDN switch
basic-net3	NET3 ISDN and New Zealand NET3 switches (covers the Euro-ISDN E-DSS1 signaling system and is ETSI-compliant)
vn3	French ISDN BRI switches
Japan	
ntt	Japanese NTT ISDN switches

continues

Table C-44 *ISDN Service Provider BRI Switch Types (Continued)*

Keywords by Area	Switch Type
North America	
basic-5ess	Lucent (AT&T) basic rate 5ESS switch
basic-dms100	Northern Telecom DMS-100 basic rate switch
basic-ni	National ISDN switches
All Users	
none	No switch defined

isdn switch-type (PRI)

To specify the central office switch type on the ISDN interface, or to configure the Cisco MC3810 PRI interface to support QSIG signaling, use the **isdn switch-type** global and interface configuration command. To disable the switch or QSIG signaling on the ISDN interface, use the **no** form of this command. Table C-45 and Table C-46 describe the syntax of the following commands:

```
isdn switch-type switch-type

no isdn switch-type switch-type
```

Table C-45 **isdn switch-type** *(PRI) Syntax Description*

Syntax	Description
switch-type	Service provider switch type; see Table C-46 for a list of supported switches.

Table C-46 *ISDN Service Provider PRI Switch Types*

Keywords by Area	Switch Type
Voice/PBX Systems	
primary-qsig	Supports QSIG signaling per Q.931. Network side functionality is assigned with the **isdn protocol-emulate** command.
Australia and Europe	
primary-net5	European, New Zealand and Asia ISDN PRI switches (covers the Euro-ISDN E-DSS1 signaling system and is ETSI-compliant).

Table C-46   *ISDN Service Provider PRI Switch Types (Continued)*

Keywords by Area	Switch Type
primary-ts014	Australia PRI switch.
Japan	
primary-ntt	Japanese ISDN PRI switch.
North America	
primary-4ess	AT&T 4ESS switch type for the United States.
primary-5ess	AT&T 5ESS switch type for the United States.
primary-dms100	NT DMS-100 switch type for the United States.
primary-ni	National ISDN switch type.
All Users	
none	No switch defined.

l2f ignore-mid-sequence

To ignore multiplex ID (MID) sequence numbers for sessions in an L2F tunnel, use the **l2f ignore-mid-sequence** command in VPDN group configuration mode. To remove the ability to ignore MID sequencing, use the **no** form of this command.

```
l2f ignore-mid-sequence
no l2f ignore-mid-sequence
```

This command has no arguments or keywords.

l2tp drop out-of-order

To instruct L2TP access concentrator (LAC) or LNS using L2TP to drop packets that are received out of order, use the **l2tp drop out-of-order** command in VPDN group configuration mode. To disable dropping of out-of-sequence packets, use the **no** form of this command.

```
l2tp drop out-of-order
no l2tp drop out-of-order
```

This command has no arguments or keywords.

l2tp flow-control backoff-queuesize

To define the maximum number of packets that can be queued locally for a session when a peer's receive window is full, use the **l2tp flow-control backoff-queuesize** command in VPDN group configuration mode. To change the value of the queue size, just reenter the command with the new queue size value. To remove a manually configured flow-control backoff value, use the **no** form of this command. Table C-47 describes the syntax of the following commands:

```
l2tp flow-control backoff-queuesize queuesize

no l2tp flow-control backoff-queuesize queuesize
```

Table C-47   l2tp flow-control backoff-queuesize *Syntax Description*

Syntax	Description
queuesize	Sets the queue size limit on a LAC or LNS so that when the remote peer's receive window is full, the LAC or LNS delays sending additional packets.

l2tp flow-control maximum-ato

To define the maximum adaptive timeout for congestion control, use the **l2tp flow-control maximum-ato** command in VPDN group configuration mode. To reset the timeout to a new value, just reenter the command with the new value. To remove a manually configured timeout value, use the **no** form of this command. Table C-48 describes the syntax of the following commands:

```
l2tp flow-control maximum-ato milliseconds

no l2tp flow-control maximum-ato milliseconds
```

Table C-48   l2tp flow-control maximum-ato *Syntax Description*

Syntax	Description
milliseconds	The wait time period, in milliseconds, before the LAC or LNS probes its remote peer's receive window to resume sending packets.

l2tp flow-control receive-window

To define the receive window on a LAC or LNS and enable either device to send sequence numbers, use the **l2tp flow-control receive-window** command in VPDN group configuration mode. Use the **no** form of this command to remove a

flow-control receive-window value and disable sequencing. Table C-49 describes the syntax of the following commands:

```
l2tp flow-control receive-window windowsize

no l2tp flow-control receive-window windowsize
```

Table C-49   **l2tp flow-control receive-window** *Syntax Description*

Syntax	Description
windowsize	The number of packets that can be received by the remote end device before backoff queueing occurs.

l2tp flow-control static-rtt

To define a static round-trip time for congestion control, use the **l2tp flow-control static-rtt** command in VPDN group configuration mode. To apply a different value, just reenter the command with the new value. To disable a static round-trip time, use the **no** form of this command. Table C-50 describes the syntax of the following commands:

```
l2tp flow-control static-rtt round-trip-time

no l2tp flow-control static-rtt round-trip-time
```

Table C-50   **l2tp flow-control static-rtt** *Syntax Description*

Syntax	Description
round-trip-time	Sets the static round-trip time in milliseconds.

l2tp hidden

To enable L2TP attribute-value (AV) pair hiding, which encrypts the AV pair value, use the **l2tp hidden** command in VPDN group configuration mode. To disable L2TP AV pair value hiding, use the **no** form of this command.

```
l2tp hidden

no l2tp hidden
```

This command has no arguments or keywords.

l2tp ip tos reflect

To configure a VPDN group to preserve the ToS field of L2TP-tunneled IP packets, use the **l2tp ip tos reflect** command in VPDN group configuration mode. To specify a ToS field of 0 for tunneled packets, use the **no** form of this command.

```
l2tp ip tos reflect
no l2tp ip tos reflect
```

This command has no arguments or keywords.

l2tp ip udp checksum

To enable IP User Data Protocol (UDP) checksums on L2TP payload packets, use the **l2tp ip udp checksum** command in VPDN group configuration mode. Use the **no** form of this command to disable IP UDP checksums.

```
l2tp ip udp checksum
no l2tp ip udp checksum
```

This command has no arguments or keywords.

l2tp offset

To enable the offset field in L2TP payload packets, use the **l2tp offset** command in VPDN group configuration mode. Use the **no** form of this command to disable the offset field.

```
l2tp offset
no l2tp offset
```

This command has no arguments or keywords.

l2tp tunnel authentication

To enable L2TP tunnel authentication, use the **l2tp tunnel authentication** command in VPDN group configuration mode. Use the **no** form of this command to disable L2TP tunnel authentication.

```
l2tp tunnel authentication
no l2tp tunnel authentication
```

This command has no arguments or keywords.

l2tp tunnel hello

To set the number of seconds between sending hello keepalive packets for a L2TP tunnel, use the **l2tp tunnel hello** command in VPDN group configuration mode. To change the tunnel hello value, just reenter the command with the new value. To disable the sending of hello keepalive packets, use the **no** form of this command. Table C-51 describes the syntax of the following commands:

```
l2tp tunnel hello hello-interval

no l2tp tunnel hello hello-interval
```

Table C-51   **l2tp tunnel hello** *Syntax Description*

Syntax	Description
hello-interval	The interval, in seconds, that the LAC and LNS wait before sending the next L2TP tunnel keepalive packet.

l2tp tunnel password

To set the password that the router will use to authenticate the tunnel, use the **l2tp tunnel password** command in VPDN group configuration mode. To remove a previously configured password, use the **no** form of this command. Table C-52 describes the syntax of the following commands:

```
l2tp tunnel password password

no l2tp tunnel password password
```

Table C-52   **l2tp tunnel password** *Syntax Description*

Syntax	Description
password	Identifies the password that the router will use for tunnel authentication.

lcp renegotiation

To allow the LNS to renegotiate the Link Control Protocol (LCP) on dialin calls, using L2TP or L2F, use the **lcp renegotiation** VPDN group configuration command. To remove LCP renegotiation, use the **no** form of this command. Table C-53 describes the syntax of the following commands:

```
lcp renegotiation {always | on-mismatch}

no lcp renegotiation
```

Table C-53   **lcp renegotiation** *Syntax Description*

Syntax	Description
always	Always renegotiate PPP LCP at the LNS.
on-mismatch	Renegotiates PPP LCP at the LNS only in the event of an LCP mismatch between the LAC and LNS.

line

To identify a specific line for configuration and begin the line configuration collection mode, use the **line** global configuration command. Table C-54 describes the syntax of the following command:

```
line [aux | console | tty | vty] line-number [ending-line-number]
```

Table C-54   **line** *Syntax Description*

Syntax	Description
aux	(Optional) Auxiliary EIA/TIA-232 DTE port. Must be addressed as relative line 0. The auxiliary port can be used for modem support and asynchronous connections.
console	(Optional) Console terminal line. The console port is DCE.
tty	(Optional) Standard asynchronous line.
vty	(Optional) Virtual terminal for remote console access.
line-number	Relative number of the terminal line (or the first line in a contiguous group) that you want to configure when the line type is specified. Numbering begins with zero.
ending-line-number	(Optional) Relative number of the last line in a contiguous group that you want to configure. If you omit the keyword, *line-number* and *ending-line-number* are absolute rather than relative line numbers.

linecode

To select the line-code type for T1 or E1 line, use the **linecode** controller configuration command. Table C-55 describes the syntax of the following command:

```
linecode {ami | b8zs | hdb3}
```

Table C-55   **linecode** *Syntax Description*

Syntax	Description
ami	Specifies alternate mark inversion (AMI) as the line-code type. Valid for T1 or E1 controllers. This is the default for T1 lines.
b8zs	Specifies B8ZS as the line-code type. Valid for T1 controller only.
hdb3	Specifies high-density bipolar 3 (hdb3) as the line-code type. Valid for E1 controller only. This is the default for E1 lines.

local name

To specify a local host name that the tunnel will use to identify itself, use the **local name** VPDN group configuration command. To remove a local name, use the **no** form of this command. Table C-56 describes the syntax of the following commands:

```
local name name
no local name name
```

Table C-56 **local name** *Syntax Description*

Syntax	Description
name	Local host name of the tunnel.

match address (CET)

To specify an extended access list for a crypto map entry, use the **match address** crypto map configuration command. To remove the extended access list from a crypto map entry, use the **no** form of this command. Table C-57 describes the syntax of the following commands:

```
match address [access-list-id | name]
no match address [access-list-id | name]
```

Table C-57 **match address** *(CET) Syntax Description*

Syntax	Description
access-list-id	(Optional) Identifies the extended access list by its name or number. This value should match the *access-list-number* or *name* argument of the extended access list being matched.
name	(Optional) Identifies the named encryption access list. This name should match the *name* argument of the named encryption access list being matched. Named access lists do not work on VIP interfaces.

match address (IPSec)

To specify an extended access list for a crypto map entry, use the **match address** crypto map configuration command. To remove the extended access list from a crypto map entry, use the **no** form of this command. Table C-58 describes the syntax of the following commands:

```
match address [access-list-id | name]
no match address [access-list-id | name]
```

Table C-58 **match address** *(IPSec) Syntax Description*

Syntax	Description
access-list-id	(Optional) Identifies the extended access list by its name or number. This value should match the *access-list-number* or *name* argument of the extended access list being matched.
name	(Optional) Identifies the named encryption access list. This name should match the *name* argument of the named encryption access list being matched.

modem inout

To configure a line for both incoming and outgoing calls, use the **modem inout** line configuration command. To disable the line, use the **no** form of this command.

```
modem inout
no modem inout
```

This command has no arguments or keywords.

multilink virtual-template

To specify a virtual template from which the specified Multilink PPP (MLP) bundle interface can clone its interface parameters, use the **multilink virtual-template** global configuration command. Table C-59 describes the syntax of the following command:

```
multilink virtual-template number
```

Table C-59 **multilink virtual-template** *Syntax Description*

Syntax	Description
number	Number of virtual templates, and is an integer in the range 1 through the largest number of virtual templates the software image supports (typically 25).

multilink-group

The **multilink-group** global configuration command is replaced by the **ppp multilink group** interface configuration command. See the description of the **ppp multilink group** interface configuration command for more information.

NOTE	The command is still recognized and accepted by the Cisco IOS software. The **show running-config** and **write memory** privileged EXEC commands will display and generate the original command in Cisco IOS Release 12.2.

peer default ip address

To specify an IP address, an address from a specific IP address pool, or an address from the Dynamic Host Configuration Protocol (DHCP) mechanism to be returned to a remote peer connecting to this interface, use the **peer default ip address** interface configuration command. To disable a prior peer IP address pooling configuration on an interface, or to remove the default address from your configuration, use the **no** form of this command. Table C-60 describes the syntax of the following commands:

```
peer default ip address {ip-address | dhcp | pool [pool-name]}
no peer default ip address
```

Table C-60 **peer default ip address** *Syntax Description*

Syntax	Description
ip-address	Specific IP address to be assigned to a remote peer dialing in to the interface. To prevent duplicate IP addresses from being assigned on more than one interface, this argument cannot be applied to a dialer rotary group or to an ISDN interface.
dhcp	Retrieves an IP address from the DHCP server.
pool	Uses the global default mechanism as defined by the **ip address-pool** command unless the optional *pool-name* argument is supplied. This is the default.
pool-name	(Optional) Name of a local address pool created using the **ip local pool** command. Retrieve an address from this pool regardless of the global default mechanism setting.

pool-member

To assign a request-dialout VPDN subgroup to a dialer pool, use the **pool-member** request-dialout configuration command. To remove the request-dialout VPDN subgroup from a dialer pool, use the **no** form of this command. Table C-61 describes the syntax of the following commands:

```
pool-member pool-number
no pool-member [pool-number]
```

Table C-61   **pool-member** *Syntax Description*

Syntax	Description
pool-number	Dialer pool that this VPDN group belongs to.

ppp authentication

To enable Challenge Handshake Authentication Protocol (CHAP) or Password Authentication Protocol (PAP) or both and to specify the order in which CHAP and PAP authentication are selected on the interface, use the **ppp authentication** command in interface configuration mode. To disable this authentication, use the **no** form of this command. Table C-62 and Table C-63 describe the syntax of the following commands:

```
ppp authentication {protocol1 [protocol2...]} [if-needed] [list-name |
   default] [callin] [one-time]
no ppp authentication
```

Table C-62   **ppp authentication** *Syntax Description*

Syntax	Description
protocol1 [*protocol2...*]	Specify at least one of the keywords described in Table C-63.
if-needed	(Optional) Used with TACACS and extended TACACS. Does not perform CHAP or PAP authentication if the user has already provided authentication. This option is available only on asynchronous interfaces.
list-name	(Optional) Used with AAA. Specifies the name of a list of methods of authentication to use. If no list name is specified, the system uses the default. The list is created with the **aaa authentication ppp** global configuration command.
default	(Optional) The name of the method list is created with the **aaa authentication ppp** global configuration command.
callin	(Optional) Specifies authentication on incoming (received) calls only.
one-time	(Optional) Accepts the username and password in the username field.

Table C-63 *ppp authentication Protocols*

Keyword	Description
chap	Enables CHAP on a serial interface.
ms-chap	Enables Microsoft's version of CHAP (MS-CHAP) on a serial interface.
pap	Enables PAP on a serial interface.

ppp chap hostname

To create a pool of dialup routers that all appear to be the same host when authenticating with CHAP, use the **ppp chap hostname** command in interface configuration mode. To disable this function, use the **no** form of the command. Table C-64 describes the syntax of the following commands:

```
ppp chap hostname hostname
no ppp chap hostname hostname
```

Table C-64   **ppp chap hostname** *Syntax Description*

Syntax	Description
hostname	The name sent in the CHAP challenge.

ppp chap password

To enable a router calling a collection of routers that do not support this command (such as routers running older Cisco IOS software images) to configure a common CHAP secret password to use in response to challenges from an unknown peer, use the **ppp chap password** command in interface configuration mode. To disable the PPP CHAP password, use the **no** form of this command. Table C-65 describes the syntax of the following commands:

```
ppp chap password secret
no ppp chap password secret
```

Table C-65   **ppp chap password** *Syntax Description*

Syntax	Description
secret	The secret used to compute the response value for any CHAP challenge from an unknown peer.

ppp encrypt mppe

To enable Microsoft Point-to-Point Encryption (MPPE) encryption on the virtual template, use the **ppp encrypt mppe** interface configuration command. Use the **no** form of this command to disable MPPE encryption. Table C-66 describes the syntax of the following commands:

```
ppp encrypt mppe {auto | 40 | 128} [passive | required] [stateful]
no ppp encrypt mppe
```

Table C-66   **ppp encrypt mppe** *Syntax Description*

Syntax	Description
auto	All available encryption strengths are allowed.
40	Only 40-bit encryption is allowed.
128	Only 128-bit encryption is allowed.
passive	(Optional) MPPE will not offer encryption, but will negotiate if the other tunnel endpoint requests encryption.
required	(Optional) MPPE must be negotiated, or the connection will be terminated.
stateful	(Optional) MPPE will negotiate only stateful encryption. If the **stateful** keyword is not used, MPPE will first attempt to negotiate stateless encryption, but will fall back to stateful if the other tunnel endpoint requests stateful.

ppp multilink group

To restrict a physical link to joining only a designated multilink-group interface, use the **ppp multilink group** interface configuration command. To remove the restrictions, use the **no** form of this command. Table C-67 describes the syntax of the following commands:

```
ppp multilink group group-number
no ppp multilink group
```

Table C-67   **ppp multilink group** *Syntax Description*

Syntax	Description
group-number	Multilink-group number (a non-0 number).

pptp flow-control receive-window

To specify how many packets the client can send before it has to wait for the tunnel server's acknowledgment, use the **pptp flow-control receive-window** VPDN configuration command. To return to the default value, use the **no** form of this command. Table C-68 describes the syntax of the following commands:

```
pptp flow-control receive-window packets
no pptp flow-control receive-window
```

Table C-68   **pptp flow-control receive-window** *Syntax Description*

Syntax	Description
packets	Number of packets the client can send before it has to wait for the tunnel server's acknowledgment. The range is 1 to 64 packets.

pptp flow-control static-rtt

To specify the timeout interval of the tunnel server between sending a packet to the client and receiving a response, use the **pptp flow-control static-rtt** VPDN configuration command. To return to the default value of 1500 milliseconds (ms), use the **no** form of this command. Table C-69 describes the syntax of the following commands:

```
pptp flow-control static-rtt milliseconds
no pptp flow-control static-rtt
```

Table C-69   **pptp flow-control static-rtt** *Syntax Description*

Syntax	Description
milliseconds	Timeout interval of the tunnel server between sending a packet to the client and receiving a response. The range is 100 to 5000 milliseconds.

pptp tunnel echo

To specify the period of idle time on the tunnel that will trigger an echo message from the tunnel server to the client, use the **pptp tunnel echo** VPDN configuration command. To return to the default value of 60 seconds, use the **no** form of this command. Table C-70 describes the syntax of the following commands:

```
pptp tunnel echo seconds
no pptp tunnel echo
```

Table C-70 **pptp tunnel echo** *Syntax Description*

Syntax	Description
seconds	Echo packet interval in seconds. The range is 0 to 1000 seconds.

pri-group timeslots nfas_d

To configure Non-Facility Associated Signaling (NFAS) and specify the channels to be controlled by the primary NFAS D channel, use the **pri-group timeslots nfas_d** controller configuration command. Table C-71 describes the syntax of the following commands:

```
pri-group timeslots range nfas_d [primary | backup | none]
    nfas_interface number nfas_group number
pri-group timeslots range
```

Table C-71 **pri-group timeslots nfas_d** *Syntax Description*

Syntax	Description
range	Channels in the range 1 to 24. A range of channels is shown with a hyphen (-).
primary	(Optional) Function of channel 24; the primary NFAS D channel.
backup	(Optional) Function of channel 24; the backup NFAS D channel.
none	(Optional) Function of channel 24; B channel.
nfas_interface *number*	Value assigned by the service provider to ensure unique identification of a PRI interface.
nfas_group *number*	Group identifier unique on the router. Multiple NFAS groups can exist on the router.

protocol (VPDN)

To specify the L2TP that VPDN subgroup will use, use the **protocol** VPDN subgroup command. To remove the protocol-specific configurations from a VPDN subgroup, use the **no** form of this command. Table C-72 describes the syntax of the following commands:

```
protocol {l2f | l2tp | pppoe | pptp | any}
no protocol
```

Table C-72   **protocol** *(VPDN) Syntax Description*

Syntax	Description
l2f	L2F tunnels.
l2tp	L2TP tunnels.
pppoe	Enables the VPDN subgroup to establish Point-to Point-Protocol over Ethernet (PPPoE) sessions.
pptp	PPTP tunnels.
any	Either L2F, L2TP, or PPTP tunnels.

radius-server host

To specify a RADIUS server host, use the **radius-server host** command in global configuration mode. To delete the specified RADIUS host, use the **no** form of this command. Table C-73 describes the syntax of the following commands:

```
radius-server host {hostname | ip-address} [auth-port port-number]
   [acct-port port-number] [timeout seconds] [retransmit retries]
   [key string] [alias {hostname | ip-address}]

no radius-server host {hostname | ip-address}
```

Table C-73   **radius-server host** *Syntax Description*

Syntax	Description
hostname	Domain Name System (DNS) name of the RADIUS server host.
ip-address	IP address of the RADIUS server host.
auth-port	(Optional) Specifies the UDP destination port for authentication requests.
port-number	(Optional) Port number for authentication requests; the host is not used for authentication if set to 0. If unspecified, the port number defaults to 1645.
acct-port	(Optional) Specifies the UDP destination port for accounting requests.
port-number	(Optional) Port number for accounting requests; the host is not used for accounting if set to 0. If unspecified, the port number defaults to 1646.

continues

Table C-73   **radius-server host** *Syntax Description (Continued)*

Syntax	Description
timeout	(Optional) The time interval (in seconds) that the router waits for the RADIUS server to reply before retransmitting. This setting overrides the global value of the **radius-server timeout** access-point configuration command. If no timeout value is specified, the global value is used. Enter a value in the range 1 to 1000.
seconds	(Optional) Specifies the **timeout** value. Enter a value in the range 1 to 1000. If no **timeout** value is specified, the global value is used.
retransmit	(Optional) The number of times a RADIUS request is re-sent to a server, if that server is not responding or responding slowly. This setting overrides the global setting of the **radius-server retransmit** access-point configuration command.
retries	(Optional) Specifies the retransmit value. Enter a value in the range 1 to 100. If no retransmit value is specified, the global value is used.
key	(Optional) Specifies the authentication and encryption key used between the router and the RADIUS daemon running on this RADIUS server. This key overrides the global setting of the **radius-server key** access-point configuration command. If no key string is specified, the global value is used. The key is a text string that must match the encryption key used on the RADIUS server. Always configure the key as the last item in the **radius-server host** access-point configuration command syntax. This is because the leading spaces are ignored, but spaces within and at the end of the key are used. If you use spaces in the key, do not enclose the key in quotation marks unless the quotation marks themselves are part of the key.
string	(Optional) Specifies the authentication and encryption key for all RADIUS communications between the router and the RADIUS server. This key must match the encryption used on the RADIUS daemon. All leading spaces are ignored, but spaces within and at the end of the key are used. If you use spaces in your key, do not enclose the key in quotation marks unless the quotation marks themselves are part of the key.
alias	(Optional) Allows up to eight aliases per line for any given RADIUS server.

radius-server key

To set the authentication and encryption key for all RADIUS communications between the router and the RADIUS daemon, use the **radius-server key** command in global configuration mode. To disable the key, use the **no** form of this command. Table C-74 describes the syntax of the following commands:

```
radius-server key {0 string | 7 string | string}
no radius-server key
```

Table C-74   **radius-server key** *Syntax Description*

Syntax	Description
0	Specifies that an unencrypted key will follow.
string	The unencrypted (clear text) shared key.
7	Specifies that a hidden key will follow.
string	The hidden shared key.
string	The unencrypted (clear text) shared key.

request dialin

To configure a LAC to request L2F or L2TP tunnels to an LNS and create a request-dialin VPDN subgroup, use the **request dialin** VPDN group configuration command. To remove the request-dialin subgroup from a VPDN group, use the **no** form of this command.

```
request dialin
no request dialin
```

This command has no arguments or keywords.

request dialout

To enable an LNS to request VPDN dialout calls by using L2TP, use the **request dialout** VPDN group configuration command. To disable L2TP dialout, use the **no** form of this command.

```
request dialout
no request dialout
```

This command has no arguments or keywords.

rotary-group

To assign a request-dialout VPDN subgroup to a dialer rotary group, use the **rotary-group** request-dialout configuration command. To remove the request-dialout VPDN subgroup from the dialer rotary group, use the **no** form of this command. Table C-75 describes the syntax of the following commands:

```
rotary-group group-number

no rotary-group [group-number]
```

Table C-75 **rotary-group** *Syntax Description*

Syntax	Description
group-number	The dialer rotary group that this VPDN group belongs to.

set peer (IPSec)

To specify an IPSec peer in a crypto map entry, use the **set peer** crypto map configuration command. To remove an IPSec peer from a crypto map entry, use the **no** form of this command. Table C-76 describes the syntax of the following commands:

```
set peer {hostname | ip-address}

no set peer {hostname | ip-address}
```

Table C-76 **set peer** *(IPSec) Syntax Description*

Syntax	Description
hostname	Specifies the IPSec peer by its host name. This is the peer's host name concatenated with its domain name (for example, myhost.example.com).
ip-address	Specifies the IPSec peer by its IP address.

set transform-set

To specify which transform sets can be used with the crypto map entry, use the **set transform-set** crypto map configuration command. To remove all transform sets from a crypto map entry, use the **no** form of this command. Table C-77 describes the syntax of the following commands:

```
set transform-set transform-set-name [transform-set-name2...transform
  set-name6]

no set transform-set
```

Table C-77   **set transform-set** *Syntax Description*

Syntax	Description
transform-set-name	Name of the transform set.
	For an **ipsec-manual** crypto map entry, you can specify only one transform set.
	For an **ipsec-isakmp** or dynamic crypto map entry, you can specify up to six transform sets.

show interfaces virtual-access

To display status, traffic data, and configuration information about a specified virtual access interface, use the **show interfaces virtual-access** privileged EXEC command. Table C-78 describes the syntax of the following command:

```
show interfaces virtual-access number [configuration]
```

Table C-78   **show interfaces virtual-access** *Syntax Description*

Syntax	Description
number	Number of the virtual access interface.
configuration	(Optional) Restricts output to configuration information.

show ppp mppe

To display MPPE information for an interface, use the **show ppp mppe** user EXEC command. Table C-79 describes the syntax of the following command:

```
show ppp mppe {serial | virtual-access}[number]
```

Table C-79   **show ppp mppe** *Syntax Description*

Syntax	Description
serial	Displays MPPE information for all serial interfaces.
virtual-access	Displays MPPE information for all virtual-access interfaces.
number	(Optional) Displays MPPE information for only the specified interface.

show vpdn

To display information about active L2F protocol tunnel and message identifiers in a VPDN, use the **show vpdn** user EXEC command. Table C-80 describes the syntax of the following command:

```
show vpdn [session][packets][tunnel][all]
```

Table C-80   show vpdn *Syntax Description*

Syntax	Description
session	(Optional) Displays a summary of the status of all active tunnels.
packets	(Optional) Displays a summary of packets coming in and going out of a session.
tunnel	(Optional) Displays information about all active L2F and L2TP tunnels in summary-style format.
all	(Optional) Displays summary information about all active L2F and L2TP tunnels.

show vpdn domain

To view all VPDN domains and DNIS groups configured on the network access server, use the **show vpdn domain** user EXEC command.

```
show vpdn domain
```

This command has no arguments or keywords.

show vpdn group

To see a summary of the relationships among VPDN groups and customer/ VPDN profiles, or to summarize the configuration of a VPDN group including domain/DNIS, load sharing information, and current session information, use the **show vpdn group** user EXEC command. Table C-81 describes the syntax of the following command:

```
show vpdn group [name] [domain | endpoint]
```

Table C-81   show vpdn group *Syntax Description*

Syntax	Description
name	(Optional) VPDN group name summarizes the configuration of the specified group.
domain	(Optional) DNIS/domain information.
endpoint	(Optional) Endpoint session information.

show vpdn history failure

To show the content of the failure history table, use the **show vpdn history failure** user EXEC command. Table C-82 describes the syntax of the following command:

```
show vpdn history failure [user-name]
```

Table C-82   **show vpdn history failure** *Syntax Description*

Syntax	Description
user-name	(Optional) Username, which displays only the entries mapped to that particular user.

source-ip

To specify an alternate IP address for a VPDN tunnel that is different from the physical IP address used to open the tunnel, use the **source-ip** group configuration command. To remove the alternate IP address, use the **no** form of this command. Table C-83 describes the syntax of the following commands:

```
source-ip ip-address

no source-ip
```

Table C-83   **source-ip** *Syntax Description*

Syntax	Description
ip-address	Alternate IP address (different from the physical IP address used to open the VPDN tunnel) that the router uses to identify the tunnel.

tacacs-server host

To specify a TACACS+ host, use the **tacacs-server host** command in global configuration mode. Use the **no** form of this command to delete the specified name or address. Table C-84 describes the syntax of the following commands:

```
tacacs-server host hostname [port integer] [timeout integer] [key
    string]

no tacacs-server host hostname
```

Table C-84 **tacacs-server host** *Syntax Description*

Syntax	Description
hostname	Name or IP address of the host.
port	(Optional) Specify a server port number. This option overrides the default, which is port 49.
integer	(Optional) Port number of the server. Valid port numbers range from 1 to 65,535.
timeout	(Optional) Specify a timeout value. This overrides the global timeout value set with the **tacacs-server timeout** global configuration command for this server only.
integer	(Optional) Integer value, in seconds, of the timeout interval.
key	(Optional) Specify an authentication and encryption key. This must match the key used by the TACACS+ daemon. Specifying this key overrides the key set by the **tacacs-server key** global configuration command for this server only.
string	(Optional) Character string specifying authentication and encryption key.

tacacs-server key

To set the authentication encryption key used for all TACACS+ communications between the access server and the TACACS+ daemon, use the **tacacs-server key** command in global configuration mode. To disable the key, use the **no** form of this command. Table C-85 describes the syntax of the following commands:

```
tacacs-server key key
no tacacs-server key [key]
```

Table C-85 **tacacs-server key** *Syntax Description*

Syntax	Description
key	Key used to set authentication and encryption. This key must match the key used on the TACACS+ daemon.

terminate-from

To specify the host name of the remote LAC or LNS that will be required when accepting a VPDN tunnel, use the **terminate-from** VPDN group configuration command. To remove the host name from the VPDN group, use the **no** form of this command. Table C-86 describes the syntax of the following commands:

```
terminate-from hostname host-name
no terminate-from [hostname host-name]
```

Table C-86   **terminate-from** *Syntax Description*

Syntax	Description
hostname *host-name*	The host name that this VPDN group will accept connections from.

username

To establish a username-based authentication system, use the **username** command in global configuration mode. Table C-87 describes the syntax of the following commands:

```
username name {nopassword | password password |
   password encryption-type encrypted-password}
username name password secret
username name [access-class number]
username name [autocommand command]
username name [callback-dialstring telephone-number]
username name [callback-rotary rotary-group-number]
username name [callback-line [tty] line-number [ending-line-number]]
username name dnis
username name [nocallback-verify]
username name [noescape] [nohangup]
username name [privilege level]
username name user-maxlinks number
```

Table C-87   **username** *Syntax Description*

Syntax	Description
name	Host name, server name, user ID, or command name. The name argument can be only one word. Blank spaces and quotation marks are not allowed.
nopassword	No password is required for this user to log in. This is usually most useful in combination with the **autocommand** keyword.
password	Specifies a possibly encrypted password for this username.

continues

Table C-87   **username** *Syntax Description (Continued)*

Syntax	Description
password	Password a user enters.
encryption-type	(Optional) Single-digit number that defines whether the text immediately following is encrypted, and, if so, what type of encryption is used. Currently defined encryption types are 0, which means that the text immediately following is not encrypted, and 7, which means that the text is encrypted using a Cisco-defined encryption algorithm.
encrypted-password	(Optional) Encrypted password a user enters.
password	Password to access the name argument. A password must be from 1 to 25 characters, can contain embedded spaces, and must be the last option specified in the **username** global configuration command.
secret	For CHAP authentication: specifies the secret for the local router or the remote device. The secret is encrypted when it is stored on the local router. The secret can consist of any string of up to 11 ASCII characters. There is no limit to the number of username and password combinations that can be specified, allowing any number of remote devices to be authenticated.
access-class	(Optional) Specifies an outgoing access list that overrides the access list specified in the **access-class** line configuration command. It is used for the duration of the user's session.
number	(Optional) Access list number.
autocommand	(Optional) Causes the specified command to be issued automatically after the user logs in. When the command is complete, the session is terminated. Because the command can be any length and contain embedded spaces, commands using the **autocommand** keyword must be the last option on the line.
command	(Optional) The command string. Because the command can be any length and contain embedded spaces, commands using the **autocommand** keyword must be the last option on the line.
callback-dialstring	(Optional) For asynchronous callback only: permits you to specify a telephone number to pass to the DCE device.
telephone-number	(Optional) For asynchronous callback only: telephone number to pass to the DCE device.

Table C-87   **username** *Syntax Description (Continued)*

Syntax	Description
callback-rotary	(Optional) For asynchronous callback only: permits you to specify a rotary group number. The next available line in the rotary group is selected.
rotary-group-number	(Optional) For asynchronous callback only: integer between 1 and 100 that identifies the group of lines on which you want to enable a specific username for callback.
callback-line	(Optional) For asynchronous callback only: specific line on which you enable a specific username for callback.
tty	(Optional) For asynchronous callback only: standard asynchronous line.
line-number	(Optional) For asynchronous callback only: relative number of the terminal line (or the first line in a contiguous group) on which you want to enable a specific username for callback. Numbering begins with 0.
ending-line-number	(Optional) Relative number of the last line in a contiguous group on which you want to enable a specific username for callback. If you omit the keyword (such as **tty**), then *line-number* and *ending-line-number* are absolute rather than relative line numbers.
dnis	Do not require password when obtained via DNIS.
nocallback-verify	(Optional) Authentication not required for EXEC callback on the specified line.
noescape	(Optional) Prevents a user from using an escape character on the host to which that user is connected.
nohangup	(Optional) Prevents Cisco IOS software from disconnecting the user after an automatic command (set up with the **autocommand** keyword) has completed. Instead, the user gets another EXEC prompt.
privilege	(Optional) Sets the privilege level for the user.
level	(Optional) Number between 0 and 15 that specifies the privilege level for the user.
user-maxlinks	Limit the user's number of inbound links.
number	**User-maxlinks** limit for inbound links.

virtual-template

To specify which virtual template will be used to clone virtual access interfaces, use the **virtual-template** accept-dialin configuration command. To remove the virtual template from an accept-dialin VPDN subgroup, use the **no** form of this command. Table C-88 describes the syntax of the following commands:

```
virtual-template template-number
no virtual-template
```

Table C-88   **virtual-template** *Syntax Description*

Syntax	Description
template-number	Number of the virtual template that will be used to clone virtual-access interfaces.

vpdn enable

To enable virtual private dialup networking on the router and inform the router to look for tunnel definitions in a local database and on a remote authorization server (home gateway), if one is present, use the **vpdn enable** global configuration command. To disable, use the **no** form of this command.

```
vpdn enable
no vpdn enable
```

This command has no arguments or keywords.

vpdn group

To associate a VPDN group to a customer or VPDN profile, use the **vpdn group** customer profile or VPDN profile configuration command. To remove the VPDN group from a customer profile or VPDN profile, use the **no** form of this command. Table C-89 describes the syntax of the following commands:

```
vpdn group name
no vpdn group name
```

Table C-89   **vpdn group** *Syntax Description*

Syntax	Description
name	Name of the VPDN group.

vpdn history failure table-size

To set the failure history table depth, use the **vpdn history failure table-size** global configuration command. Table C-90 describes the syntax of the following commands:

```
vpdn history failure table-size entries
```

Table C-90   **vpdn history failure table-size** *Syntax Description*

Syntax	Description
entries	Number of entries. Valid entries are 20 to 50.

vpdn logging

To enable the logging of VPDN events, use the **vpdn logging** global configuration command. To disable the logging of VPDN events, use the **no** form of this command. Table C-91 describes the syntax of the following commands:

```
vpdn logging [local | remote]

no vpdn logging [local | remote]
```

Table C-91   **vpdn logging** *Syntax Description*

Syntax	Description
local	(Optional) Logs VPDN events locally.
remote	(Optional) Logs VPDN events to a remote tunnel endpoint.

vpdn logging history failure

To enable the logging of failure events to the failure history table, use the **vpdn logging history failure** global configuration command. To disable the logging of failure events, use the **no** form of this command.

```
vpdn logging history failure

no vpdn logging history failure
```

This command has no arguments or keywords.

vpdn search-order

To specify how the service provider network access server is to perform VPDN tunnel authorization searches, use the **vpdn search-order** global configuration command. To remove a prior specification, use the **no** form of this command. Table C-92 describes the syntax of the following commands:

```
vpdn search-order {dnis domain | domain dnis | domain | dnis}
no vpdn search-order
```

Table C-92   **vpdn search-order** *Syntax Description*

Syntax	Description
dnis domain	Searches first on the DNIS information provided on ISDN lines and then searches on the domain name.
domain dnis	Searches first on the domain name and then searches on the DNIS information.
domain	Searches on the domain name only.
dnis	Searches on the DNIS information only.

vpdn session-limit

To limit the number of simultaneous VPN sessions that can be established on a router, use the **vpdn session-limit** global configuration command. To allow an unlimited number of simultaneous VPN sessions, use the **no** form of this command. Table C-93 describes the syntax of the following commands:

```
vpdn session-limit sessions
no vpdn session-limit
```

Table C-93   **vpdn session-limit** *Syntax Description*

Syntax	Description
sessions	Maximum number of simultaneous VPN sessions that are allowed on a router.

vpdn softshut

To prevent new sessions from being established on a VPN tunnel without disturbing existing sessions, use the **vpdn softshut** global configuration command. To return the VPN tunnel to active service, use the **no** form of this command.

```
vpdn softshut
no vpdn softshut
```

This command has no arguments or keywords.

Debug Output

This appendix contains comprehensive **debug** command output from the three end-to-end solutions and from the L2TP Dial-Out feature. Debug output is detailed output from the Cisco IOS software that describes the messages the devices send and receive and the internal processes the devices perform. Debug output is a powerful tool that can help you understand the entire process of how an access VPDN is established.

WARNING Because debug output is assigned high priority in the CPU process, it can render the system unusable. For this reason, use **debug** commands only to troubleshoot specific problems or during troubleshooting sessions with Cisco technical support staff. Moreover, it is best to use **debug** commands while testing the network or during periods of lower network traffic and fewer users. Debugging during these periods decreases the likelihood that increased debug command processing overhead will affect system use.

This appendix contains the following sections:

- **L2F Solution Debug Output**—This is debug output from the three implementation phases of the network described in Chapter 2, "Access VPDN Dial-In Using L2F Solution."

- **L2TP Solution Debug Output**—This is debug output from the network described in Chapter 3, "Access VPDN Dial-In Using L2TP Solution."

- **IPSec over L2TP Solution Debug Output**—This is debug output from the network described in Chapter 4, "Access VPDN Dial-In Using IPSec over L2TP Solution."

- **L2TP Dial-Out Debug Output**—This is debug output from the network described in Appendix A, "New Access VPDN Services: L2TP Dial-Out."

For information on the topologies and configurations that produced this debug output, see the appropriate chapter or appendix. This appendix breaks up the debug output to include explanations of important lines of output. These important lines are shaded for emphasis.

NOTE   If you are accessing the devices through a Telnet connection, you need to enable the **terminal monitor** user EXEC command. This command ensures that your EXEC session is receiving the logging and debug output from the devices.

L2F Solution Debug Output

This section contains debug output from the three implementation phases of the L2F solution:

- Debug Output from Configuring Basic Dial Access for the NAS
- Debug Output from Configuring Access VPDN with Local AAA
- Debug Output from Configuring Access VPDN with Remote AAA

For more information on this solution, see Chapter 2, "Access VPDN Dial-In Using L2F Solution."

Debug Output from Configuring Basic Dial Access for the NAS

The following debug output is produced when a client dials in to the NAS via the Public Switched Telephone Network (PSTN) and is authenticated locally on the NAS. Enable the following **debug** commands on the NAS:

```
debug isdn q931
debug ppp negotiation
debug ppp authentication
debug modem csm
debug ip peer
```

From the client, dial the PRI telephone number assigned to the NAS T1 trunks. In this example, the username is jeremy; the password is subaru. The user is locally authenticated by the NAS.

As the NAS receives the modem call from the client, the following **debug** command output appears on the NAS terminal screen:

```
ISP_NAS#
```

A modem call comes in to the access server on TTY line 14. Interface async 4 comes up. After PPP launches, TTY line 14 becomes async interface 14. An incoming PPP frame is recognized. PPP is launched on TTY line 14.

```
*Jan  1 21:22:16.410: TTY14: destroy timer type 1
*Jan  1 21:22:16.410: TTY14: destroy timer type 0
*Jan  1 21:22:16.410: tty14: Modem: IDLE->READY
*Jan  1 21:22:18.410: %LINK-3-UPDOWN: Interface Async14, changed state to up
*Jan  1 21:22:18.410: As14 PPP: Treating connection as a dedicated line
*Jan  1 21:22:18.410: As14 PPP: Phase is ESTABLISHING, Active Open
*Jan  1 21:22:18.410: As14 LCP: O CONFREQ [Closed] id 1 len 25
*Jan  1 21:22:18.410: As14 LCP:    ACCM 0x000A0000 (0x0206000A0000)
*Jan  1 21:22:18.410: As14 LCP:    AuthProto CHAP (0x0305C22305)
*Jan  1 21:22:18.410: As14 LCP:    MagicNumber 0x151213B2 (0x0506151213B2)
*Jan  1 21:22:18.410: As14 LCP:    PFC (0x0702)
*Jan  1 21:22:18.410: As14 LCP:    ACFC (0x0802)
*Jan  1 21:22:18.542: As14 LCP: I CONFACK [REQsent] id 1 len 25
*Jan  1 21:22:18.542: As14 LCP:    ACCM 0x000A0000 (0x0206000A0000)
*Jan  1 21:22:18.542: As14 LCP:    AuthProto CHAP (0x0305C22305)
*Jan  1 21:22:18.542: As14 LCP:    MagicNumber 0x151213B2 (0x0506151213B2)
*Jan  1 21:22:18.542: As14 LCP:    PFC (0x0702)
*Jan  1 21:22:18.542: As14 LCP:    ACFC (0x0802)
```

Incoming config request (I CONFREQ). The remote test PC requests a set of options to be negotiated. The PC asks the NAS to support the callback option.

```
*Jan  1 21:22:19.262: As14 LCP: I CONFREQ [ACKrcvd] id 2 len 23
*Jan  1 21:22:19.262: As14 LCP:    ACCM 0x000A0000 (0x0206000A0000)
*Jan  1 21:22:19.262: As14 LCP:    MagicNumber 0x001A9072 (0x0506001A9072)
*Jan  1 21:22:19.262: As14 LCP:    PFC (0x0702)
*Jan  1 21:22:19.262: As14 LCP:    ACFC (0x0802)
*Jan  1 21:22:19.262: As14 LCP:    Callback 6  (0x0D0306)
```

Outgoing config reject (O CONFREJ). The NAS rejects the callback option. The access server is not configured to support Microsoft Callback in this solution.

```
*Jan  1 21:22:19.262: As14 LCP: O CONFREJ [ACKrcvd] id 2 len 7
*Jan  1 21:22:19.262: As14 LCP:    Callback 6  (0x0D0306)
```

Incoming config request (I CONFREQ). The test PC resends the request for options, but without the last line requesting callback.

```
*Jan  1 21:22:19.374: As14 LCP: I CONFREQ [ACKrcvd] id 3 len 20
*Jan  1 21:22:19.374: As14 LCP:    ACCM 0x000A0000 (0x0206000A0000)
*Jan  1 21:22:19.374: As14 LCP:    MagicNumber 0x001A9072 (0x0506001A9072)
*Jan  1 21:22:19.374: As14 LCP:    PFC (0x0702)
*Jan  1 21:22:19.374: As14 LCP:    ACFC (0x0802)
```

Outgoing config acknowledgment (O CONFACK). The NAS accepts the new set of options.

```
*Jan  1 21:22:19.374: As14 LCP: O CONFACK [ACKrcvd] id 3 len 20
*Jan  1 21:22:19.374: As14 LCP:    ACCM 0x000A0000 (0x0206000A0000)
*Jan  1 21:22:19.374: As14 LCP:    MagicNumber 0x001A9072 (0x0506001A9072)
*Jan  1 21:22:19.374: As14 LCP:    PFC (0x0702)
*Jan  1 21:22:19.374: As14 LCP:    ACFC (0x0802)
```

LCP is now open (LCP: State is Open). Both sides have acknowledged (CONFACK) the other side's configuration request (CONFREQ).

```
*Jan  1 21:22:19.374: As14 LCP: State is Open
```

After LCP negotiates, authentication starts. Authentication must take place before any network protocols, such as IP, are delivered. Both sides authenticate with the method negotiated during LCP. The NAS authenticates the client using CHAP. The client does not authenticate the access server.

```
*Jan  1 21:22:19.374: As14 PPP: Phase is AUTHENTICATING, by this end
```

Outgoing challenge sent from ISP_NAS.

```
*Jan  1 21:22:19.374: As14 CHAP: O CHALLENGE id 1 len 28 from "ISP_NAS"
```

Incoming CHAP response from the test PC, which shows the username jeremy.

```
*Jan  1 21:22:19.518: As14 CHAP: I RESPONSE id 1 len 27 from "jeremy"
```

An outgoing success message is sent from the NAS—authentication is successful.

```
*Jan  1 21:22:19.518: As14 CHAP: O SUCCESS id 1 len 4
```

PPP is up. The NAS PPP link is now open and available to negotiate any network protocols supported by both peers.

```
*Jan  1 21:22:19.518: As14 PPP: Phase is UP
*Jan  1 21:22:19.518: As14 IPCP: O CONFREQ [Closed] id 1 len 10
*Jan  1 21:22:19.518: As14 IPCP:    Address 172.22.66.23 (0x0306AC164217)
*Jan  1 21:22:19.630: As14 IPCP: I CONFREQ [REQsent] id 1 len 40
*Jan  1 21:22:19.630: As14 IPCP:    CompressType VJ 15 slots CompressSlotID
  (0x0206002D0F01)
*Jan  1 21:22:19.630: As14 IPCP:    Address 0.0.0.0 (0x030600000000)
*Jan  1 21:22:19.630: As14 IPCP:    PrimaryDNS 0.0.0.0 (0x810600000000)
*Jan  1 21:22:19.630: As14 IPCP:    PrimaryWINS 0.0.0.0 (0x820600000000)
*Jan  1 21:22:19.630: As14 IPCP:    SecondaryDNS 0.0.0.0 (0x830600000000)
```

```
*Jan  1 21:22:19.630: As14 IPCP:    SecondaryWINS 0.0.0.0 (0x840600000000)
*Jan  1 21:22:19.630: As14 IPCP: Using pool 'dialin_pool'
*Jan  1 21:22:19.630: ip_get_pool: As14: using pool dialin_pool
*Jan  1 21:22:19.630: ip_get_pool: As14: returning address = 172.22.66.55
*Jan  1 21:22:19.630: As14 IPCP: Pool returned 172.22.66.55
*Jan  1 21:22:19.630: As14 IPCP: O CONFREJ [REQsent] id 1 len 22
*Jan  1 21:22:19.630: As14 IPCP:    CompressType VJ 15 slots CompressSlotID
  (0x0206002D0F01)
*Jan  1 21:22:19.630: As14 IPCP:    PrimaryWINS 0.0.0.0 (0x820600000000)
*Jan  1 21:22:19.630: As14 IPCP:    SecondaryWINS 0.0.0.0 (0x840600000000)
```

The client requests support for Microsoft Point-to-Point Compression (MPPC). The NAS rejects this request. The access server's integrated modems already support hardware compression, and the Cisco IOS is not configured to support software compression.

```
*Jan  1 21:22:19.646: As14 CCP: I CONFREQ [Not negotiated] id 1 len 15
*Jan  1 21:22:19.646: As14 CCP:    MS-PPC supported bits 0x00000001
  (0x120600000001)
*Jan  1 21:22:19.646: As14 CCP:    Stacker history 1 check mode EXTENDED
  (0x1105000104)
*Jan  1 21:22:19.646: As14 LCP: O PROTREJ [Open] id 2 len 21 protocol CCP
*Jan  1 21:22:19.646: As14 LCP:    (0x80FD0101000F1206000000111050001)
*Jan  1 21:22:19.646: As14 LCP:    (0x04)
*Jan  1 21:22:19.646: As14 IPCP: I CONFACK [REQsent] id 1 len 10
*Jan  1 21:22:19.646: As14 IPCP:    Address 172.22.66.23 (0x0306AC164217)
*Jan  1 21:22:20.518: %LINEPROTO-5-UPDOWN: Line protocol on Interface
  Async14, changed state to up
*Jan  1 21:22:21.518: As14 IPCP: TIMEout: State ACKrcvd
*Jan  1 21:22:21.518: As14 IPCP: O CONFREQ [ACKrcvd] id 2 len 10
*Jan  1 21:22:21.518: As14 IPCP:    Address 172.22.66.23 (0x0306AC164217)
*Jan  1 21:22:21.626: As14 IPCP: I CONFACK [REQsent] id 2 len 10
*Jan  1 21:22:21.626: As14 IPCP:    Address 172.22.66.23 (0x0306AC164217)
```

The primary and secondary DNS addresses are negotiated. At first, the client asks for 0.0.0.0. addresses. The access server sends out a CONFNAK and supplies the correct values, which include an IP address from the pool, the primary DNS address, and the backup DNS address.

```
*Jan  1 21:22:22.634: As14 IPCP: I CONFREQ [ACKrcvd] id 2 len 34
*Jan  1 21:22:22.634: As14 IPCP:    Address 0.0.0.0 (0x030600000000)
*Jan  1 21:22:22.634: As14 IPCP:    PrimaryDNS 0.0.0.0 (0x810600000000)
*Jan  1 21:22:22.634: As14 IPCP:    PrimaryWINS 0.0.0.0 (0x820600000000)
*Jan  1 21:22:22.634: As14 IPCP:    SecondaryDNS 0.0.0.0 (0x830600000000)
*Jan  1 21:22:22.634: As14 IPCP:    SecondaryWINS 0.0.0.0 (0x840600000000)
*Jan  1 21:22:22.634: As14 IPCP: O CONFREJ [ACKrcvd] id 2 len 16
*Jan  1 21:22:22.634: As14 IPCP:    PrimaryWINS 0.0.0.0 (0x820600000000)
*Jan  1 21:22:22.634: As14 IPCP:    SecondaryWINS 0.0.0.0 (0x840600000000)
*Jan  1 21:22:22.742: As14 IPCP: I CONFREQ [ACKrcvd] id 3 len 22
```

```
*Jan  1 21:22:22.746: As14 IPCP:    Address 0.0.0.0 (0x030600000000)
*Jan  1 21:22:22.746: As14 IPCP:    PrimaryDNS 0.0.0.0 (0x810600000000)
*Jan  1 21:22:22.746: As14 IPCP:    SecondaryDNS 0.0.0.0 (0x830600000000)
*Jan  1 21:22:22.746: As14 IPCP: O CONFNAK [ACKrcvd] id 3 len 22
*Jan  1 21:22:22.746: As14 IPCP:    Address 172.22.66.55 (0x0306AC164237)
*Jan  1 21:22:22.746: As14 IPCP:    PrimaryDNS 171.68.10.70 (0x8106AB440A46)
*Jan  1 21:22:22.746: As14 IPCP:    SecondaryDNS 171.68.10.140
  (0x8306AB440A8C)
```

The client sends an incoming request saying that the new values are accepted. Whenever the access server sends out a CONFNAK that includes values, the client still has to accept the new values.

```
*Jan  1 21:22:22.854: As14 IPCP: I CONFREQ [ACKrcvd] id 4 len 22
*Jan  1 21:22:22.854: As14 IPCP:    Address 172.22.66.55 (0x0306AC164237)
```

An outgoing CONFACK is sent for IPCP.

```
*Jan  1 21:22:22.858: As14 IPCP:    PrimaryDNS 171.68.10.70 (0x8106AB440A46)
*Jan  1 21:22:22.858: As14 IPCP:    SecondaryDNS 171.68.10.140
  (0x8306AB440A8C)
*Jan  1 21:22:22.858: ip_get_pool: As14: validate address = 172.22.66.55
*Jan  1 21:22:22.858: ip_get_pool: As14: using pool dialin_pool
*Jan  1 21:22:22.858: ip_get_pool: As14: returning address = 172.22.66.55
*Jan  1 21:22:22.858: set_ip_peer_addr: As14: address = 172.22.66.55 (3) is
  redundant
*Jan  1 21:22:22.858: As14 IPCP: O CONFACK [ACKrcvd] id 4 len 22
*Jan  1 21:22:22.858: As14 IPCP:    Address 172.22.66.55 (0x0306AC164237)
*Jan  1 21:22:22.858: As14 IPCP:    PrimaryDNS 171.68.10.70 (0x8106AB440A46)
*Jan  1 21:22:22.858: As14 IPCP:    SecondaryDNS 171.68.10.140
  (0x8306AB440A8C)
```

The state is open for IPCP. A route is negotiated and installed for the IPCP peer, which is assigned IP address 172.22.66.55.

```
*Jan  1 21:22:22.858: As14 IPCP: State is Open
*Jan  1 21:22:22.858: As14 IPCP: Install route to 172.22.66.55
ISP_NAS#
```

Debug Output from Configuring Access VPDN with Local AAA

The following debug output is produced by an access VPDN that is using local AAA. The client dials in to the NAS, is forwarded to the home gateway using L2F, and the tunnel and username are authenticated using local AAA. Enable the following **debug** commands on the NAS:

```
debug isdn q931
debug modem csm
```

```
debug ppp authentication
debug ppp negotiation
debug vpdn event
debug vpdn l2x-events
```

Enable the following debug commands on the home gateway:

```
debug vpdn events
debug vpdn l2x-events
debug ppp negotiation
debug ppp authentication
debug vtemplate
debug ip peer
```

Local AAA Debug Output on the NAS

Send an asynchronous PPP modem call in to the access server. The following is debug output from successful L2F negotiation using local AAA on the NAS, ISP_NAS:

```
ISP_NAS#
```

The inbound call is received from the PRI TDM stream. The ISDN bearer capability reports that the call is an analog call (0x8090A2).

```
*Jan  2 01:04:48.817: ISDN Se0:23: RX <-  SETUP pd = 8  callref = 0x0266
*Jan  2 01:04:48.817:           Bearer Capability i = 0x8090A2
*Jan  2 01:04:48.817:           Channel ID i = 0xA98381
*Jan  2 01:04:48.821:           Progress Ind i = 0x8283 - Origination address
  is non-ISDN
*Jan  2 01:04:48.821:         Calling Party Number i = '!', 0x83, '4089548042'
*Jan  2 01:04:48.821:           Called Party Number i = 0xC1, '5550945'
*Jan  2 01:04:48.821: ISDN Se0:23: TX ->  CALL_PROC pd = 8  callref = 0x8266
*Jan  2 01:04:48.821:           Channel ID i = 0xA98381
*Jan  2 01:04:48.821: ISDN Se0:23: TX ->  ALERTING pd = 8  callref = 0x8266
*Jan  2 01:04:48.821: EVENT_FROM_ISDN::dchan_idb=0x60E9DD98, call_id=0x2E,
  ces=0x1
    bchan=0x0, event=0x1, cause=0x0

*Jan  2 01:04:48.821: VDEV_ALLOCATE: slot 1 and port 21 is allocated.

*Jan  2 01:04:48.821: EVENT_FROM_ISDN:(002E): DEV_INCALL at slot 1 and port
  21

*Jan  2 01:04:48.825: CSM_PROC_IDLE: CSM_EVENT_ISDN_CALL at slot 1, port 21
```

The access server routes the call to the onboard MICA modem at 1/21 and begins negotiation with the remote site.

```
*Jan  2 01:04:48.825: Mica Modem(1/21): Configure(0x1 = 0x0)
*Jan  2 01:04:48.825: Mica Modem(1/21): Configure(0x23 = 0x0)
*Jan  2 01:04:48.825: Mica Modem(1/21): Call Setup
*Jan  2 01:04:48.913: Mica Modem(1/21): State Transition to Call Setup
```

```
*Jan  2 01:04:48.913: Mica Modem(1/21): Went offhook
*Jan  2 01:04:48.913: CSM_PROC_IC1_RING: CSM_EVENT_MODEM_OFFHOOK at slot 1,
  port 21
*Jan  2 01:04:48.913: ISDN Se0:23: TX ->  CONNECT pd = 8  callref = 0x8266
*Jan  2 01:04:48.945: ISDN Se0:23: RX <-  CONNECT_ACK pd = 8  callref = 0x0266
*Jan  2 01:04:48.945: EVENT_FROM_ISDN::dchan_idb=0x60E9DD98, call_id=0x2E,
  ces=0
x1 bchan=0x0, event=0x4, cause=0x0

*Jan  2 01:04:48.949: EVENT_FROM_ISDN:(002E): DEV_CONNECTED at slot 1 and
  port 21

*Jan  2 01:04:48.949: CSM_PROC_IC4_WAIT_FOR_CARRIER:
  CSM_EVENT_ISDN_CONNECTED at slot 1, port 21
```

Both sides successfully negotiate, and asynchronous interface 22 comes up. At
this point, the NAS still does not know that the call is an access VPDN call.

```
*Jan  2 01:04:48.949: Mica Modem(1/21): Link Initiate
*Jan  2 01:04:50.049: Mica Modem(1/21): State Transition to Connect
*Jan  2 01:04:55.201: Mica Modem(1/21): State Transition to Link
*Jan  2 01:05:12.753: Mica Modem(1/21): State Transition to Trainup
*Jan  2 01:05:14.489: Mica Modem(1/21): State Transition to EC Negotiating
*Jan  2 01:05:15.149: Mica Modem(1/21): State Transition to Steady State
*Jan  2 01:05:17.969: %LINK-3-UPDOWN: Interface Async22, changed state to up
```

The first phase of PPP negotiation begins, which is link control protocol (LCP)
negotiation. In this phase, the remote peers negotiate what type of authentication
to use. The NAS demands that the client authenticate with CHAP.

```
*Jan  2 01:05:17.969: As22 PPP: Treating connection as a dedicated line
*Jan  2 01:05:17.969: As22 PPP: Phase is ESTABLISHING, Active Open
*Jan  2 01:05:17.969: As22 LCP: O CONFREQ [Closed] id 1 len 39
*Jan  2 01:05:17.969: As22 LCP:    ACCM 0x000A0000 (0x0206000A0000)
*Jan  2 01:05:17.969: As22 LCP:    AuthProto CHAP (0x0305C22305)
*Jan  2 01:05:17.969: As22 LCP:    MagicNumber 0x15DE3BBE (0x050615DE3BBE)
*Jan  2 01:05:17.969: As22 LCP:    PFC (0x0702)
*Jan  2 01:05:17.969: As22 LCP:    ACFC (0x0802)
*Jan  2 01:05:17.969: As22 LCP:    MRRU 1524 (0x110405F4)
*Jan  2 01:05:17.969: As22 LCP:    EndpointDisc 1 Local
  (0x130A014953505F4E4153)
*Jan  2 01:05:18.101: As22 LCP: I CONFREJ [REQsent] id 1 len 18
*Jan  2 01:05:18.101: As22 LCP:    MRRU 1524 (0x110405F4)
*Jan  2 01:05:18.101: As22 LCP:    EndpointDisc 1 Local
  (0x130A014953505F4E4153)
*Jan  2 01:05:18.105: As22 LCP: O CONFREQ [REQsent] id 2 len 25
*Jan  2 01:05:18.105: As22 LCP:    ACCM 0x000A0000 (0x0206000A0000)
*Jan  2 01:05:18.105: As22 LCP:    AuthProto CHAP (0x0305C22305)
```

```
*Jan  2 01:05:18.105: As22 LCP:    MagicNumber 0x15DE3BBE (0x050615DE3BBE)
*Jan  2 01:05:18.105: As22 LCP:    PFC (0x0702)
*Jan  2 01:05:18.105: As22 LCP:    ACFC (0x0802)
```

The client asks the NAS to support call back. The NAS denies the request. The client now resends the same request without the rejected option.

```
*Jan  2 01:05:18.213: As22 LCP: I CONFREQ [REQsent] id 2 len 23
*Jan  2 01:05:18.213: As22 LCP:    ACCM 0x000A0000 (0x0206000A0000)
*Jan  2 01:05:18.213: As22 LCP:    MagicNumber 0x00E6BDE9 (0x050600E6BDE9)
*Jan  2 01:05:18.213: As22 LCP:    PFC (0x0702)
*Jan  2 01:05:18.213: As22 LCP:    ACFC (0x0802)
*Jan  2 01:05:18.217: As22 LCP:    Callback 6  (0x0D0306)
*Jan  2 01:05:18.217: As22 LCP: O CONFREJ [REQsent] id 2 len 7
*Jan  2 01:05:18.217: As22 LCP:    Callback 6  (0x0D0306)
*Jan  2 01:05:18.229: As22 LCP: I CONFACK [REQsent] id 2 len 25
*Jan  2 01:05:18.229: As22 LCP:    ACCM 0x000A0000 (0x0206000A0000)
*Jan  2 01:05:18.229: As22 LCP:    AuthProto CHAP (0x0305C22305)
*Jan  2 01:05:18.229: As22 LCP:    MagicNumber 0x15DE3BBE (0x050615DE3BBE)
*Jan  2 01:05:18.233: As22 LCP:    PFC (0x0702)
*Jan  2 01:05:18.233: As22 LCP:    ACFC (0x0802)
*Jan  2 01:05:18.325: As22 LCP: I CONFREQ [ACKrcvd] id 3 len 20
*Jan  2 01:05:18.325: As22 LCP:    ACCM 0x000A0000 (0x0206000A0000)
*Jan  2 01:05:18.325: As22 LCP:    MagicNumber 0x00E6BDE9 (0x050600E6BDE9)
*Jan  2 01:05:18.325: As22 LCP:    PFC (0x0702)
*Jan  2 01:05:18.325: As22 LCP:    ACFC (0x0802)
*Jan  2 01:05:18.325: As22 LCP: O CONFACK [ACKrcvd] id 3 len 20
*Jan  2 01:05:18.325: As22 LCP:    ACCM 0x000A0000 (0x0206000A0000)
*Jan  2 01:05:18.329: As22 LCP:    MagicNumber 0x00E6BDE9 (0x050600E6BDE9)
*Jan  2 01:05:18.329: As22 LCP:    PFC (0x0702)
*Jan  2 01:05:18.329: As22 LCP:    ACFC (0x0802)
```

The NAS sends the authentication CHAP challenge to the client.

```
*Jan  2 01:05:18.329: As22 LCP: State is Open
*Jan  2 01:05:18.329: As22 PPP: Phase is AUTHENTICATING, by this end
*Jan  2 01:05:18.329: As22 CHAP: O CHALLENGE id 1 len 28 from "ISP_NAS"
```

The client responds with "jeremy@hgw.com." The NAS saves the client's response and later forwards it to the home gateway.

```
*Jan  2 01:05:18.469: As22 CHAP: I RESPONSE id 1 len 35 from "jeremy@hgw.com"
```

The NAS found a DNIS string. VPDN authorization is about to begin.

```
*Jan  2 01:05:18.469: VPDN: Got DNIS string 5550945
*Jan  2 01:05:18.469: As22 VPDN: Looking for tunnel -- hgw.com --
```

Tunnel information is found for the domain name hgw.com, tunnel name ISP_NAS, and the tunnel IP endpoint 172.22.66.25.

```
*Jan   2 01:05:18.473:  L2F: Tunnel state closed
*Jan   2 01:05:18.473: As22 VPDN: Get tunnel info for hgw.com with NAS
  ISP_NAS, I
P 172.22.66.25
*Jan   2 01:05:18.473: As22 VPDN: Forward to address 172.22.66.25
*Jan   2 01:05:18.473: As22 VPDN: Forwarding...
*Jan   2 01:05:18.473: As22 VPDN: Bind interface direction=1
*Jan   2 01:05:18.473:  L2F: MID  state closed
```

A UDP socket interface is opened to the home gateway's IP address. Because L2F is a UDP packet, a socket interface needs to be created.

```
*Jan   2 01:05:18.473: L2F: Open UDP socket to 172.22.66.25
*Jan   2 01:05:18.473:  L2F: Tunnel state opening
```

The L2F protocol begins. A bidirectional authentication takes place between the NAS and the home gateway. Because no tunnel currently exists for jeremy@hgw.com, the message "waiting_for_tunnel" appears. After the tunnel is established, the message "jeremy@hgw.com is forwarded" appears.

```
*Jan   2 01:05:18.473: As22 L2F: MID jeremy@hgw.com state waiting_for_tunnel
*Jan   2 01:05:18.473: As22 VPDN: jeremy@hgw.com is forwarded
```

The tunnel is authenticated and established between the NAS and home gateway. CHAP is the default tunnel authentication method.

```
*Jan   2 01:05:18.477: L2F: L2F_CONF received
*Jan   2 01:05:18.477: L2F: Removing resend packet (L2F_CONF)
*Jan   2 01:05:18.477: ISP_NAS L2F: Tunnel state open
*Jan   2 01:05:18.481: L2F: L2F_OPEN received
*Jan   2 01:05:18.481: L2F: Removing resend packet (L2F_OPEN)
*Jan   2 01:05:18.481: L2F: Building nas2gw_mid0
```

Cisco proprietary L2F client information is forwarded to the home gateway. This information is used by the home gateway for accounting purposes. L2F uses standard AV pairs to forward this information.

```
*Jan   2 01:05:18.481: L2F: L2F_CLIENT_INFO: CLID/DNIS 4089548042/5550945
*Jan   2 01:05:18.481: L2F: L2F_CLIENT_INFO: NAS-Port Async22
*Jan   2 01:05:18.481: L2F: L2F_CLIENT_INFO: Client-Bandwidth-Kbps 115
*Jan   2 01:05:18.481: L2F: L2F_CLIENT_INFO: NAS-Rate L2F/0/0
*Jan   2 01:05:18.481: As22 L2F: MID jeremy@hgw.com state opening
*Jan   2 01:05:18.481: VPDN: Chap authentication succeeded for ISP_NAS
*Jan   2 01:05:18.569: L2F: L2F_OPEN received
```

```
*Jan  2 01:05:18.569: L2F: Got a MID management packet
*Jan  2 01:05:18.569: L2F: Removing resend packet (L2F_OPEN)
*Jan  2 01:05:18.569: As22 L2F: MID jeremy@hgw.com state open
*Jan  2 01:05:18.569: As22 L2F: MID synced NAS/HG Clid=8/8 Mid=1
```

The PPP session is forwarded to the home gateway. Notice that IPCP negotiation does not occur on the NAS, but occurs on the home gateway. See the home gateway's debug output.

```
*Jan  2 01:05:18.569: As22 PPP: Phase is FORWARDED
```

The asynchronous line protocol is up, which enables network layer communication.

```
*Jan  2 01:05:19.473: %LINEPROTO-5-UPDOWN: Line protocol on Interface
   Async22, changed state to up
```

Local AAA Debug Output on the Home Gateway

The following is debug output from successful L2F negotiation using local AAA on the home gateway, ENT_HGW:

```
ENT_HGW#
```

The home gateway receives the request from the NAS to open an L2F tunnel. The home gateway authenticates the tunnel and opens it.

```
*Feb  4 14:14:40.413: L2F: L2F_CONF received
*Feb  4 14:14:40.413: L2F: Creating new tunnel for ISP_NAS
*Feb  4 14:14:40.413:  L2F: Tunnel state closed
*Feb  4 14:14:40.413: L2F: Got a tunnel named ISP_NAS, responding
*Feb  4 14:14:40.417: L2F: Open UDP socket to 172.22.66.23
*Feb  4 14:14:40.417: ISP_NAS L2F: Tunnel state opening
*Feb  4 14:14:40.417: L2F: L2F_OPEN received
*Feb  4 14:14:40.417: L2F: Removing resend packet (L2F_CONF)
*Feb  4 14:14:40.417: VPDN: Chap authentication succeeded for ISP_NAS
*Feb  4 14:14:40.417: ISP_NAS L2F: Tunnel state open
```

The home gateway receives the client information forwarded from the NAS.

```
*Feb  4 14:14:40.421: L2F: L2F_OPEN received
*Feb  4 14:14:40.421: L2F: L2F_CLIENT_INFO: CLID/DNIS 4089548042/5550945
*Feb  4 14:14:40.421: L2F: L2F_CLIENT_INFO: NAS-Port Async21
*Feb  4 14:14:40.421: L2F: L2F_CLIENT_INFO: Client-Bandwidth-Kbps 115
*Feb  4 14:14:40.421: L2F: L2F_CLIENT_INFO: NAS-Rate L2F/0/0
*Feb  4 14:14:40.421: L2F: Got a MID management packet
*Feb  4 14:14:40.421:  L2F: MID  state closed
*Feb  4 14:14:40.421: L2F: Start create mid intf process for jeremy@hgw.com
```

A virtual access interface is cloned from virtual template 1, which is not a physical interface, but it is treated like a regular interface that uses the IP address of the Fast Ethernet 0/0 interface.

The debug output following "interface Virtual-Access1" lists every command that has been configured for virtual template 1. Enter the **clear vtemplate** privileged EXEC command to reset the command history.

```
*Feb  4 14:14:40.421: Vi1 VTEMPLATE: Reuse Vi1, recycle queue size 0
*Feb  4 14:14:40.421: Vi1 VTEMPLATE: Hardware address 0050.d193.e000
*Feb  4 14:14:40.421: Vi1 VPDN: Virtual interface created for jeremy@hgw.com
*Feb  4 14:14:40.421: Vi1 VPDN: Set to Async interface
*Feb  4 14:14:40.425: Vi1 PPP: Phase is DOWN, Setup
*Feb  4 14:14:40.425: Vi1 VPDN: Clone from Vtemplate 1 filterPPP=0 blocking
*Feb  4 14:14:40.425: Vi1 VTEMPLATE: Has a new cloneblk vtemplate, now it
  has vtemplate
*Feb  4 14:14:40.425: Vi1 VTEMPLATE: ************* CLONE VACCESS1
  **************
***
*Feb  4 14:14:40.425: Vi1 VTEMPLATE: Clone from Virtual-Template1
interface Virtual-Access1
default ip address
no ip address
encap ppp
ip unnumbered fastethernet 0/0
no ip directed-broadcast
ip unnumbered fastethernet 0/0
no ip directed-broadcast
ppp authentication chap
peer default ip address pool default
encapsulation ppp
ppp multilink
end

1d02h: %LINK-3-UPDOWN: Interface Virtual-Access1, changed state to up
*Feb  4 14:14:40.505: Vi1 PPP: Treating connection as a dedicated line
*Feb  4 14:14:40.505: Vi1 PPP: Phase is ESTABLISHING, Active Open
*Feb  4 14:14:40.505: Vi1 LCP: O CONFREQ [Closed] id 1 len 39
*Feb  4 14:14:40.505: Vi1 LCP:    ACCM 0x000A0000 (0x0206000A0000)
*Feb  4 14:14:40.505: Vi1 LCP:    AuthProto CHAP (0x0305C22305)
*Feb  4 14:14:40.505: Vi1 LCP:    MagicNumber 0x566F3EA8 (0x0506566F3EA8)
*Feb  4 14:14:40.505: Vi1 LCP:    PFC (0x0702)
*Feb  4 14:14:40.505: Vi1 LCP:    ACFC (0x0802)
*Feb  4 14:14:40.505: Vi1 LCP:    MRRU 1524 (0x110405F4)
*Feb  4 14:14:40.505: Vi1 LCP:    EndpointDisc 1 Local
  (0x130A01454E545F484757)
*Feb  4 14:14:40.505: Vi1 VPDN: Bind interface direction=2
*Feb  4 14:14:40.505: Vi1 PPP: Treating connection as a dedicated line
```

The NAS forces the information from the LCP negotiation with the client onto the virtual-access interface.

```
*Feb  4 14:14:40.505: Vi1 LCP: I FORCED CONFREQ len 21
*Feb  4 14:14:40.505: Vi1 LCP:    ACCM 0x000A0000 (0x0206000A0000)
*Feb  4 14:14:40.505: Vi1 LCP:    AuthProto CHAP (0x0305C22305)
*Feb  4 14:14:40.505: Vi1 LCP:    MagicNumber 0x15B7E4FD (0x050615B7E4FD)
*Feb  4 14:14:40.505: Vi1 LCP:    PFC (0x0702)
*Feb  4 14:14:40.505: Vi1 LCP:    ACFC (0x0802)
*Feb  4 14:14:40.505: Vi1 VPDN: PPP LCP accepted rcv CONFACK
*Feb  4 14:14:40.505: Vi1 VPDN: PPP LCP accepted sent CONFACK
*Feb  4 14:14:40.505: Vi1 PPP: Phase is AUTHENTICATING, by this end
```

The home gateway sends a CHAP challenge to the client. The client responds and is authenticated by the home gateway.

```
*Feb  4 14:14:40.505: Vi1 CHAP: O CHALLENGE id 2 len 28 from "ENT_HGW"
*Feb  4 14:14:40.505: Vi1 L2F: Transfer NAS-Rate L2F/0/0 to LCP
*Feb  4 14:14:40.509: Vi1 CHAP: I RESPONSE id 1 len 35 from "jeremy@hgw.com"
*Feb  4 14:14:40.509: Vi1 L2F: Finish create mid intf for jeremy@hgw.com
*Feb  4 14:14:40.509: Vi1 L2F: MID jeremy@hgw.com state open
*Feb  4 14:14:40.509: Vi1 CHAP: O SUCCESS id 1 len 4
*Feb  4 14:14:40.509: Vi1 PPP: Phase is UP
*Feb  4 14:14:40.509: Vi1 IPCP: O CONFREQ [Closed] id 1 len 10
*Feb  4 14:14:40.509: Vi1 IPCP:    Address 172.22.66.25 (0x0306AC164219)
*Feb  4 14:14:40.617: Vi1 IPCP: I CONFREQ [REQsent] id 1 len 40
*Feb  4 14:14:40.617: Vi1 IPCP:    CompressType VJ 15 slots CompressSlotID
    (0x0206002D0F01)
*Feb  4 14:14:40.617: Vi1 IPCP:    Address 0.0.0.0 (0x030600000000)
*Feb  4 14:14:40.617: Vi1 IPCP:    PrimaryDNS 0.0.0.0 (0x810600000000)
*Feb  4 14:14:40.617: Vi1 IPCP:    PrimaryWINS 0.0.0.0 (0x820600000000)
*Feb  4 14:14:40.621: Vi1 IPCP:    SecondaryDNS 0.0.0.0 (0x830600000000)
*Feb  4 14:14:40.621: Vi1 IPCP:    SecondaryWINS 0.0.0.0 (0x840600000000)
```

The home gateway assigns the client the IP address 172.30.2.1 from the default pool.

```
*Feb  4 14:14:40.621: Vi1 IPCP: Using pool 'default'
*Feb  4 14:14:40.621: ip_get_pool: Vi1: using pool default
*Feb  4 14:14:40.621: ip_get_pool: Vi1: returning address = 172.30.2.1
*Feb  4 14:14:40.621: Vi1 IPCP: Pool returned 172.30.2.1
*Feb  4 14:14:40.621: Vi1 IPCP: O CONFREJ [REQsent] id 1 len 10
*Feb  4 14:14:40.621: Vi1 IPCP:    CompressType VJ 15 slots CompressSlotID
    (0x0206002D0F01)
*Feb  4 14:14:40.633: Vi1 CCP: I CONFREQ [Not negotiated] id 1 len 15
*Feb  4 14:14:40.633: Vi1 CCP:    MS-PPC supported bits 0x00000001
    (0x120600000001)
```

```
*Feb  4 14:14:40.633: Vi1 CCP:    Stacker history 1 check mode EXTENDED
  (0x1105000104)
*Feb  4 14:14:40.633: Vi1 LCP: O PROTREJ [Open] id 2 len 21 protocol CCP
*Feb  4 14:14:40.633: Vi1 LCP:   (0x80FD0101000F12060000000111050001)
*Feb  4 14:14:40.633: Vi1 LCP:   (0x04)
*Feb  4 14:14:40.633: Vi1 IPCP: I CONFACK [REQsent] id 1 len 10
```

The line protocol on interface Virtual-Access1 is changed to the up state.

```
*Feb  4 14:14:40.637: Vi1 IPCP:    Address 172.22.66.25 (0x0306AC164219)
1d02h: %LINEPROTO-5-UPDOWN: Line protocol on Interface Virtual-Access1,
  changed state to up
*Feb  4 14:14:42.505: Vi1 LCP: TIMEout: State Open
*Feb  4 14:14:42.509: Vi1 IPCP: TIMEout: State ACKrcvd
*Feb  4 14:14:42.509: Vi1 IPCP: O CONFREQ [ACKrcvd] id 2 len 10
*Feb  4 14:14:42.509: Vi1 IPCP:    Address 172.22.66.25 (0x0306AC164219)
*Feb  4 14:14:42.613: Vi1 IPCP: I CONFACK [REQsent] id 2 len 10
*Feb  4 14:14:42.617: Vi1 IPCP:    Address 172.22.66.25 (0x0306AC164219)
```

The client requests IP addresses of DNS and WINS servers.

```
*Feb  4 14:14:43.621: Vi1 IPCP: I CONFREQ [ACKrcvd] id 2 len 34
*Feb  4 14:14:43.621: Vi1 IPCP:    Address 0.0.0.0 (0x030600000000)
*Feb  4 14:14:43.621: Vi1 IPCP:    PrimaryDNS 0.0.0.0 (0x810600000000)
*Feb  4 14:14:43.621: Vi1 IPCP:    PrimaryWINS 0.0.0.0 (0x820600000000)
*Feb  4 14:14:43.621: Vi1 IPCP:    SecondaryDNS 0.0.0.0 (0x830600000000)
*Feb  4 14:14:43.621: Vi1 IPCP:    SecondaryWINS 0.0.0.0 (0x840600000000)
*Feb  4 14:14:43.621: Vi1 IPCP: O CONFNAK [ACKrcvd] id 2 len 34
*Feb  4 14:14:43.621: Vi1 IPCP:    Address 172.30.2.1 (0x0306AC1E0201)
*Feb  4 14:14:43.621: Vi1 IPCP:    PrimaryDNS 172.23.1.10 (0x8106AC17010A)
*Feb  4 14:14:43.621: Vi1 IPCP:    PrimaryWINS 172.23.1.11 (0x8206AC17010B)
*Feb  4 14:14:43.621: Vi1 IPCP:    SecondaryDNS 172.23.2.10 (0x8306AC17020A)
*Feb  4 14:14:43.621: Vi1 IPCP:    SecondaryWINS 172.23.2.11
  (0x8406AC17020B)
*Feb  4 14:14:43.749: Vi1 IPCP: I CONFREQ [ACKrcvd] id 3 len 34
*Feb  4 14:14:43.749: Vi1 IPCP:    Address 172.30.2.1 (0x0306AC1E0201)
*Feb  4 14:14:43.749: Vi1 IPCP:    PrimaryDNS 172.23.1.10 (0x8106AC17010A)
*Feb  4 14:14:43.749: Vi1 IPCP:    PrimaryWINS 172.23.1.11 (0x8206AC17010B)
*Feb  4 14:14:43.749: Vi1 IPCP:    SecondaryDNS 172.23.2.10 (0x8306AC17020A)
*Feb  4 14:14:43.749: Vi1 IPCP:    SecondaryWINS 172.23.2.11
  (0x8406AC17020B)
*Feb  4 14:14:43.749: ip_get_pool: Vi1: validate address = 172.30.2.1
*Feb  4 14:14:43.749: ip_get_pool: Vi1: using pool default
*Feb  4 14:14:43.749: ip_get_pool: Vi1: returning address = 172.30.2.1
*Feb  4 14:14:43.749: set_ip_peer_addr: Vi1: address = 172.30.2.1 (3) is
  redundant
```

The home gateway receives a positive acknowledgment from the client confirming the IP addresses of the DNS and WNIS servers.

```
*Feb  4 14:14:43.749: Vi1 IPCP: O CONFACK [ACKrcvd] id 3 len 34
*Feb  4 14:14:43.749: Vi1 IPCP:    Address 172.30.2.1 (0x0306AC1E0201)
*Feb  4 14:14:43.749: Vi1 IPCP:    PrimaryDNS 172.23.1.10 (0x8106AC17010A)
*Feb  4 14:14:43.749: Vi1 IPCP:    PrimaryWINS 172.23.1.11 (0x8206AC17010B)
*Feb  4 14:14:43.753: Vi1 IPCP:    SecondaryDNS 172.23.2.10 (0x8306AC17020A)
*Feb  4 14:14:43.753: Vi1 IPCP:    SecondaryWINS 172.23.2.11
    (0x8406AC17020B)
```

The home gateway installs the route to the client's IP address, 172.30.2.1.

```
*Feb  4 14:14:43.753: Vi1 IPCP: State is Open
*Feb  4 14:14:43.753: Vi1 IPCP: Install route to 172.30.2.1
ENT_HGW#
```

Debug Output from Configuring Access VPDN with Remote AAA

The following debug output is produced by an access VPDN using remote AAA. The client dials in to the NAS and is forwarded to the home gateway using L2F. The NAS authenticates the tunnel using a Cisco Secure UNIX RADIUS server, and the home gateway authenticates the username using a Cisco Secure NT RADIUS server. Enable the following **debug** commands on the NAS:

```
debug isdn q931
debug modem csm
debug radius
debug aaa authentication
debug aaa authorization
debug ppp authentication
debug ppp negotiation
debug vpdn event
debug vpdn l2x-event
```

Enable the following **debug** commands on the home gateway:

```
debug radius
debug aaa authentication
debug aaa authorization
debug ppp negotiation
debug ppp authentication
debug vtemplate
debug ip peer
debug vpdn l2x-errors
debug vpdn l2x-events
debug vpdn events
```

Remote AAA Debug Output on the NAS

Launch an asynchronous PPP modem call in to the NAS. The following is debug output from successful L2F negotiation using remote AAA on the NAS, ISP_NAS:

```
ISP_NAS#
Jan  7 19:29:15.775: ISDN Se0:23: RX <-  SETUP pd = 8  callref = 0x0301
Jan  7 19:29:15.775:         Bearer Capability i = 0x9090A2
Jan  7 19:29:15.775:         Channel ID i = 0xA98381
Jan  7 19:29:15.775:         Calling Party Number i = 0x0083, '408'
Jan  7 19:29:15.775:         Called Party Number i = 0xC1, '5550945'
Jan  7 19:29:15.779: ISDN Se0:23: TX ->  CALL_PROC pd = 8  callref = 0x8301
Jan  7 19:29:15.779:         Channel ID i = 0xA98381
Jan  7 19:29:15.779: ISDN Se0:23: TX ->  ALERTING pd = 8  callref = 0x8301
Jan  7 19:29:15.779: EVENT_FROM_ISDN::dchan_idb=0x60E97CDC, call_id=0x53,
  ces=0x1 bchan=0x0, event=0x1, cause=0x0

Jan  7 19:29:15.779: VDEV_ALLOCATE: slot 1 and port 10 is allocated.

Jan  7 19:29:15.779: EVENT_FROM_ISDN:(0053): DEV_INCALL at slot 1 and port
  10

Jan  7 19:29:15.779: CSM_PROC_IDLE: CSM_EVENT_ISDN_CALL at slot 1, port 10
Jan  7 19:29:15.779: Mica Modem(1/10): Configure(0x1 = 0x0)
Jan  7 19:29:15.779: Mica Modem(1/10): Configure(0x23 = 0x0)
Jan  7 19:29:15.779: Mica Modem(1/10): Call Setup
Jan  7 19:29:15.923: Mica Modem(1/10): State Transition to Call Setup
Jan  7 19:29:15.923: Mica Modem(1/10): Went offhook
Jan  7 19:29:15.923: CSM_PROC_IC1_RING: CSM_EVENT_MODEM_OFFHOOK at slot 1,
  port 10
Jan  7 19:29:15.923: ISDN Se0:23: TX ->  CONNECT pd = 8  callref = 0x8301
Jan  7 19:29:15.939: ISDN Se0:23: RX <-  CONNECT_ACK pd = 8  callref = 0x0301
Jan  7 19:29:15.943: EVENT_FROM_ISDN::dchan_idb=0x60E97CDC, call_id=0x53,
  ces=0x1 bchan=0x0, event=0x4, cause=0x0

Jan  7 19:29:15.943: EVENT_FROM_ISDN:(0053): DEV_CONNECTED at slot 1 and
  port 10

Jan  7 19:29:15.943: CSM_PROC_IC4_WAIT_FOR_CARRIER: CSM_EVENT_ISDN_
  CONNECTED at slot 1, port 10
Jan  7 19:29:15.943: Mica Modem(1/10): Link Initiate
Jan  7 19:29:17.059: Mica Modem(1/10): State Transition to Connect
Jan  7 19:29:22.211: Mica Modem(1/10): State Transition to Link
Jan  7 19:29:33.715: Mica Modem(1/10): State Transition to Trainup
Jan  7 19:29:36.951: Mica Modem(1/10): State Transition to EC Negotiating
Jan  7 19:29:37.491: Mica Modem(1/10): State Transition to Steady State
Jan  7 19:29:40.339: %LINK-3-UPDOWN: Interface Async11, changed state to up
Jan  7 19:29:40.339: As11 PPP: Treating connection as a dedicated line
Jan  7 19:29:40.339: As11 PPP: Phase is ESTABLISHING, Active Open
Jan  7 19:29:40.339: As11 AAA/AUTHOR/FSM: (0): LCP succeeds trivially
Jan  7 19:29:40.339: As11 LCP: O CONFREQ [Closed] id 3 len 25
Jan  7 19:29:40.339: As11 LCP:    ACCM 0x000A0000 (0x0206000A0000)
Jan  7 19:29:40.339: As11 LCP:    AuthProto CHAP (0x0305C22305)
Jan  7 19:29:40.339: As11 LCP:    MagicNumber 0x33911E0F (0x050633911E0F)
Jan  7 19:29:40.339: As11 LCP:    PFC (0x0702)
Jan  7 19:29:40.339: As11 LCP:    ACFC (0x0802)
Jan  7 19:29:40.443: As11 LCP: I CONFACK [REQsent] id 3 len 25
Jan  7 19:29:40.443: As11 LCP:    ACCM 0x000A0000 (0x0206000A0000)
Jan  7 19:29:40.443: As11 LCP:    AuthProto CHAP (0x0305C22305)
Jan  7 19:29:40.443: As11 LCP:    MagicNumber 0x33911E0F (0x050633911E0F)
Jan  7 19:29:40.443: As11 LCP:    PFC (0x0702)
```

```
Jan  7 19:29:40.443: As11 LCP:    ACFC (0x0802)
Jan  7 19:29:40.859: As11 LCP: I CONFREQ [ACKrcvd] id 2 len 23
Jan  7 19:29:40.859: As11 LCP:    ACCM 0x000A0000 (0x0206000A0000)
Jan  7 19:29:40.859: As11 LCP:    MagicNumber 0x0002D813 (0x05060002D813)
Jan  7 19:29:40.859: As11 LCP:    PFC (0x0702)
Jan  7 19:29:40.859: As11 LCP:    ACFC (0x0802)
Jan  7 19:29:40.859: As11 LCP:    Callback 6  (0x0D0306)
Jan  7 19:29:40.859: As11 LCP: O CONFREJ [ACKrcvd] id 2 len 7
Jan  7 19:29:40.859: As11 LCP:    Callback 6  (0x0D0306)
Jan  7 19:29:42.339: As11 LCP: TIMEout: State ACKrcvd
Jan  7 19:29:42.339: As11 LCP: O CONFREQ [ACKrcvd] id 4 len 25
Jan  7 19:29:42.339: As11 LCP:    ACCM 0x000A0000 (0x0206000A0000)
Jan  7 19:29:42.339: As11 LCP:    AuthProto CHAP (0x0305C22305)
Jan  7 19:29:42.339: As11 LCP:    MagicNumber 0x33911E0F (0x050633911E0F)
Jan  7 19:29:42.339: As11 LCP:    PFC (0x0702)
Jan  7 19:29:42.339: As11 LCP:    ACFC (0x0802)
Jan  7 19:29:42.439: As11 LCP: I CONFACK [REQsent] id 4 len 25
Jan  7 19:29:42.439: As11 LCP:    ACCM 0x000A0000 (0x0206000A0000)
Jan  7 19:29:42.439: As11 LCP:    AuthProto CHAP (0x0305C22305)
Jan  7 19:29:42.439: As11 LCP:    MagicNumber 0x33911E0F (0x050633911E0F)
Jan  7 19:29:42.439: As11 LCP:    PFC (0x0702)
Jan  7 19:29:42.439: As11 LCP:    ACFC (0x0802)
Jan  7 19:29:43.859: As11 LCP: I CONFREQ [ACKrcvd] id 3 len 23
Jan  7 19:29:43.859: As11 LCP:    ACCM 0x000A0000 (0x0206000A0000)
Jan  7 19:29:43.859: As11 LCP:    MagicNumber 0x0002D813 (0x05060002D813)
Jan  7 19:29:43.863: As11 LCP:    PFC (0x0702)
Jan  7 19:29:43.863: As11 LCP:    ACFC (0x0802)
Jan  7 19:29:43.863: As11 LCP:    Callback 6  (0x0D0306)
Jan  7 19:29:43.863: As11 LCP: O CONFREJ [ACKrcvd] id 3 len 7
Jan  7 19:29:43.863: As11 LCP:    Callback 6  (0x0D0306)
Jan  7 19:29:44.003: As11 LCP: I CONFREQ [ACKrcvd] id 4 len 20
Jan  7 19:29:44.003: As11 LCP:    ACCM 0x000A0000 (0x0206000A0000)
Jan  7 19:29:44.003: As11 LCP:    MagicNumber 0x0002D813 (0x05060002D813)
Jan  7 19:29:44.003: As11 LCP:    PFC (0x0702)
Jan  7 19:29:44.003: As11 LCP:    ACFC (0x0802)
Jan  7 19:29:44.007: As11 LCP: O CONFACK [ACKrcvd] id 4 len 20
Jan  7 19:29:44.007: As11 LCP:    ACCM 0x000A0000 (0x0206000A0000)
Jan  7 19:29:44.007: As11 LCP:    MagicNumber 0x0002D813 (0x05060002D813)
Jan  7 19:29:44.007: As11 LCP:    PFC (0x0702)
Jan  7 19:29:44.007: As11 LCP:    ACFC (0x0802)
Jan  7 19:29:44.007: As11 LCP: State is Open
```

LCP negotiation is finished. The NAS sends a CHAP challenge to the client. The client sends a CHAP response with the username jeremy@hgw.com.

```
Jan  7 19:29:44.007: As11 PPP: Phase is AUTHENTICATING, by this end
Jan  7 19:29:44.007: As11 CHAP: O CHALLENGE id 2 len 28 from "ISP_NAS"
Jan  7 19:29:44.115: As11 CHAP: I RESPONSE id 2 len 35 from "jeremy@hgw.com"
Jan  7 19:29:44.115: As11 PPP: Phase is FORWARDING
Jan  7 19:29:44.115: sVPDN: Got DNIS string As11
```

The NAS is searching for tunnel information.

```
Jan  7 19:29:44.119: As11 VPDN: Looking for tunnel -- hgw.com --
```

AAA displays the call-path information. The current call uses TTY line 11, asynchronous interface 11, and serial B channel 0:0.

```
Jan  7 19:29:44.119: AAA: parse name=Async11 idb type=10 tty=11
Jan  7 19:29:44.119: AAA: name=Async11 flags=0x11 type=4 shelf=0 slot=0
  adapter=0 port=11 channel=0
Jan  7 19:29:44.119: AAA: parse name=Serial0:0 idb type=12 tty=-1
Jan  7 19:29:44.119: AAA: name=Serial0:0 flags=0x51 type=1 shelf=0 slot=0
  adapter=0 port=0 channel=0
Jan  7 19:29:44.119: AAA/AUTHEN: create_user (0x6118F250) user='hgw.com'
  ruser='
' port='Async11' rem_addr='' authen_type=NONE service=LOGIN priv=0
```

The local authorization module is accessed. The running configuration wants authorization for PPP and VPDN services, and a AAA list called default. The default authorization method is RADIUS.

```
Jan  7 19:29:44.119: AAA/AUTHOR/VPDN (338468652): Port='Async11'
  list='default' service=NET
Jan  7 19:29:44.119: AAA/AUTHOR/VPDN:  (338468652) send AV service=ppp
Jan  7 19:29:44.119: AAA/AUTHOR/VPDN:  (338468652) send AV protocol=vpdn
Jan  7 19:29:44.119: AAA/AUTHOR/VPDN (338468652) found list "default"
Jan  7 19:29:44.119: AAA/AUTHOR/VPDN:  (338468652) Method=RADIUS
Jan  7 19:29:44.119: RADIUS: authenticating to get author data
Jan  7 19:29:44.119: RADIUS: ustruct sharecount=2
```

The RADIUS module in the Cisco IOS software transmits authentication and authorization attributes to the remote RADIUS server. The server is located at IP address 172.22.66.18. RADIUS authentication on UNIX platforms listens to port 1645. All authentication packets go out this port. The NAS requests RADIUS attributes to be negotiated by the AAA server.

```
Jan  7 19:29:44.119: RADIUS: Initial Transmit Async11 id 52
  172.22.66.18:1645, Access-Request, len 71
Jan  7 19:29:44.119:         Attribute 4 6 AC164217
Jan  7 19:29:44.119:         Attribute 5 6 0000000B
Jan  7 19:29:44.119:         Attribute 61 6 00000000
Jan  7 19:29:44.119:         Attribute 1 9 6867772E
Jan  7 19:29:44.119:         Attribute 2 18 99DFD8F8
Jan  7 19:29:44.119:         Attribute 6 6 00000005
```

The remote RADIUS server performs its authentication and authorization for hgw.com. The NAS receives vendor specific AV pairs from the AAA server.

```
Jan  7 19:29:44.123: RADIUS: Received from id 52 172.22.66.18:1645, Access-
  Accept, len 153
Jan  7 19:29:44.123:         Attribute 26 31 0000000901197670
Jan  7 19:29:44.123:         Attribute 26 32 00000009011A7670
```

```
Jan  7 19:29:44.123:        Attribute 26 31 0000000901197670
Jan  7 19:29:44.123:        Attribute 26 39 0000000901217670
Jan  7 19:29:44.123: RADIUS: saved authorization data for user 6118F250 at
   61075 698
```

The RADIUS module transfers the attribute information to the local AAA subsystem. The post authorization status is equal to pass. The domain name hgw.com has been authenticated (see the free_user field).

```
Jan  7 19:29:44.127: RADIUS: cisco AVPair "vpdn:gw-password=cisco"
Jan  7 19:29:44.127: RADIUS: cisco AVPair "vpdn:nas-password=cisco"
Jan  7 19:29:44.127: RADIUS: cisco AVPair "vpdn:tunnel-id=ISP_NAS"
Jan  7 19:29:44.127: RADIUS: cisco AVPair "vpdn:ip-addresses=172.22.66.25"
Jan  7 19:29:44.127: AAA/AUTHOR (338468652): Post authorization status =
   PASS_ADD
Jan  7 19:29:44.127: AAA/AUTHOR/VPDN: Processing AV service=ppp
Jan  7 19:29:44.127: AAA/AUTHOR/VPDN: Processing AV protocol=vpdn
Jan  7 19:29:44.127: AAA/AUTHOR/VPDN: Processing AV gw-password=cisco
Jan  7 19:29:44.127: AAA/AUTHOR/VPDN: Processing AV nas-password=cisco
Jan  7 19:29:44.127: AAA/AUTHOR/VPDN: Processing AV tunnel-id=ISP_NAS
Jan  7 19:29:44.127: AAA/AUTHOR/VPDN: Processing AV ip-
   addresses=172.22.66.25
Jan  7 19:29:44.127: As11 VPDN: Get tunnel info for hgw.com with NAS ISP_NAS,
   IP 172.22.66.25
Jan  7 19:29:44.127: AAA/AUTHEN: free_user (0x6118F250) user='hgw.com'
   ruser=''
port='Async11' rem_addr='' authen_type=NONE service=LOGIN priv=0
Jan  7 19:29:44.127:  L2F: Tunnel state closed
Jan  7 19:29:44.127: As11 VPDN: Forward to address 172.22.66.25
Jan  7 19:29:44.127: As11 VPDN: Forwarding...
Jan  7 19:29:44.127: AAA: parse name=Async11 idb type=10 tty=11
Jan  7 19:29:44.127: AAA: name=Async11 flags=0x11 type=4 shelf=0 slot=0
   adapter=0 port=11 channel=0
Jan  7 19:29:44.127: AAA: parse name=Serial0:0 idb type=12 tty=-1
Jan  7 19:29:44.127: AAA: name=Serial0:0 flags=0x51 type=1 shelf=0 slot=0
   adapter=0 port=0 channel=0
```

The NAS attempts to forward the L2F tunnel to the home gateway at IP address 172.22.66.25. The home gateway authenticates the tunnel. A UDP socket is opened from the NAS to 172.22.66.25. The first IP connection is made between the NAS and the home gateway.

```
Jan  7 19:29:44.127: AAA/AUTHEN: create_user (0x612B7E1C)
   user='jeremy@hgw.com'
ruser='' port='Async11' rem_addr='408/5550945' authen_type=CHAP service=PPP
   priv=1
Jan  7 19:29:44.127: As11 VPDN: Bind interface direction=1
Jan  7 19:29:44.127:  L2F: MID  state closed
Jan  7 19:29:44.127:  L2F: Open UDP socket to 172.22.66.25
```

```
Jan  7 19:29:44.131:  L2F: Tunnel state opening
Jan  7 19:29:44.131: As11 L2F: MID jeremy@hgw.com state waiting_for_tunnel
Jan  7 19:29:44.131: As11 VPDN: jeremy@hgw.com is forwarded
Jan  7 19:29:44.135: L2F: L2F_CONF received
Jan  7 19:29:44.135: L2F: Removing resend packet (L2F_CONF)
Jan  7 19:29:44.135: ENT_HGW L2F: Tunnel state open
Jan  7 19:29:44.135: L2F: L2F_OPEN received
Jan  7 19:29:44.139: L2F: Removing resend packet (L2F_OPEN)
Jan  7 19:29:44.139: L2F: Building nas2gw_mid0
Jan  7 19:29:44.139: L2F: L2F_CLIENT_INFO: CLID/DNIS 408/5550945
Jan  7 19:29:44.139: L2F: L2F_CLIENT_INFO: NAS-Port Async11
Jan  7 19:29:44.139: L2F: L2F_CLIENT_INFO: Client-Bandwidth-Kbps 115
Jan  7 19:29:44.139: L2F: L2F_CLIENT_INFO: NAS-Rate L2F/28800/50000
Jan  7 19:29:44.139: As11 L2F: MID jeremy@hgw.com state opening
Jan  7 19:29:44.139: RADIUS: ustruct sharecount=3
```

An accounting packet is sent to the AAA RADIUS server at IP address
172.22.66.18. RADIUS accounting listens on port 1646 on UNIX platforms. All
accounting packets go out this port.

```
Jan  7 19:29:44.139: RADIUS: Initial Transmit Async11 id 53
  172.22.66.18:1646, Accounting-Request, len 108
Jan  7 19:29:44.139:          Attribute 4 6 AC164217
Jan  7 19:29:44.139:          Attribute 5 6 0000000B
Jan  7 19:29:44.139:          Attribute 61 6 00000000
Jan  7 19:29:44.139:          Attribute 1 16 6A657265
Jan  7 19:29:44.139:          Attribute 30 9 35373130
Jan  7 19:29:44.139:          Attribute 31 5 34303828
Jan  7 19:29:44.139:          Attribute 40 6 00000001
Jan  7 19:29:44.139:          Attribute 45 6 00000002
Jan  7 19:29:44.139:          Attribute 6 6 00000002
Jan  7 19:29:44.139:          Attribute 44 10 30303030
Jan  7 19:29:44.139:          Attribute 7 6 00000001
Jan  7 19:29:44.139:          Attribute 41 6 00000000
Jan  7 19:29:44.227: L2F: L2F_OPEN received
Jan  7 19:29:44.227: L2F: Got a MID management packet
Jan  7 19:29:44.227: L2F: Removing resend packet (L2F_OPEN)
Jan  7 19:29:44.227: As11 L2F: MID jeremy@hgw.com state open
Jan  7 19:29:44.227: As11 L2F: MID synced NAS/HG Clid=64/34 Mid=1
```

The line protocol on asynchronous interface 11 is up, which means the L2F tunnel
is established between the NAS and the home gateway.

```
Jan  7 19:29:44.227: As11 PPP: Phase is FORWARDED
Jan  7 19:29:44.795: RADIUS: Received from id 53 172.22.66.18:1646,
  Accounting-response, len 20
Jan  7 19:29:45.131: %LINEPROTO-5-UPDOWN: Line protocol on Interface
  Async11, changed state to up
```

Remote AAA Debug Output on the Home Gateway

The following is debug output from successful L2F negotiation using remote AAA on the home gateway, ENT_HGW:

```
ENT_HGW#
```

The home gateway receives a request from the NAS to open an L2F tunnel. The home gateway authenticates the tunnel and opens it.

```
Jan  7 19:29:44.132: L2F: L2F_CONF received
Jan  7 19:29:44.132: L2F: Creating new tunnel for ISP_NAS
Jan  7 19:29:44.132:  L2F: Tunnel state closed
Jan  7 19:29:44.132: L2F: Got a tunnel named ISP_NAS, responding
Jan  7 19:29:44.132: AAA: parse name=<no string> idb type=-1 tty=-1
```

The home gateway receives a SENDAUTH packet from the NAS, which wants to authenticate the home gateway. The home gateway authenticates the tunnel using local AAA.

```
Jan  7 19:29:44.132: AAA/AUTHEN: create_user (0x612D550C) user='ENT_HGW'
  ruser='' port='' rem_addr='' authen_type=CHAP service=PPP priv=1
Jan  7 19:29:44.132: AAA/AUTHEN/START (384300079): port='' list='default'
  action=SENDAUTH service=PPP
Jan  7 19:29:44.132: AAA/AUTHEN/START (384300079): found list default
Jan  7 19:29:44.132: AAA/AUTHEN/START (384300079): Method=LOCAL
Jan  7 19:29:44.132: AAA/AUTHEN (384300079): status = PASS
Jan  7 19:29:44.132: AAA/AUTHEN: free_user (0x612D550C) user='ENT_HGW'
  ruser='' port='' rem_addr='' authen_type=CHAP service=PPP priv=1
Jan  7 19:29:44.132: AAA: parse name=<no string> idb type=-1 tty=-1
Jan  7 19:29:44.132: AAA/AUTHEN: create_user (0x612D550C) user='ISP_NAS'
  ruser='' port='' rem_addr='' authen_type=CHAP service=PPP priv=1
Jan  7 19:29:44.132: AAA/AUTHEN/START (2545876944): port='' list='default'
  action=SENDAUTH service=PPP
Jan  7 19:29:44.132: AAA/AUTHEN/START (2545876944): found list default
Jan  7 19:29:44.132: AAA/AUTHEN/START (2545876944): Method=LOCAL
Jan  7 19:29:44.132: AAA/AUTHEN (2545876944): status = PASS
Jan  7 19:29:44.132: AAA/AUTHEN: free_user (0x612D550C) user='ISP_NAS'
  ruser='' port='' rem_addr='' authen_type=CHAP service=PPP priv=1
Jan  7 19:29:44.132: L2F: Open UDP socket to 172.22.66.23
```

The NAS authenticates the home gateway and sends an L2F_OPEN packet to open the tunnel.

```
Jan  7 19:29:44.132: ISP_NAS L2F: Tunnel state opening
Jan  7 19:29:44.136: L2F: L2F_OPEN received
Jan  7 19:29:44.136: L2F: Removing resend packet (L2F_CONF)
Jan  7 19:29:44.136: AAA: parse name=<no string> idb type=-1 tty=-1
Jan  7 19:29:44.136: AAA/AUTHEN: create_user (0x612D550C) user='ISP_NAS'
```

```
     ruser='' port='' rem_addr='' authen_type=CHAP service=PPP priv=1
Jan  7 19:29:44.136: AAA/AUTHEN/START (1465065509): port='' list='default'
  action=LOGIN service=PPP
Jan  7 19:29:44.136: AAA/AUTHEN/START (1465065509): found list default
Jan  7 19:29:44.136: AAA/AUTHEN/START (1465065509): Method=LOCAL
Jan  7 19:29:44.136: AAA/AUTHEN (1465065509): status = PASS
```

The home gateway authenticates the NAS and opens the L2F tunnel.

```
Jan  7 19:29:44.136: VPDN: Chap authentication succeeded for ISP_NAS
Jan  7 19:29:44.136: AAA/AUTHEN: free_user (0x612D550C) user='ISP_NAS'
  ruser='' port='' rem_addr='' authen_type=CHAP service=PPP priv=1
Jan  7 19:29:44.136: ISP_NAS L2F: Tunnel state open
Jan  7 19:29:44.140: L2F: L2F_OPEN received
```

The home gateway receives the client information forwarded from the NAS.

```
Jan  7 19:29:44.140: L2F: L2F_CLIENT_INFO: CLID/DNIS 408/5550945
Jan  7 19:29:44.140: L2F: L2F_CLIENT_INFO: NAS-Port Async11
Jan  7 19:29:44.140: L2F: L2F_CLIENT_INFO: Client-Bandwidth-Kbps 115
Jan  7 19:29:44.140: L2F: L2F_CLIENT_INFO: NAS-Rate L2F/28800/50000
Jan  7 19:29:44.140: L2F: Got a MID management packet
Jan  7 19:29:44.140:  L2F: MID  state closed
Jan  7 19:29:44.140: L2F: Start create mid intf process for jeremy@hgw.com
Jan  7 19:29:44.140: Vi1 VTEMPLATE: Reuse Vi1, recycle queue size 0
Jan  7 19:29:44.140: Vi1 VTEMPLATE: Hardware address 0050.d193.e000
```

A virtual access interface is cloned from virtual template 1, which is not a physical interface, but is treated like a regular interface that uses the IP address of the Fast Ethernet 0/0 interface.

The debug output following "interface Virtual-Access1" lists every command that has been configured for virtual template 1. Enter the **clear vtemplate** privileged EXEC command to reset the command history.

```
Jan  7 19:29:44.140: Vi1 VPDN: Virtual interface created for jeremy@hgw.com
Jan  7 19:29:44.140: Vi1 VPDN: Set to Async interface
Jan  7 19:29:44.140: Vi1 PPP: Phase is DOWN, Setup
Jan  7 19:29:44.140: Vi1 VPDN: Clone from Vtemplate 1 filterPPP=0 blocking
Jan  7 19:29:44.140: Vi1 VTEMPLATE: Has a new cloneblk vtemplate, now
  it has vtemplate
Jan  7 19:29:44.140: Vi1 VTEMPLATE: ************* CLONE VACCESS1
  *****************
Jan  7 19:29:44.144: Vi1 VTEMPLATE: Clone from Virtual-Template1
interface Virtual-Access1
default ip address
no ip address
encap ppp
```

```
ip unnumbered fastethernet 0/0
no ip directed-broadcast
ip unnumbered fastethernet 0/0
no ip directed-broadcast
ppp authentication chap
peer default ip address pool default
encapsulation ppp
ppp multilink
end


6w5d: %LINK-3-UPDOWN: Interface Virtual-Access1, changed state to up
Jan  7 19:29:44.224: Vi1 PPP: Treating connection as a dedicated line
Jan  7 19:29:44.224: Vi1 PPP: Phase is ESTABLISHING, Active Open
Jan  7 19:29:44.224: Vi1 AAA/AUTHOR/FSM: (0): LCP succeeds trivially
Jan  7 19:29:44.224: Vi1 LCP: O CONFREQ [Closed] id 1 len 39
Jan  7 19:29:44.224: Vi1 LCP:    ACCM 0x000A0000 (0x0206000A0000)
Jan  7 19:29:44.224: Vi1 LCP:    AuthProto CHAP (0x0305C22305)
Jan  7 19:29:44.224: Vi1 LCP:    MagicNumber 0x47ADAD67 (0x050647ADAD67)
Jan  7 19:29:44.224: Vi1 LCP:    PFC (0x0702)
Jan  7 19:29:44.224: Vi1 LCP:    ACFC (0x0802)
Jan  7 19:29:44.224: Vi1 LCP:    MRRU 1524 (0x110405F4)
Jan  7 19:29:44.224: Vi1 LCP:    EndpointDisc 1 Local
  (0x130A01454E545F484757)
Jan  7 19:29:44.224: Vi1 VPDN: Bind interface direction=2
Jan  7 19:29:44.224: Vi1 PPP: Treating connection as a dedicated line
```

The NAS forces the information from the LCP negotiation with the client onto the virtual access interface.

```
Jan  7 19:29:44.224: Vi1 LCP: I FORCED CONFREQ len 21
Jan  7 19:29:44.224: Vi1 LCP:    ACCM 0x000A0000 (0x0206000A0000)
Jan  7 19:29:44.224: Vi1 LCP:    AuthProto CHAP (0x0305C22305)
Jan  7 19:29:44.224: Vi1 LCP:    MagicNumber 0x33911E0F (0x050633911E0F)
Jan  7 19:29:44.224: Vi1 LCP:    PFC (0x0702)
Jan  7 19:29:44.224: Vi1 LCP:    ACFC (0x0802)
Jan  7 19:29:44.224: Vi1 VPDN: PPP LCP accepted rcv CONFACK
Jan  7 19:29:44.224: Vi1 VPDN: PPP LCP accepted sent CONFACK
Jan  7 19:29:44.224: Vi1 PPP: Phase is AUTHENTICATING, by this end
```

The home gateway sends a CHAP challenge to the client, which replies with a CHAP response.

```
Jan  7 19:29:44.224: Vi1 CHAP: O CHALLENGE id 3 len 28 from "ENT_HGW"
Jan  7 19:29:44.224: Vi1 L2F: Transfer NAS-Rate L2F/28800/50000 to LCP
Jan  7 19:29:44.228: Vi1 CHAP: I RESPONSE id 2 len 35 from "jeremy@hgw.com"
Jan  7 19:29:44.228: Vi1 L2F: Finish create mid intf for jeremy@hgw.com
Jan  7 19:29:44.228: Vi1 L2F: MID jeremy@hgw.com state open
Jan  7 19:29:44.228: AAA: parse name=Virtual-Access1 idb type=21 tty=-1
Jan  7 19:29:44.228: AAA: name=Virtual-Access1 flags=0x11 type=5 shelf=0
  slot=0 adapter=0 port=1 channel=0
```

```
Jan  7 19:29:44.228: AAA/AUTHEN: create_user (0x612F1F78)
  user='jeremy@hgw.com'
ruser='' port='Virtual-Access1' rem_addr='408/5550945' authen_type=CHAP
  service=PPPpriv=1
Jan  7 19:29:44.228: AAA/AUTHEN/START (101773535): port='Virtual-Access1'
  list='' action=LOGIN service=PPP
Jan  7 19:29:44.228: AAA/AUTHEN/START (101773535): using "default" list
Jan  7 19:29:44.228: AAA/AUTHEN/START (101773535): Method=LOCAL
Jan  7 19:29:44.228: AAA/AUTHEN (101773535): status = ERROR
```

The home gateway forwards the user information to its RADIUS server, and the
RADIUS server authenticates and authorizes the user.

```
Jan  7 19:29:44.228: AAA/AUTHEN/START (101773535): Method=RADIUS
Jan  7 19:29:44.228: RADIUS: ustruct sharecount=1
Jan  7 19:29:44.228: RADIUS: Initial Transmit Virtual-Access1 id 119
  172.22.66.13:1645, Access-Request, len 99
Jan  7 19:29:44.228:        Attribute 4 6 AC164219
Jan  7 19:29:44.228:        Attribute 5 6 00000001
Jan  7 19:29:44.228:        Attribute 61 6 00000005
Jan  7 19:29:44.228:        Attribute 1 16 6A657265
Jan  7 19:29:44.228:        Attribute 30 9 35373130
Jan  7 19:29:44.228:        Attribute 31 5 34303803
Jan  7 19:29:44.228:        Attribute 3 19 02A4F6DD
Jan  7 19:29:44.228:        Attribute 6 6 00000002
Jan  7 19:29:44.228:        Attribute 7 6 00000001
Jan 7 19:29:44.692: RADIUS: Received from id 119 172.22.66.13:1645, Access-
  Accept, len 38
Jan  7 19:29:44.692:        Attribute 6 6 00000002
Jan  7 19:29:44.692:        Attribute 7 6 00000001
Jan  7 19:29:44.692:        Attribute 8 6 FFFFFFFE
Jan  7 19:29:44.692: AAA/AUTHEN (101773535): status = PASS
Jan  7 19:29:44.692: Vi1 AAA/AUTHOR/LCP: Authorize LCP
Jan  7 19:29:44.692: AAA/AUTHOR/LCP Vi1 (3630870259): Port='Virtual-
  Access1' list='' service=NET
Jan  7 19:29:44.692: AAA/AUTHOR/LCP: Vi1 (3630870259) user='jeremy@hgw.com'
Jan  7 19:29:44.692: AAA/AUTHOR/LCP: Vi1 (3630870259) send AV service=ppp
Jan  7 19:29:44.692: AAA/AUTHOR/LCP: Vi1 (3630870259) send AV protocol=lcp
Jan  7 19:29:44.692: AAA/AUTHOR/LCP (3630870259) found list "default"
Jan  7 19:29:44.692: AAA/AUTHOR/LCP: Vi1 (3630870259) Method=RADIUS
Jan  7 19:29:44.692: AAA/AUTHOR (3630870259): Post authorization status =
  PASS_REPL
Jan  7 19:29:44.692: Vi1 AAA/AUTHOR/LCP: Processing AV service=ppp
Jan  7 19:29:44.692: Vi1 CHAP: O SUCCESS id 2 len 4
Jan  7 19:29:44.692: Vi1 PPP: Phase is UP
Jan  7 19:29:44.696: Vi1 AAA/AUTHOR/FSM: (0): Can we start IPCP?
Jan  7 19:29:44.696: AAA/AUTHOR/FSM Vi1 (2925705703): Port='Virtual-
  Access1' list='' service=NET
Jan  7 19:29:44.696: AAA/AUTHOR/FSM: Vi1 (2925705703) user='jeremy@hgw.com'
Jan  7 19:29:44.696: AAA/AUTHOR/FSM: Vi1 (2925705703) send AV service=ppp
Jan  7 19:29:44.696: AAA/AUTHOR/FSM: Vi1 (2925705703) send AV protocol=ip
```

```
Jan  7 19:29:44.696: AAA/AUTHOR/FSM (2925705703) found list "default"
Jan  7 19:29:44.696: AAA/AUTHOR/FSM: Vi1 (2925705703) Method=RADIUS
Jan  7 19:29:44.696: RADIUS: Using NAS default peer
Jan  7 19:29:44.696: RADIUS: Authorize IP address 0.0.0.0
Jan  7 19:29:44.696: AAA/AUTHOR (2925705703): Post authorization status =
   PASS_REPL
Jan  7 19:29:44.696: Vi1 AAA/AUTHOR/FSM: We can start IPCP
Jan  7 19:29:44.696: Vi1 IPCP: O CONFREQ [Closed] id 1 len 10
Jan  7 19:29:44.696: Vi1 IPCP:    Address 172.22.66.25 (0x0306AC164219)
Jan  7 19:29:44.696: RADIUS: ustruct sharecount=2
Jan  7 19:29:44.696: RADIUS: Initial Transmit Virtual-Access1 id 120
   172.22.66.13:1646, Accounting-Request, len 108
Jan  7 19:29:44.696:          Attribute 4 6 AC164219
Jan  7 19:29:44.696:          Attribute 5 6 00000001
Jan  7 19:29:44.696:          Attribute 61 6 00000005
Jan  7 19:29:44.696:          Attribute 1 16 6A657265
Jan  7 19:29:44.696:          Attribute 30 9 35373130
Jan  7 19:29:44.696:          Attribute 31 5 34303828
Jan  7 19:29:44.696:          Attribute 40 6 00000001
Jan  7 19:29:44.696:          Attribute 45 6 00000001
Jan  7 19:29:44.696:          Attribute 6 6 00000002
Jan  7 19:29:44.700:          Attribute 44 10 30303030
Jan  7 19:29:44.700:          Attribute 7 6 00000001
Jan  7 19:29:44.700:          Attribute 41 6 00000000
Jan  7 19:29:44.740: RADIUS: Received from id 120 172.22.66.13:1646,
   Accounting-response, len 20
Jan  7 19:29:44.804: Vi1 IPCP: I CONFREQ [REQsent] id 1 len 40
Jan  7 19:29:44.804: Vi1 IPCP:    CompressType VJ 15 slots CompressSlotID
   (0x0206002D0F01)
Jan  7 19:29:44.804: Vi1 IPCP:    Address 0.0.0.0 (0x030600000000)
Jan  7 19:29:44.804: Vi1 IPCP:    PrimaryDNS 171.68.10.70 (0x8106AB440A46)
Jan  7 19:29:44.804: Vi1 IPCP:    PrimaryWINS 171.68.235.228
   (0x8206AB44EBE4)
Jan  7 19:29:44.804: Vi1 IPCP:    SecondaryDNS 171.68.10.140
   (0x8306AB440A8C)
Jan  7 19:29:44.808: Vi1 IPCP:    SecondaryWINS 171.68.235.229
   (0x8406AB44EBE5)
Jan  7 19:29:44.808: Vi1 AAA/AUTHOR/IPCP: Start.  Her address 0.0.0.0, we
   want 0.0.0.0
Jan  7 19:29:44.808: Vi1 AAA/AUTHOR/IPCP: Processing AV service=ppp
Jan  7 19:29:44.808: Vi1 AAA/AUTHOR/IPCP: Processing AV addr=0.0.0.0
Jan  7 19:29:44.808: Vi1 AAA/AUTHOR/IPCP: Authorization succeeded
Jan  7 19:29:44.808: Vi1 AAA/AUTHOR/IPCP: Done.  Her address 0.0.0.0, we
   want 0.0.0.0
```

The home gateway assigns the client the IP address 172.30.2.1 from the default pool.

```
Jan  7 19:29:44.808: Vi1 IPCP: Using pool 'default'
Jan  7 19:29:44.808: ip_get_pool: Vi1: using pool default
Jan  7 19:29:44.808: ip_get_pool: Vi1: returning address = 172.30.2.1
Jan  7 19:29:44.808: Vi1 IPCP: Pool returned 172.30.2.1
```

```
Jan  7 19:29:44.808: Vi1 IPCP: O CONFREJ [REQsent] id 1 len 10
Jan  7 19:29:44.808: Vi1 IPCP:    CompressType VJ 15 slots CompressSlotID
  (0x0206002D0F01)
Jan  7 19:29:44.808: Vi1 CCP: I CONFREQ [Not negotiated] id 1 len 15
Jan  7 19:29:44.808: Vi1 CCP:    MS-PPC supported bits 0x00000001
  (0x120600000001)
Jan  7 19:29:44.808: Vi1 CCP:    Stacker history 1 check mode EXTENDED
  (0x1105000104)
Jan  7 19:29:44.808: Vi1 LCP: O PROTREJ [Open] id 2 len 21 protocol CCP
Jan  7 19:29:44.808: Vi1 LCP:    (0x80FD0101000F120600000000111050001)
Jan  7 19:29:44.808: Vi1 LCP:    (0x04)
Jan  7 19:29:44.808: Vi1 IPCP: I CONFACK [REQsent] id 1 len 10
Jan  7 19:29:44.808: Vi1 IPCP:    Address 172.22.66.25 (0x0306AC164219)
```

The line protocol on interface Virtual-Access1 changes to the up state.

```
6w5d: %LINEPROTO-5-UPDOWN: Line protocol on Interface Virtual-Access1,
  changed state to up
Jan  7 19:29:46.224: Vi1 LCP: TIMEout: State Open
Jan  7 19:29:46.696: Vi1 IPCP: TIMEout: State ACKrcvd
Jan  7 19:29:46.696: Vi1 IPCP: O CONFREQ [ACKrcvd] id 2 len 10
Jan  7 19:29:46.696: Vi1 IPCP:    Address 172.22.66.25 (0x0306AC164219)
Jan  7 19:29:46.784: Vi1 IPCP: I CONFACK [REQsent] id 2 len 10
Jan  7 19:29:46.784: Vi1 IPCP:    Address 172.22.66.25 (0x0306AC164219)
```

The client requests IP addresses of DNS and WINS servers.

```
Jan  7 19:29:47.792: Vi1 IPCP: I CONFREQ [ACKrcvd] id 2 len 34
Jan  7 19:29:47.792: Vi1 IPCP:    Address 0.0.0.0 (0x030600000000)
Jan  7 19:29:47.792: Vi1 IPCP:    PrimaryDNS 171.68.10.70 (0x8106AB440A46)
Jan  7 19:29:47.792: Vi1 IPCP:    PrimaryWINS 171.68.235.228
  (0x8206AB44EBE4)
Jan  7 19:29:47.792: Vi1 IPCP:    SecondaryDNS 171.68.10.140
  (0x8306AB440A8C)
Jan  7 19:29:47.792: Vi1 IPCP:    SecondaryWINS 171.68.235.229
  (0x8406AB44EBE5)
Jan  7 19:29:47.792: Vi1 AAA/AUTHOR/IPCP: Start.  Her address 0.0.0.0, we
  want 172.30.2.1
Jan  7 19:29:47.792: Vi1 AAA/AUTHOR/IPCP: Processing AV service=ppp
Jan  7 19:29:47.792: Vi1 AAA/AUTHOR/IPCP: Processing AV addr=0.0.0.0
Jan  7 19:29:47.792: Vi1 AAA/AUTHOR/IPCP: Authorization succeeded
Jan  7 19:29:47.792: Vi1 AAA/AUTHOR/IPCP: Done.  Her address 0.0.0.0, we
  want 172.30.2.1
Jan  7 19:29:47.792: Vi1 IPCP: O CONFNAK [ACKrcvd] id 2 len 34
Jan  7 19:29:47.792: Vi1 IPCP:    Address 172.30.2.1 (0x0306AC1E0201)
Jan  7 19:29:47.792: Vi1 IPCP:    PrimaryDNS 172.23.1.10 (0x8106AC17010A)
```

```
Jan  7 19:29:47.792: Vi1 IPCP:     PrimaryWINS 172.23.1.11 (0x8206AC17010B)
Jan  7 19:29:47.792: Vi1 IPCP:     SecondaryDNS 172.23.2.10 (0x8306AC17020A)
Jan  7 19:29:47.792: Vi1 IPCP:     SecondaryWINS 172.23.2.11 (0x8406AC17020B)
```

The home gateway receives a positive acknowledgment from the client confirming the IP addresses of the DNS and WNIS servers.

```
Jan  7 19:29:47.952: Vi1 IPCP: I CONFREQ [ACKrcvd] id 3 len 34
Jan  7 19:29:47.952: Vi1 IPCP:     Address 172.30.2.1 (0x0306AC1E0201)
Jan  7 19:29:47.952: Vi1 IPCP:     PrimaryDNS 172.23.1.10 (0x8106AC17010A)
Jan  7 19:29:47.952: Vi1 IPCP:     PrimaryWINS 172.23.1.11 (0x8206AC17010B)
Jan  7 19:29:47.952: Vi1 IPCP:     SecondaryDNS 172.23.2.10 (0x8306AC17020A)
Jan  7 19:29:47.952: Vi1 IPCP:     SecondaryWINS 172.23.2.11 (0x8406AC17020B)
Jan  7 19:29:47.952: Vi1 AAA/AUTHOR/IPCP: Start.  Her address 172.30.2.1,
  we want 172.30.2.1
Jan  7 19:29:47.952: AAA/AUTHOR/IPCP Vi1 (1744344778): Port='Virtual-
  Access1' list='' service=NET
Jan  7 19:29:47.952: AAA/AUTHOR/IPCP: Vi1 (1744344778)
  user='jeremy@hgw.com'
Jan  7 19:29:47.952: AAA/AUTHOR/IPCP: Vi1 (1744344778) send AV service=ppp
Jan  7 19:29:47.952: AAA/AUTHOR/IPCP: Vi1 (1744344778) send AV protocol=ip
Jan  7 19:29:47.952: AAA/AUTHOR/IPCP: Vi1 (1744344778) send AV
  addr*172.30.2.1
Jan  7 19:29:47.952: AAA/AUTHOR/IPCP (1744344778) found list "default"
Jan  7 19:29:47.952: AAA/AUTHOR/IPCP: Vi1 (1744344778) Method=RADIUS
Jan  7 19:29:47.952: RADIUS: Using NAS default peer
Jan  7 19:29:47.952: RADIUS: Authorize IP address 172.30.2.1
Jan  7 19:29:47.952: AAA/AUTHOR (1744344778): Post authorization status =
  PASS_REPL
Jan  7 19:29:47.952: set_ip_peer_addr: Vi1: address = 172.30.2.1 (4) is
  redundant
Jan  7 19:29:47.952: Vi1 AAA/AUTHOR/IPCP: Processing AV service=ppp
Jan  7 19:29:47.952: Vi1 AAA/AUTHOR/IPCP: Processing AV addr=172.30.2.1
Jan  7 19:29:47.952: Vi1 AAA/AUTHOR/IPCP: Authorization succeeded
Jan  7 19:29:47.952: Vi1 AAA/AUTHOR/IPCP: Done.  Her address 172.30.2.1, we
  want 172.30.2.1
Jan  7 19:29:47.952: Vi1 IPCP: O CONFACK [ACKrcvd] id 3 len 34
Jan  7 19:29:47.956: Vi1 IPCP:     Address 172.30.2.1 (0x0306AC1E0201)
Jan  7 19:29:47.956: Vi1 IPCP:     PrimaryDNS 172.23.1.10 (0x8106AC17010A)
Jan  7 19:29:47.956: Vi1 IPCP:     PrimaryWINS 172.23.1.11 (0x8206AC17010B)
Jan  7 19:29:47.956: Vi1 IPCP:     SecondaryDNS 172.23.2.10 (0x8306AC17020A)
Jan  7 19:29:47.956: Vi1 IPCP:     SecondaryWINS 172.23.2.11 (0x8406AC17020B)
Jan  7 19:29:47.956: Vi1 IPCP: State is Open
```

The home gateway installs the route to the client's IP address, 172.30.2.1.

```
Jan  7 19:29:47.956: Vi1 IPCP: Install route to 172.30.2.1
ENT_HGW#
```

L2TP Solution Debug Output

The following sections contain comprehensive debug output for an L2TP tunnel
and session that is created between ISP-LAC-1 and SER-LNS-1:

- Debug Output on ISP-LAC-1
- Debug Output on SER-LNS-1

For more information on this solution, see Chapter 3, "Access VPDN Dial-In
Using L2TP Solution."

Debug Output on ISP-LAC-1

To view the following debug output, enable the following debug commands on
ISP-LAC-1 and dial in to ISP-LAC-1 using username ser-test-1@service.com and
password pass2me:

```
debug isdn q931
debug modem csm
debug ppp authentication
debug ppp negotiation
debug vpdn event
debug vpdn 12x-events
```

The following is debug output from successful L2TP negotiation on the LAC,
ISP-LAC-1:

```
ISP-LAC-1#
```

The call is received:

```
*May 16 21:35:25.659: ISDN Se0:23: RX <-  SETUP pd = 8  callref = 0x17
```

Bearer capability 0x8090A2 indicates that it is an analog call:

```
*May 16 21:35:25.659:          Bearer Capability i = 0x8090A2
*May 16 21:35:25.659:          Channel ID i = 0xA98393
*May 16 21:35:25.659:          Called Party Number i = 0x80, '1123',
  Plan:Unknown
*May 16 21:35:25.659: VDEV_ALLOCATE: 1/7 is allocated
*May 16 21:35:25.663: ISDN Se0:23: TX -> CALL_PROC pd = 8  callref = 0x8017
*May 16 21:35:25.663:          Channel ID i = 0xA98393
*May 16 21:35:25.663: EVENT_FROM_ISDN::dchan_idb=0x62171A04, call_id=0x1F,
  ces=1
  bchan=0x12, event=0x1, cause=0x0
*May 16 21:35:25.663: EVENT_FROM_ISDN:(001F): DEV_INCALL at slot 1 and port
  7
*May 16 21:35:25.663: CSM_PROC_IDLE: CSM_EVENT_ISDN_CALL at slot 1, port 7
```

These MICA technologies modem debug lines indicate that the call is sent to MICA modem 1/7:

```
*May 16 21:35:25.663: Mica Modem(1/7): Configure(0x1 = 0x0)
*May 16 21:35:25.663: Mica Modem(1/7): Configure(0x23 = 0x0)
*May 16 21:35:25.663: Mica Modem(1/7): Call Setup
*May 16 21:35:25.663:  Enter csm_connect_pri_vdev function
*May 16 21:35:25.663: csm_connect_pri_vdev:tdm_allocate_bp_ts() call. BP TS
  all0
*May 16 21:35:25.663: ISDN Se0:23: TX -> ALERTING pd = 8  callref = 0x8017
*May 16 21:35:25.763: Mica Modem(1/7): State Transition to Call Setup
*May 16 21:35:25.763: Mica Modem(1/7): Went offhook
*May 16 21:35:25.763: CSM_PROC_IC2_RING: CSM_EVENT_MODEM_OFFHOOK at slot 1,
  port 7
*May 16 21:35:25.763: ISDN Se0:23: TX -> CONNECT pd = 8  callref = 0x8017
*May 16 21:35:25.819: ISDN Se0:23: RX <- CONNECT_ACK pd = 8  callref = 0x17
*May 16 21:35:25.823: ISDN Se0:23: CALL_PROGRESS: CALL_CONNECTED call id
  0x1F, 0
*May 16 21:35:25.823: EVENT_FROM_ISDN::dchan_idb=0x62171A04, call_id=0x1F,
  ces=1
  bchan=0x12, event=0x4, cause=0x0
*May 16 21:35:25.823: EVENT_FROM_ISDN:(001F): DEV_CONNECTED at slot 1 and
  port 7
*May 16 21:35:25.823: CSM_PROC_IC6_WAIT_FOR_CONNECT: CSM_EVENT_ISDN_
  CONNECTED at
slot 1 and port 7
*May 16 21:35:25.823: Mica Modem(1/7): Link Initiate
*May 16 21:35:26.903: Mica Modem(1/7): State Transition to Connect
*May 16 21:35:31.407: Mica Modem(1/7): State Transition to Link
*May 16 21:35:42.815: Mica Modem(1/7): State Transition to Trainup
*May 16 21:35:46.775: Mica Modem(1/7): State Transition to EC Negotiating
*May 16 21:35:47.375: Mica Modem(1/7): State Transition to Steady State
```

ISP-LAC-1 and the client have successfully negotiated, and asynchronous interface 8 is assigned to the call and brought up:

```
*May 16 21:35:52.595: %LINK-3-UPDOWN: Interface Async8, changed state to up
```

PPP negotiation begins on asynchronous interface 8 with Link Control Protocol (LCP) negotiation:

```
*May 16 21:35:52.595: As8 PPP: Treating connection as a dedicated line
*May 16 21:35:52.595: As8 PPP: Phase is ESTABLISHING, Active Open
*May 16 21:35:52.595: As8 LCP: O CONFREQ [Closed] id 1 len 25
*May 16 21:35:52.595: As8 LCP:    ACCM 0x000A0000 (0x0206000A0000)
```

ISP-LAC-1 requires that the client authenticate with CHAP:

```
*May 16 21:35:52.595: As8 LCP:   AuthProto CHAP (0x0305C22305)
*May 16 21:35:52.595: As8 LCP:   MagicNumber 0x28C9DAF1 (0x050628C9DAF1)
*May 16 21:35:52.595: As8 LCP:   PFC (0x0702)
*May 16 21:35:52.595: As8 LCP:   ACFC (0x0802)
*May 16 21:35:53.471: As8 LCP: I CONFREQ [REQsent] id 3 len 23
*May 16 21:35:53.471: As8 LCP:   ACCM 0x000A0000 (0x0206000A0000)
*May 16 21:35:53.471: As8 LCP:   MagicNumber 0x3D675D0F (0x05063D675D0F)
*May 16 21:35:53.471: As8 LCP:   PFC (0x0702)
*May 16 21:35:53.471: As8 LCP:   ACFC (0x0802)
*May 16 21:35:53.471: As8 LCP:   Callback 6  (0x0D0306)
```

ISP-LAC-1 rejects the client request for callback service, and the client then resends its request without the rejected callback option:

```
*May 16 21:35:53.475: As8 LCP: O CONFREJ [REQsent] id 3 len 7
*May 16 21:35:53.475: As8 LCP:   Callback 6  (0x0D0306)
*May 16 21:35:54.595: As8 LCP: TIMEout: State REQsent
*May 16 21:35:54.595: As8 LCP: O CONFREQ [REQsent] id 2 len 25
*May 16 21:35:54.595: As8 LCP:   ACCM 0x000A0000 (0x0206000A0000)
*May 16 21:35:54.595: As8 LCP:   AuthProto CHAP (0x0305C22305)
*May 16 21:35:54.595: As8 LCP:   MagicNumber 0x28C9DAF1 (0x050628C9DAF1)
*May 16 21:35:54.595: As8 LCP:   PFC (0x0702)
*May 16 21:35:54.595: As8 LCP:   ACFC (0x0802)
*May 16 21:35:54.703: As8 LCP: I CONFACK [REQsent] id 2 len 25
*May 16 21:35:54.703: As8 LCP:   ACCM 0x000A0000 (0x0206000A0000)
*May 16 21:35:54.703: As8 LCP:   AuthProto CHAP (0x0305C22305)
*May 16 21:35:54.707: As8 LCP:   MagicNumber 0x28C9DAF1 (0x050628C9DAF1)
*May 16 21:35:54.707: As8 LCP:   PFC (0x0702)
*May 16 21:35:54.707: As8 LCP:   ACFC (0x0802)
*May 16 21:35:56.483: As8 LCP: I CONFREQ [ACKrcvd] id 4 len 23
*May 16 21:35:56.483: As8 LCP:   ACCM 0x000A0000 (0x0206000A0000)
*May 16 21:35:56.483: As8 LCP:   MagicNumber 0x3D675D0F (0x05063D675D0F)
*May 16 21:35:56.483: As8 LCP:   PFC (0x0702)
*May 16 21:35:56.483: As8 LCP:   ACFC (0x0802)
*May 16 21:35:56.483: As8 LCP:   Callback 6  (0x0D0306)
*May 16 21:35:56.483: As8 LCP: O CONFREJ [ACKrcvd] id 4 len 7
*May 16 21:35:56.483: As8 LCP:   Callback 6  (0x0D0306)
*May 16 21:35:56.579: As8 LCP: I CONFREQ [ACKrcvd] id 5 len 20
*May 16 21:35:56.579: As8 LCP:   ACCM 0x000A0000 (0x0206000A0000)
*May 16 21:35:56.579: As8 LCP:   MagicNumber 0x3D675D0F (0x05063D675D0F)
*May 16 21:35:56.579: As8 LCP:   PFC (0x0702)
*May 16 21:35:56.579: As8 LCP:   ACFC (0x0802)
*May 16 21:35:56.579: As8 LCP: O CONFACK [ACKrcvd] id 5 len 20
*May 16 21:35:56.579: As8 LCP:   ACCM 0x000A0000 (0x0206000A0000)
*May 16 21:35:56.579: As8 LCP:   MagicNumber 0x3D675D0F (0x05063D675D0F)
*May 16 21:35:56.579: As8 LCP:   PFC (0x0702)
*May 16 21:35:56.579: As8 LCP:   ACFC (0x0802)
```

LCP negotiation is complete:

```
*May 16 21:35:56.579: As8 LCP: State is Open
*May 16 21:35:56.579: As8 PPP: Phase is AUTHENTICATING, by this end
```

ISP-LAC-1 sends a CHAP challenge, and the client replies with a CHAP response:

```
*May 16 21:35:56.579: As8 CHAP: O CHALLENGE id 1 len 30 from "ISP-LAC-1"
*May 16 21:35:56.707: As8 CHAP: I RESPONSE id 1 len 40 from
 "ser-test-1@service.com"
*May 16 21:35:56.707: As8 PPP: Phase is FORWARDING
*May 16 21:35:56.707: As8 VPDN: Got DNIS string 1123
```

VPDN determines the domain name of the username and searches the VPDN groups for a matching domain name:

```
*May 16 21:35:56.707: As8 VPDN: Looking for tunnel -- service.com --
*May 16 21:35:56.707: As8 VPDN/ISP-LAC-1/1: Got tunnel info for service.com
*May 16 21:35:56.707: As8 VPDN/ISP-LAC-1/1:   LAC ISP-LAC-1
*May 16 21:35:56.707: As8 VPDN/ISP-LAC-1/1:   l2tp-busy-disconnect yes
```

ISP-LAC-1 sends the L2TP tunnel password to SER-LNS-1 at IP address 192.168.48.1:

```
*May 16 21:35:56.707: As8 VPDN/ISP-LAC-1/1:   l2tp-tunnel-password xxxxxx
*May 16 21:35:56.707: As8 VPDN/ISP-LAC-1/1:   IP 192.168.48.1
*May 16 21:35:56.711: As8 VPDN/1: curlvl 1 Address 0: 192.168.48.1,
 priority 1
*May 16 21:35:56.711: As8 VPDN/1: Select non-active address 192.168.48.1,
 priority 1
```

ISP-LAC-1 assigns the tunnel the local tunnel ID 8173:

```
*May 16 21:35:56.711: Tnl 8173 L2TP: SM State idle
```

ISP-LAC-1 sends a Start-Control-Connection-Request (SCCRQ) message to SER-LNS-1 to begin L2TP tunnel negotiation:

```
*May 16 21:35:56.711: Tnl 8173 L2TP: O SCCRQ
*May 16 21:35:56.711: Tnl 8173 L2TP: Tunnel state change from idle
 to wait-ctl-reply
*May 16 21:35:56.711: Tnl 8173 L2TP: SM State wait-ctl-reply
*May 16 21:35:56.711: As8 VPDN: Find LNS process created
*May 16 21:35:56.711: As8 VPDN: Forward to address 192.168.48.1
*May 16 21:35:56.711: As8 VPDN: Pending
*May 16 21:35:56.711: As8 VPDN: Process created
```

ISP-LAC-1 receives a Start-Control-Connection-Reply (SCCRP) message from
SER-LNS-1, which indicates that SER-LNS-1 received the SCCRQ message:

```
*May 16 21:35:56.715: Tnl 8173 L2TP: I SCCRP from SER-LNS-1
```

ISP-LAC-1 and SER-LNS-1 successfully authenticate their L2TP tunnel
passwords, and ISP-LAC-1 changes the tunnel state to established:

```
*May 16 21:35:56.715: Tnl 8173 L2TP: Got a challenge from remote peer, SER-
 LNS-1
*May 16 21:35:56.715: Tnl 8173 L2TP: Got a response from remote peer, SER-
 LNS-1
*May 16 21:35:56.715: Tnl 8173 L2TP: Tunnel Authentication success
*May 16 21:35:56.715: Tnl 8173 L2TP: Tunnel state change from wait-ctl-reply
 to established
```

ISP-LAC-1 sends a Start-Control-Connection-Connected (SCCN) message to
SER-LNS-1, which completes L2TP tunnel negotiation. This debug line also
contains tunnel ID 15991 from SER-LNS-1 for this tunnel:

```
*May 16 21:35:56.715: Tnl 8173 L2TP: O SCCCN  to SER-LNS-1 tnlid 15991
*May 16 21:35:56.715: Tnl 8173 L2TP: SM State established
*May 16 21:35:56.719: As8 VPDN: Forwarding...
*May 16 21:35:56.719: As8 VPDN: Bind interface direction=1
*May 16 21:35:56.719: Tnl/Cl 8173/6 L2TP: Session FS enabled
*May 16 21:35:56.719: Tnl/Cl 8173/6 L2TP: Session state change from idle
 to wait-for-tunnel
*May 16 21:35:56.719: As8 Tnl/Cl 8173/6 L2TP: Create session
*May 16 21:35:56.719: Tnl 8173 L2TP: SM State established
```

ISP-LAC-1 sends an Incoming-Call-Request (ICRQ) message to L2TP tunnel
15991 on SER-LNS-1, which begins L2TP session negotiation. ISP-LAC-1
assigns local session ID 6 to this session:

```
*May 16 21:35:56.719: As8 Tnl/Cl 8173/6 L2TP: O ICRQ to SER-LNS-1 15991/0
*May 16 21:35:56.719: As8 Tnl/Cl 8173/6 L2TP: Session state change
 from wait-for-tunnel to wait-reply
```

ISP-LAC-1 has received an Incoming-Call-Reply (ICRP) message from SER-
LNS-1 (not shown in the debug output), which indicates that it has accepted the
ICRQ message:

```
*May 16 21:35:56.719: As8 VPDN: ser-test-1@service.com is forwarded
```

ISP-LAC-1 sends an Incoming-Call-Connected (ICCN) message to SER-LNS-1, which completes the L2TP session negotiation. SER-LNS-1 has assigned the local session ID 4 to this session:

```
*May 16 21:35:56.723: As8 Tnl/Cl 8173/6 L2TP: O ICCN to SER-LNS-1 15991/4
```

The L2TP session is now established, and the line protocol on asynchronous interface 8 is brought up:

```
*May 16 21:35:56.723: As8 Tnl/Cl 8173/6 L2TP: Session state change from
 wait-reply to
established
*May 16 21:35:57.719: %LINEPROTO-5-UPDOWN: Line protocol on Interface
 Async8,
 changed state to up
*May 16 21:35:57.823: Mica Modem(1/7): State Transition to Steady State
 Speedshg
*May 16 21:35:59.083: Mica Modem(1/7): State Transition to Steady State
ISP-LAC-1#
```

Debug Output on SER-LNS-1

To view the following debug output, enable the following debug commands on SER-LNS-1 and dial in to ISP-LAC-1 using username ser-test-1@service.com and password pass2me:

```
debug vpdn events
debug vpdn l2x-events
debug ppp negotiation
debug ppp authentication
debug vtemplate
```

The following is debug output from successful L2TP negotiation on the LNS, SER-LNS-1.

SER-LNS-1 receives an SCCRQ message from ISP-LAC-1, which identifies the tunnel with ID 8173. SER-LNS-1 considers ID 8173 to be the remote ID and ISP-LAC-1 considers it to be the local ID:

```
May 16 21:38:02.313: L2TP: I SCCRQ from ISP-LAC-1 tnl 8173
```

SER-LNS-1 identifies this tunnel with the local ID 15991:

```
May 16 21:38:02.313: Tnl 15991 L2TP: Got a challenge in SCCRQ, ISP-LAC-1
May 16 21:38:02.313: Tnl 15991 L2TP: New tunnel created for remote
 ISP-LAC-1, address 172.22.16.1
```

SER-LNS-1 replies to ISP-LAC-1 with a SCCRP message:

```
May 16 21:38:02.313: Tnl 15991 L2TP: O SCCRP  to ISP-LAC-1 tnlid 8173
May 16 21:38:02.313: Tnl 15991 L2TP: Tunnel state change from idle to wait-
  ctl-reply
```

SER-LNS-1 receives an SCCN message from ISP-LAC-1 containing its L2TP tunnel password. SER-LNS-1 successfully authenticates the tunnel and changes the tunnel state to established:

```
May 16 21:38:02.317: Tnl 15991 L2TP: I SCCCN from ISP-LAC-1 tnl 8173
May 16 21:38:02.317: Tnl 15991 L2TP: Got a Challenge Response in SCCCN
  from ISP-LAC-1
May 16 21:38:02.321: Tnl 15991 L2TP: Tunnel Authentication success
May 16 21:38:02.321: Tnl 15991 L2TP: Tunnel state change from wait-ctl-reply
  to established
May 16 21:38:02.321: Tnl 15991 L2TP: SM State established
```

SER-LNS-1 receives an ICRQ message from ISP-LAC-1. SER-LNS-1 assigns local session ID 4 to this session:

```
May 16 21:38:02.321: Tnl 15991 L2TP: I ICRQ from ISP-LAC-1 tnl 8173
May 16 21:38:02.321: Tnl/Cl 15991/4 L2TP: Session FS enabled
May 16 21:38:02.321: Tnl/Cl 15991/4 L2TP: Session state change from idle
  to wait-for-tunnel
May 16 21:38:02.321: Tnl/Cl 15991/4 L2TP: New session created
```

SER-LNS-1 replies with an ICRP message to ISP-LAC-1, and then receives an ICCN message confirming the session establishment:

```
May 16 21:38:02.321: Tnl/Cl 15991/4 L2TP: O ICRP to ISP-LAC-1 8173/6
May 16 21:38:02.325: Tnl/Cl 15991/4 L2TP: I ICCN from ISP-LAC-1 tnl 8173,
  cl 6
May 16 21:38:02.325: Tnl/Cl 15991/4 L2TP: Session state change from wait-
  connect to established
May 16 21:38:02.325: ser-test-1@service.comTnl/Cl 15991/4 L2TP: Session
  sequencing
```

SER-LNS-1 now creates a virtual access interface for the L2TP session. Virtual access interface 1 is reused:

```
May 16 21:38:02.325: Vt1 VTEMPLATE: Unable to create and clone vaccess
May 16 21:38:02.325: Vi1 VTEMPLATE: Reuse Vi1, recycle queue size 0
```

Virtual access interface 1 is assigned the MAC address 0090.ab09.c000:

```
May 16 21:38:02.325: Vi1 VTEMPLATE: Hardware address 0090.ab09.c000
```

VPDN acknowledges the creation of the virtual access interface for
ser-test-1@service.com. SER-LNS-1 designates virtual access interface 1
as an asynchronous interface and clones the configuration from virtual
template 1:

```
May 16 21:38:02.325: Vi1 VPDN: Virtual interface created for ser-test-
  1@service.com
May 16 21:38:02.325: Vi1 VPDN: Set to Async interface
May 16 21:38:02.325: Vi1 PPP: Phase is DOWN, Setup
May 16 21:38:02.325: Vi1 VPDN: Clone from Vtemplate 1 filterPPP=0 blocking
May 16 21:38:02.325: Vi1 VTEMPLATE: Has a new cloneblk vtemplate, now it has
  vtemplate
May 16 21:38:02.325: Vi1 VTEMPLATE: ************* CLONE VACCESS1
  ***************
May 16 21:38:02.329: Vi1 VTEMPLATE: Clone from Virtual-Template1
interface Virtual-Access1
default ip address
no ip address
encap ppp
ip unnumbered Serial2/0
peer default ip address pool default
ppp authentication chap
ip unnum fas 0/0
peer default ip address pool default
end
```

The following message indicates that SER-LNS-1 first erroneously attempted to
configure the **ip unnumbered serial 2/0** interface configuration command, which
is not allowed because serial interface 2/0 is also unnumbered. Instead, virtual
access interface is configured with the **ip unnumbered fastethernet 0/0** interface
configuration command:

```
May 16 21:38:02.385: Vi1 VTEMPLATE: Messages from (un)cloning ...
Cannot use an unnumbered interface: Serial2/0
```

Virtual access interface 1 is brought up:

```
3w0d: %LINK-3-UPDOWN: Interface Virtual-Access1, changed state to up
May 16 21:38:02.385: Vi1 PPP: Treating connection as a dedicated line
May 16 21:38:02.385: Vi1 PPP: Phase is ESTABLISHING, Active Open
May 16 21:38:02.385: Vi1 LCP: O CONFREQ [Closed] id 1 len 25
May 16 21:38:02.385: Vi1 LCP:    ACCM 0x000A0000 (0x0206000A0000)
May 16 21:38:02.385: Vi1 LCP:    AuthProto CHAP (0x0305C22305)
May 16 21:38:02.385: Vi1 LCP:    MagicNumber 0xFD07FFBB (0x0506FD07FFBB)
May 16 21:38:02.385: Vi1 LCP:    PFC (0x0702)
May 16 21:38:02.385: Vi1 LCP:    ACFC (0x0802)
May 16 21:38:02.385: Vi1 VPDN: Bind interface direction=2
May 16 21:38:02.389: Vi1 PPP: Treating connection as a dedicated line
```

ISP-LAC-1 has forwarded information from the LCP negotiation with the client,
and SER-LNS-1 then forces this information onto virtual access interface 1:

```
May 16 21:38:02.389: Vi1 LCP: I FORCED CONFREQ len 21
May 16 21:38:02.389: Vi1 LCP:    ACCM 0x000A0000 (0x0206000A0000)
```

```
May 16 21:38:02.389: Vi1 LCP:    AuthProto CHAP (0x0305C22305)
May 16 21:38:02.389: Vi1 LCP:    MagicNumber 0x28C9DAF1 (0x050628C9DAF1)
May 16 21:38:02.389: Vi1 LCP:    PFC (0x0702)
May 16 21:38:02.389: Vi1 LCP:    ACFC (0x0802)
May 16 21:38:02.389: Vi1 VPDN: PPP LCP accepted rcv CONFACK
May 16 21:38:02.389: Vi1 VPDN: PPP LCP accepted sent CONFACK
May 16 21:38:02.389: Vi1 PPP: Phase is AUTHENTICATING, by this end
```

SER-LNS-1 sends a CHAP challenge to ser-test-1@service.com which replies with a CHAP response. SER-LNS-1 then authenticates the CHAP response and sends a CHAP success:

```
May 16 21:38:02.389: Vi1 CHAP: O CHALLENGE id 2 len 30 from "SER-LNS-1"
May 16 21:38:02.389: Vi1 CHAP: I RESPONSE id 1 len 40 from
  "ser-test-1@service.com"
May 16 21:38:02.389: Vi1 CHAP: O SUCCESS id 1 len 4
May 16 21:38:02.389: Vi1 PPP: Phase is UP
May 16 21:38:02.389: Vi1 IPCP: O CONFREQ [Closed] id 1 len 10
May 16 21:38:02.389: Vi1 IPCP:    Address 192.168.48.1 (0x0306C0A83001)
May 16 21:38:02.501: Vi1 IPCP: I CONFREQ [REQsent] id 1 len 40
May 16 21:38:02.501: Vi1 IPCP:    CompressType VJ 15 slots CompressSlotID
  (0x02)
May 16 21:38:02.501: Vi1 IPCP:    Address 0.0.0.0 (0x030600000000)
May 16 21:38:02.501: Vi1 IPCP:    PrimaryDNS 0.0.0.0 (0x810600000000)
May 16 21:38:02.501: Vi1 IPCP:    PrimaryWINS 0.0.0.0 (0x820600000000)
May 16 21:38:02.501: Vi1 IPCP:    SecondaryDNS 0.0.0.0 (0x830600000000)
May 16 21:38:02.501: Vi1 IPCP:    SecondaryWINS 0.0.0.0 (0x840600000000)
May 16 21:38:02.501: Vi1 AAA/AUTHOR/IPCP: Start.  Her address 0.0.0.0,
  we want 0.0.0.0
May 16 21:38:02.501: Vi1 AAA/AUTHOR/IPCP: Done.  Her address 0.0.0.0,
  we want 0.0.0.0
```

SER-LNS-1 assigns the IP address 192.168.49.1 to the client from the default IP address pool:

```
May 16 21:38:02.501: Vi1 IPCP: Pool returned 192.168.49.1
May 16 21:38:02.501: Vi1 IPCP: O CONFREJ [REQsent] id 1 len 10
May 16 21:38:02.501: Vi1 IPCP:    CompressType VJ 15 slots CompressSlotID
  (0x02)
May 16 21:38:02.501: Vi1 CCP: I CONFREQ [Not negotiated] id 1 len 15
May 16 21:38:02.501: Vi1 CCP:    MS-PPC supported bits 0x00000001
  (0x1206000000)
May 16 21:38:02.501: Vi1 CCP:    Stacker history 1 check mode EXTENDED
  (0x11050)
May 16 21:38:02.501: Vi1 LCP: O PROTREJ [Open] id 2 len 21 protocol CCP
May 16 21:38:02.501: Vi1 LCP:    (0x80FD0101000F1206000000111050001)
May 16 21:38:02.501: Vi1 LCP:    (0x04)
May 16 21:38:02.517: Vi1 IPCP: I CONFACK [REQsent] id 1 len 10
May 16 21:38:02.517: Vi1 IPCP:    Address 192.168.48.1 (0x0306C0A83001)
```

The line protocol on virtual access interface 1 is brought up:

```
3w0d: %LINEPROTO-5-UPDOWN: Line protocol on Interface Virtual-Access1,
changed state to up
May 16 21:38:04.385: Vi1 LCP: TIMEout: State Open
May 16 21:38:04.389: Vi1 IPCP: TIMEout: State ACKrcvd
May 16 21:38:04.389: Vi1 IPCP: O CONFREQ [ACKrcvd] id 2 len 10
May 16 21:38:04.389: Vi1 IPCP:    Address 192.168.48.1 (0x0306C0A83001)
May 16 21:38:04.821: Vi1 IPCP: I CONFACK [REQsent] id 2 len 10
May 16 21:38:04.821: Vi1 IPCP:    Address 192.168.48.1 (0x0306C0A83001)
```

The client requests IP addresses for DNS and WINS servers:

```
May 16 21:38:05.477: Vi1 IPCP: I CONFREQ [ACKrcvd] id 2 len 34
May 16 21:38:05.477: Vi1 IPCP:    Address 0.0.0.0 (0x030600000000)
May 16 21:38:05.477: Vi1 IPCP:    PrimaryDNS 0.0.0.0 (0x810600000000)
May 16 21:38:05.477: Vi1 IPCP:    PrimaryWINS 0.0.0.0 (0x820600000000)
May 16 21:38:05.477: Vi1 IPCP:    SecondaryDNS 0.0.0.0 (0x830600000000)
May 16 21:38:05.477: Vi1 IPCP:    SecondaryWINS 0.0.0.0 (0x840600000000)
May 16 21:38:05.477: Vi1 AAA/AUTHOR/IPCP: Start.  Her address 0.0.0.0,
we want 192.168.49.1
May 16 21:38:05.477: Vi1 AAA/AUTHOR/IPCP: Done.  Her address 0.0.0.0,
we want 192.168.49.1
```

SER-LNS-1 replies with the IP addresses of the DNS and WINS servers:

```
May 16 21:38:05.477: Vi1 IPCP: O CONFNAK [ACKrcvd] id 2 len 34
May 16 21:38:05.477: Vi1 IPCP:    Address 192.168.49.1 (0x0306C0A83101)
May 16 21:38:05.477: Vi1 IPCP:    PrimaryDNS 172.23.1.10 (0x8106AC17010A)
May 16 21:38:05.477: Vi1 IPCP:    PrimaryWINS 172.23.1.11 (0x8206AC17010B)
May 16 21:38:05.477: Vi1 IPCP:    SecondaryDNS 172.23.2.10 (0x8306AC17020A)
May 16 21:38:05.481: Vi1 IPCP:    SecondaryWINS 172.23.2.11 (0x8406AC17020B)
May 16 21:38:05.589: Vi1 IPCP: I CONFREQ [ACKrcvd] id 3 len 34
May 16 21:38:05.589: Vi1 IPCP:    Address 192.168.49.1 (0x0306C0A83101)
May 16 21:38:05.589: Vi1 IPCP:    PrimaryDNS 172.23.1.10 (0x8106AC17010A)
May 16 21:38:05.589: Vi1 IPCP:    PrimaryWINS 172.23.1.11 (0x8206AC17010B)
May 16 21:38:05.589: Vi1 IPCP:    SecondaryDNS 172.23.2.10 (0x8306AC17020A)
May 16 21:38:05.589: Vi1 IPCP:    SecondaryWINS 172.23.2.11 (0x8406AC17020B)
May 16 21:38:05.589: Vi1 AAA/AUTHOR/IPCP: Start.  Her address 192.168.49.1,
we want 192.168.49.1
May 16 21:38:05.589: Vi1 AAA/AUTHOR/IPCP: Reject 192.168.49.1, using
  192.168.49.1
May 16 21:38:05.589: Vi1 AAA/AUTHOR/IPCP: Done.  Her address 192.168.49.1,
we want 192.168.49.1
```

SER-LNS-1 receives positive acknowledgment that the client received the IP addresses for the DNS and WINS servers:

```
May 16 21:38:05.593: Vi1 IPCP: O CONFACK [ACKrcvd] id 3 len 34
May 16 21:38:05.593: Vi1 IPCP:    Address 192.168.49.1 (0x0306C0A83101)
```

```
May 16 21:38:05.593: Vi1 IPCP:    PrimaryDNS 172.23.1.10 (0x8106AC17010A)
May 16 21:38:05.593: Vi1 IPCP:    PrimaryWINS 172.23.1.11 (0x8206AC17010B)
May 16 21:38:05.593: Vi1 IPCP:    SecondaryDNS 172.23.2.10 (0x8306AC17020A)
May 16 21:38:05.593: Vi1 IPCP:    SecondaryWINS 172.23.2.11 (0x8406AC17020B)
May 16 21:38:05.593: Vi1 IPCP: State is Open
```

SER-LNS-1 installs the route to 192.168.49.1, the IP address of the client:

```
May 16 21:38:05.593: Vi1 IPCP: Install route to 192.168.49.1
SER-LNS-1#
```

IPSec over L2TP Solution Debug Output

The following sections show debug output from successful IPSec negotiation between the peer and LNS:

- Peer Debug Output from Successful IPSec Negotiation
- LNS Debug Output From Successful IPSec Negotiation

For more information on this solution, see Chapter 4, "Access VPDN Dial-In Using IPSec over L2TP Solution."

Peer Debug Output from Successful IPSec Negotiation

To view the following debug output, enable the following commands on the peer and dial in to the peer:

```
debug crypto engine
debug crypto ipsec
debug crypto isakmp
```

The following is debug output from successful IPSec negotiation on the peer isdn4:

```
isdn4#
```

IPSec requests SAs between 192.232.1.25 and 192.250.3.2. It prefers to use the transform set ah-md5-hmac, but it also will consider esp-des with esp-md5-hmac:

```
*Mar  1 16:22:53 PDT: IPSEC(sa_request): ,
  (key eng. msg.) src= 192.232.1.25, dest= 192.250.3.2,
    src_proxy= 192.232.1.24/255.255.255.248/0/0 (type=4),
    dest_proxy= 192.250.3.0/255.255.255.248/0/0 (type=4),
    protocol= AH, transform= ah-md5-hmac ,
    lifedur= 3600s and 4608000kb,
    spi= 0x87E2ABDD(2279779293), conn_id= 0, keysize= 0, flags= 0x4004
*Mar  1 16:22:53 PDT: IPSEC(sa_request): ,
  (key eng. msg.) src= 192.232.1.25, dest= 192.250.3.2,
    src_proxy= 192.232.1.24/255.255.255.248/0/0 (type=4),
    dest_proxy= 192.250.3.0/255.255.255.248/0/0 (type=4),
```

```
    protocol= ESP, transform= esp-des esp-md5-hmac ,
    lifedur= 3600s and 4608000kb,
    spi= 0x9400618(155190808), conn_id= 0, keysize= 0, flags= 0x4004
*Mar  1 16:22:53 PDT: ISAKMP: received ke message (1/2)
*Mar  1 16:22:53 PDT: ISAKMP: local port 500, remote port 500
*Mar  1 16:22:53 PDT: ISAKMP (0:1): beginning Main Mode exchange
*Mar  1 16:22:53 PDT: ISAKMP (0:1): sending packet to 192.250.3.2 (I)
  MM_NO_STATE
.
```

The following lines show that BRI interface 0:1 has been brought up, which indicates that L2TP session and tunnel negotiations were successfully completed, and the peer is now connected to the LNS:

```
*Mar  1 16:22:56 PDT: %LINK-3-UPDOWN: Interface BRI0:1, changed state to up.
*Mar  1 16:22:56 PDT: %DIALER-6-BIND: Interface BR0:1 bound to profile
  Di6...
Success rate is 0 percent (0/5)
isdn4#
*Mar  1 16:23:02 PDT: %ISDN-6-CONNECT: Interface BRI0:1 is now connected to
  50127 unknown
*Mar  1 16:23:02 PDT: %LINEPROTO-5-UPDOWN: Line protocol on Interface
  BRI0:1, changed state to up
*Mar  1 16:23:02 PDT: %CRYPTO-4-RECVD_PKT_INV_SPI: decaps: rec'd IPSEC
  packet has invalid spi for destaddr=192.232.1.25, prot=51,
  spi=0x1C080522(470287650)
*Mar  1 16:23:03 PDT: ISAKMP (0:1): retransmitting phase 1 MM_NO_STATE...
*Mar  1 16:23:03 PDT: ISAKMP (0:1): incrementing error counter on sa:
  retransmit phase 1
*Mar  1 16:23:03 PDT: ISAKMP (0:1): retransmitting phase 1 MM_NO_STATE
*Mar  1 16:23:03 PDT: ISAKMP (0:1): sending packet to 192.250.3.2 (I)
  MM_NO_STATE
*Mar  1 16:23:03 PDT: ISAKMP (0:1): received packet from 192.250.3.2 (I)
  MM_NO_STATE
*Mar  1 16:23:03 PDT: ISAKMP (0:1): processing SA payload. message ID = 0
```

The peer determines that the LNS wants to perform pre-shared key authentication:

```
*Mar  1 16:23:03 PDT: ISAKMP (0:1): found peer pre-shared key matching
  192.250.3.2
```

IKE receives the IKE policy from the LNS and determines that it is acceptable:

```
*Mar  1 16:23:03 PDT: ISAKMP (0:1): Checking ISAKMP transform 1
  against priority 1 policy
*Mar  1 16:23:03 PDT: ISAKMP:      encryption DES-CBC
*Mar  1 16:23:03 PDT: ISAKMP:      hash SHA
*Mar  1 16:23:03 PDT: ISAKMP:      default group 1
```

```
*Mar  1 16:23:03 PDT: ISAKMP:      auth pre-share
*Mar  1 16:23:03 PDT: ISAKMP (0:1): atts are acceptable. Next payload is 0
*Mar  1 16:23:03 PDT: CryptoEngine0: generate alg parameter
*Mar  1 16:23:03 PDT: CRYPTO_ENGINE: Dh phase 1 status: 0
*Mar  1 16:23:03 PDT: CRYPTO_ENGINE: Dh phase 1 status: 0
```

The IKE SA is used to authenticate the LNS:

```
*Mar  1 16:23:03 PDT: ISAKMP (0:1): SA is doing pre-shared key authentication
  using id type ID_IPV4_ADDR
*Mar  1 16:23:03 PDT: ISAKMP (0:1): sending packet to 192.250.3.2 (I)
  MM_SA_SETUP
*Mar  1 16:23:03 PDT: ISAKMP (0:1): received packet from 192.250.3.2 (I)
  MM_SA_SETUP
*Mar  1 16:23:03 PDT: ISAKMP (0:1): processing KE payload. message ID = 0
*Mar  1 16:23:03 PDT: CryptoEngine0: generate alg parameter
*Mar  1 16:23:03 PDT: ISAKMP (0:1): processing NONCE payload. message ID = 0
*Mar  1 16:23:03 PDT: ISAKMP (0:1): found peer pre-shared key matching
  192.250.3.2
*Mar  1 16:23:03 PDT: CryptoEngine0: create ISAKMP SKEYID for conn id 1
*Mar  1 16:23:03 PDT: ISAKMP (0:1): SKEYID state generated
*Mar  1 16:23:03 PDT: ISAKMP (0:1): processing vendor id payload
*Mar  1 16:23:03 PDT: ISAKMP (0:1): speaking to another IOS box!
*Mar  1 16:23:03 PDT: ISAKMP (1): ID payload
        next-payload : 8
        type         : 1
        protocol     : 17
        port         : 500
        length       : 8
*Mar  1 16:23:03 PDT: ISAKMP (1): Total payload length: 12
*Mar  1 16:23:03 PDT: CryptoEngine0: generate hmac context for conn id 1
*Mar  1 16:23:03 PDT: ISAKMP (0:1): sending packet to 192.250.3.2 (I)
  MM_KEY_EXCH
*Mar  1 16:23:03 PDT: ISAKMP (0:1): received packet from 192.250.3.2 (I)
  MM_KEY_EXCH
*Mar  1 16:23:03 PDT: ISAKMP (0:1): processing ID payload. message ID = 0
*Mar  1 16:23:03 PDT: ISAKMP (0:1): processing HASH payload. message ID = 0
*Mar  1 16:23:03 PDT: CryptoEngine0: generate hmac context for conn id 1
*Mar  1 16:23:03 PDT: ISAKMP (0:1): SA has been authenticated with
  192.250.3.2
*Mar  1 16:23:03 PDT: ISAKMP (0:1): beginning Quick Mode exchange,
  M-ID of 211899060
*Mar  1 16:23:03 PDT: CryptoEngine0: generate hmac context for conn id 1
*Mar  1 16:23:03 PDT: ISAKMP (0:1): sending packet to 192.250.3.2 (I) QM_IDLE

*Mar  1 16:23:03 PDT: CryptoEngine0: clear dh number for conn id 1
*Mar  1 16:23:03 PDT: ISAKMP (0:1): received packet from 192.250.3.2 (I)
  QM_IDLE

*Mar  1 16:23:03 PDT: CryptoEngine0: generate hmac context for conn id 1
```

```
*Mar  1 16:23:03 PDT: ISAKMP (0:1): processing HASH payload. message
 ID = 211899060
*Mar  1 16:23:03 PDT: ISAKMP (0:1): processing SA payload. message ID =
  211899060
```

IKE negotiates to set up the IPSec SA by searching for a matching transform set.
It determines that both the ah-md5-hmac transform set and the esp-des with
esp-md5-hmac transform set are acceptable:

```
*Mar  1 16:23:03 PDT: ISAKMP (0:1): Checking IPSec proposal 1
*Mar  1 16:23:03 PDT: ISAKMP: transform 1, AH_MD5
*Mar  1 16:23:03 PDT: ISAKMP:    attributes in transform:
*Mar  1 16:23:03 PDT: ISAKMP:      encaps is 1
*Mar  1 16:23:03 PDT: ISAKMP:      SA life type in seconds
*Mar  1 16:23:03 PDT: ISAKMP:      SA life duration (basic) of 3600
*Mar  1 16:23:03 PDT: ISAKMP:      SA life type in kilobytes
*Mar  1 16:23:03 PDT: ISAKMP:      SA life duration (VPI) of  0x0 0x46 0x50 0x0
*Mar  1 16:23:03 PDT: ISAKMP:      authenticator is HMAC-MD5
*Mar  1 16:23:03 PDT: validate proposal 0
*Mar  1 16:23:03 PDT: ISAKMP (0:1): atts are acceptable.
*Mar  1 16:23:03 PDT: ISAKMP (0:1): Checking IPSec proposal 1
*Mar  1 16:23:03 PDT: ISAKMP: transform 1, ESP_DES
*Mar  1 16:23:03 PDT: ISAKMP:    attributes in transform:
*Mar  1 16:23:03 PDT: ISAKMP:      encaps is 1
*Mar  1 16:23:03 PDT: ISAKMP:      SA life type in seconds
*Mar  1 16:23:03 PDT: ISAKMP:      SA life duration (basic) of 3600
*Mar  1 16:23:03 PDT: ISAKMP:      SA life type in kilobytes
*Mar  1 16:23:03 PDT: ISAKMP:      SA life duration (VPI) of  0x0 0x46 0x50 0x0
*Mar  1 16:23:03 PDT: ISAKMP:      authenticator is HMAC-MD5
*Mar  1 16:23:03 PDT: validate proposal 0
*Mar  1 16:23:03 PDT: ISAKMP (0:1): atts are acceptable.
```

IPSec validates that the SAs negotiated by IKE are acceptable:

```
*Mar  1 16:23:03 PDT: IPSEC(validate_proposal_request): proposal part #1,
  (key eng. msg.) dest= 192.250.3.2, src= 192.232.1.25,
    dest_proxy= 192.250.3.0/255.255.255.248/0/0 (type=4),
    src_proxy= 192.232.1.24/255.255.255.248/0/0 (type=4),
    protocol= AH, transform= ah-md5-hmac ,
    lifedur= 0s and 0kb,
    spi= 0x0(0), conn_id= 0, keysize= 0, flags= 0x4
*Mar  1 16:23:03 PDT: IPSEC(validate_proposal_request): proposal part #2,
  (key eng. msg.) dest= 192.250.3.2, src= 192.232.1.25,
    dest_proxy= 192.250.3.0/255.255.255.248/0/0 (type=4),
    src_proxy= 192.232.1.24/255.255.255.248/0/0 (type=4),
    protocol= ESP, transform= esp-des esp-md5-hmac ,
    lifedur= 0s and 0kb,
    spi= 0x0(0), conn_id= 0, keysize= 0, flags= 0x4
*Mar  1 16:23:03 PDT: validate proposal request 0
```

```
*Mar   1 16:23:04 PDT: ISAKMP (0:1): processing NONCE payload. message ID
  = 211899060
*Mar   1 16:23:04 PDT: ISAKMP (0:1): processing ID payload. message ID =
  211899060
*Mar   1 16:23:04 PDT: ISAKMP (0:1): processing ID payload. message ID =
  211899060
*Mar   1 16:23:04 PDT: CryptoEngine0: generate hmac context for conn id 1
*Mar   1 16:23:04 PDT: ipsec allocate flow 0
*Mar   1 16:23:04 PDT: ipsec allocate flow 0
```

Now that a matching transform set has been established, IKE creates the
IPSec SAs:

```
*Mar   1 16:23:04 PDT: ISAKMP (0:1): Creating IPSec SAs
*Mar   1 16:23:04 PDT:            inbound SA from 192.250.3.2 to 192.232.1.25
        (proxy 192.250.3.0 to 192.232.1.24)
*Mar   1 16:23:04 PDT:            has spi 0x87E2ABDD and conn_id 2000 and flags 4
*Mar   1 16:23:04 PDT:            lifetime of 3600 seconds
*Mar   1 16:23:04 PDT:            lifetime of 4608000 kilobytes
*Mar   1 16:23:04 PDT:            outbound SA from 192.232.1.25   to 192.250.3.2
      (proxy 192.232.1.24    to 192.250.3.0    )
*Mar   1 16:23:04 PDT:            has spi -213910971 and conn_id 2001 and flags 4
*Mar   1 16:23:04 PDT:            lifetime of 3600 seconds
*Mar   1 16:23:04 PDT:            lifetime of 4608000 kilobytes
*Mar   1 16:23:04 PDT: ISAKMP (0:1): Creating IPSec SAs
*Mar   1 16:23:04 PDT:            inbound SA from 192.250.3.2 to 192.232.1.25
        (proxy 192.250.3.0 to 192.232.1.24)
*Mar   1 16:23:04 PDT:            has spi 0x9400618 and conn_id 2002 and flags 4
*Mar   1 16:23:04 PDT:            lifetime of 3600 seconds
*Mar   1 16:23:04 PDT:            lifetime of 4608000 kilobytes
*Mar   1 16:23:04 PDT:            outbound SA from 192.232.1.25   to 192.250.3.2
      (proxy 192.232.1.24    to 192.250.3.0    )
*Mar   1 16:23:04 PDT:            has spi -1518012306 and conn_id 2003 and flags 4
*Mar   1 16:23:04 PDT:            lifetime of 3600 seconds
*Mar   1 16:23:04 PDT:            lifetime of 4608000 kilobytes
*Mar   1 16:23:04 PDT: ISAKMP (0:1): sending packet to 192.250.3.2 (I) QM_IDLE

*Mar   1 16:23:04 PDT: ISAKMP (0:1): deleting node 211899060 error FALSE
  reason " "
```

Now that the proposal has been accepted, and IKE has finished the negotiations
and generated the keying material, IKE notifies IPSec of the new SA:

```
*Mar   1 16:23:04 PDT: IPSEC(key_engine): got a queue event...
```

The following output pertains to the inbound SA. The connection ID value in the
second shaded line references an entry in the crypto engine connection table:

```
*Mar   1 16:23:04 PDT: IPSEC(initialize_sas): ,
  (key eng. msg.) dest= 192.232.1.25, src= 192.250.3.2,
    dest_proxy= 192.232.1.24/255.255.255.248/0/0 (type=4),
```

```
    src_proxy= 192.250.3.0/255.255.255.248/0/0 (type=4),
    protocol= AH, transform= ah-md5-hmac ,
    lifedur= 3600s and 4608000kb,
    spi= 0x87E2ABDD(2279779293), conn_id= 2000, keysize= 0, flags= 0x4
```

The following output pertains to the outbound SA:

```
*Mar  1 16:23:04 PDT: IPSEC(initialize_sas): ,
   (key eng. msg.) src= 192.232.1.25, dest= 192.250.3.2,
    src_proxy= 192.232.1.24/255.255.255.248/0/0 (type=4),
    dest_proxy= 192.250.3.0/255.255.255.248/0/0 (type=4),
    protocol= AH, transform= ah-md5-hmac ,
    lifedur= 3600s and 4608000kb,
    spi= 0xF33FFA45(4081056325), conn_id= 2001, keysize= 0, flags= 0x4
*Mar  1 16:23:04 PDT: IPSEC(initialize_sas): ,
   (key eng. msg.) dest= 192.232.1.25, src= 192.250.3.2,
    dest_proxy= 192.232.1.24/255.255.255.248/0/0 (type=4),
    src_proxy= 192.250.3.0/255.255.255.248/0/0 (type=4),
    protocol= ESP, transform= esp-des esp-md5-hmac ,
    lifedur= 3600s and 4608000kb,
    spi= 0x9400618(155190808), conn_id= 2002, keysize= 0, flags= 0x4
*Mar  1 16:23:04 PDT: IPSEC(initialize_sas): ,
   (key eng. msg.) src= 192.232.1.25, dest= 192.250.3.2,
    src_proxy= 192.232.1.24/255.255.255.248/0/0 (type=4),
    dest_proxy= 192.250.3.0/255.255.255.248/0/0 (type=4),
    protocol= ESP, transform= esp-des esp-md5-hmac ,
    lifedur= 3600s and 4608000kb,
    spi= 0xA584F86E(2776954990), conn_id= 2003, keysize= 0, flags= 0x4
```

IPSec now installs the SA information into its SA database:

```
*Mar  1 16:23:04 PDT: IPSEC(create_sa): sa created,
   (sa) sa_dest= 192.232.1.25, sa_prot= 51,
    sa_spi= 0x87E2ABDD(2279779293),
    sa_trans= ah-md5-hmac , sa_conn_id= 2000
*Mar  1 16:23:04 PDT: IPSEC(create_sa): sa created,
   (sa) sa_dest= 192.250.3.2, sa_prot= 51,
    sa_spi= 0xF33FFA45(4081056325),
    sa_trans= ah-md5-hmac , sa_conn_id= 2001
*Mar  1 16:23:04 PDT: IPSEC(create_sa): sa created,
   (sa) sa_dest= 192.232.1.25, sa_prot= 50,
    sa_spi= 0x9400618(155190808),
    sa_trans= esp-des esp-md5-hmac , sa_conn_id= 2002
*Mar  1 16:23:04 PDT: IPSEC(create_sa): sa created,
   (sa) sa_dest= 192.250.3.2, sa_prot= 50,
    sa_spi= 0xA584F86E(2776954990),
    sa_trans= esp-des esp-md5-hmac , sa_conn_id= 2003
isdn4#
```

LNS Debug Output from Successful IPSec Negotiation

To view the following debug output, enable the following commands on the LNS and dial in to the peer:

```
debug crypto engine
debug crypto ipsec
debug crypto isakmp
debug crypto key-exchange
```

The following is debug output from successful IPSec negotiation on the LNS, ISP3AC5:

```
ISP3AC5#
```

The first two lines show that the virtual access interface has been created and brought online, which indicates that L2TP session and tunnel negotiations were successfully completed:

```
Oct  3 13:05:41 PST: %LINK-3-UPDOWN: Interface Virtual-Access152,
  changed state to up
Oct  3 13:05:47 PST: %LINEPROTO-5-UPDOWN: Line protocol on Interface
  Virtual-Access152, changed state to up
Oct  3 13:05:48 PST: ISAKMP (0:0): received packet from 192.232.1.25 (N) NEW
  SA
Oct  3 13:05:48 PST: ISAKMP: local port 500, remote port 500
Oct  3 13:05:48 PST: ISAKMP (0:1365): processing SA payload. message ID = 0
```

The LNS determines that the peer wants to perform pre-shared key authentication:

```
Oct  3 13:05:48 PST: ISAKMP (0:1365): found peer pre-shared key matching
  192.232.1.25
```

IKE first negotiates its own SAs by checking for a matching IKE policy:

```
Oct  3 13:05:48 PST: ISAKMP (0:1365): Checking ISAKMP transform 1 against
  priority 1 policy
Oct  3 13:05:48 PST: ISAKMP:      encryption DES-CBC
Oct  3 13:05:48 PST: ISAKMP:      hash SHA
Oct  3 13:05:48 PST: ISAKMP:      default group 1
Oct  3 13:05:48 PST: ISAKMP:      auth pre-share
Oct  3 13:05:48 PST: ISAKMP (0:1365): atts are acceptable. Next payload is 0
Oct  3 13:05:48 PST: CryptoEngine0: generate alg parameter
Oct  3 13:05:48 PST: CRYPTO_ENGINE: Dh phase 1 status: 0
Oct  3 13:05:48 PST: CRYPTO_ENGINE: Dh phase 1 status: 0
```

IKE has found a matching policy. IKE now uses the SA to authenticate the peer:

```
Oct  3 13:05:48 PST: ISAKMP (0:1365): SA is doing pre-shared key
  authentication using id type ID_IPV4_ADDR
Oct  3 13:05:48 PST: ISAKMP (0:1365): sending packet to 192.232.1.25 (R)
  MM_SA_SETUP
Oct  3 13:05:48 PST: ISAKMP (0:1365): received packet from 192.232.1.25 (R)
  MM_SA_SETUP
```

```
Oct  3 13:05:48 PST: ISAKMP (0:1365): processing KE payload. message ID = 0
Oct  3 13:05:48 PST: CryptoEngine0: generate alg parameter
Oct  3 13:05:48 PST: ISAKMP (0:1365): processing NONCE payload. message ID
  = 0
Oct  3 13:05:48 PST: ISAKMP (0:1365): found peer pre-shared key matching
  192.232.1.25
Oct  3 13:05:48 PST: CryptoEngine0: create ISAKMP SKEYID for conn id 1365
Oct  3 13:05:48 PST: ISAKMP (0:1365): SKEYID state generated
Oct  3 13:05:48 PST: ISAKMP (0:1365): processing vendor id payload
Oct  3 13:05:48 PST: ISAKMP (0:1365): speaking to another IOS box!
Oct  3 13:05:48 PST: ISAKMP (0:1365): sending packet to 192.232.1.25 (R)
  MM_KEY_EXCH
Oct  3 13:05:48 PST: ISAKMP (0:1365): received packet from 192.232.1.25 (R)
  MM_KEY_EXCH
Oct  3 13:05:48 PST: ISAKMP (0:1365): processing ID payload. message ID = 0
Oct  3 13:05:48 PST: ISAKMP (0:1365): processing HASH payload. message ID = 0
Oct  3 13:05:48 PST: CryptoEngine0: generate hmac context for conn id 1365
Oct  3 13:05:48 PST: ISAKMP (0:1365): SA has been authenticated with
  192.232.1.25
Oct  3 13:05:48 PST: ISAKMP (1365): ID payload
                     next-payload : 8
                     type         : 1
                     protocol     : 17
                     port         : 500
                     length       : 8
Oct  3 13:05:48 PST: ISAKMP (1365): Total payload length: 12
Oct  3 13:05:48 PST: CryptoEngine0: generate hmac context for conn id 1365
Oct  3 13:05:48 PST: CryptoEngine0: clear dh number for conn id 1
Oct  3 13:05:48 PST: ISAKMP (0:1365): sending packet to 192.232.1.25 (R)
  QM_IDLE

Oct  3 13:05:48 PST: ISAKMP (0:1365): received packet from 192.232.1.25 (R)
  QM_IDLE
Oct  3 13:05:48 PST: CryptoEngine0: generate hmac context for conn id 1365
Oct  3 13:05:48 PST: ISAKMP (0:1365): processing HASH payload. message
  ID = 211899060
Oct  3 13:05:48 PST: ISAKMP (0:1365): processing SA payload. message
  ID = 211899060
```

IKE negotiates to set up the IPSec SA by searching for a matching transform set:

```
Oct  3 13:05:48 PST: ISAKMP (0:1365): Checking IPSec proposal 1
Oct  3 13:05:48 PST: ISAKMP: transform 1, AH_MD5
Oct  3 13:05:48 PST: ISAKMP:    attributes in transform:
Oct  3 13:05:48 PST: ISAKMP:      encaps is 1
Oct  3 13:05:48 PST: ISAKMP:      SA life type in seconds
Oct  3 13:05:48 PST: ISAKMP:      SA life duration (basic) of 3600
Oct  3 13:05:48 PST: ISAKMP:      SA life type in kilobytes
Oct  3 13:05:48 PST: ISAKMP:      SA life duration (VPI) of  0x0 0x46 0x50 0x0
Oct  3 13:05:48 PST: ISAKMP:      authenticator is HMAC-MD5
Oct  3 13:05:48 PST: validate proposal 0
```

```
Oct  3 13:05:48 PST: ISAKMP (0:1365): atts are acceptable.
Oct  3 13:05:48 PST: ISAKMP (0:1365): Checking IPSec proposal 1
Oct  3 13:05:48 PST: ISAKMP: transform 1, ESP_DES
Oct  3 13:05:48 PST: ISAKMP:    attributes in transform:
Oct  3 13:05:48 PST: ISAKMP:       encaps is 1
Oct  3 13:05:48 PST: ISAKMP:       SA life type in seconds
Oct  3 13:05:48 PST: ISAKMP:       SA life duration (basic) of 3600
Oct  3 13:05:48 PST: ISAKMP:       SA life type in kilobytes
Oct  3 13:05:48 PST: ISAKMP:       SA life duration (VPI) of  0x0 0x46 0x50 0x0
Oct  3 13:05:48 PST: ISAKMP:       authenticator is HMAC-MD5
Oct  3 13:05:48 PST: validate proposal 0
Oct  3 13:05:48 PST: ISAKMP (0:1365): atts are acceptable.
```

IPSec validates that the SAs negotiated by IKE are acceptable:

```
Oct  3 13:05:48 PST: IPSEC(validate_proposal_request): proposal part #1,
   (key eng. msg.) dest= 192.250.3.2, src= 192.232.1.25,
     dest_proxy= 192.250.3.0/255.255.255.248/0/0 (type=4),
     src_proxy= 192.232.1.24/255.255.255.248/0/0 (type=4),
     protocol= AH, transform= ah-md5-hmac ,
     lifedur= 0s and 0kb,
     spi= 0x0(0), conn_id= 0, keysize= 0, flags= 0x4
Oct  3 13:05:48 PST: IPSEC(validate_proposal_request): proposal part #2,
   (key eng. msg.) dest= 192.250.3.2, src= 192.232.1.25,
     dest_proxy= 192.250.3.0/255.255.255.248/0/0 (type=4),
     src_proxy= 192.232.1.24/255.255.255.248/0/0 (type=4),
     protocol= ESP, transform= esp-des esp-md5-hmac ,
     lifedur= 0s and 0kb,
     spi= 0x0(0), conn_id= 0, keysize= 0, flags= 0x4
Oct  3 13:05:48 PST: validate proposal request 0
Oct  3 13:05:48 PST: ISAKMP (0:1365): processing NONCE payload.
 message ID = 211899060
Oct  3 13:05:48 PST: ISAKMP (0:1365): processing ID payload.
 message ID = 211899060
Oct  3 13:05:48 PST: ISAKMP (1365): ID_IPV4_ADDR_SUBNET src 192.232.1.24/
   255.255.
255.248 prot 0 port 0
Oct  3 13:05:48 PST: ISAKMP (0:1365): processing ID payload.
 message ID = 211899060
Oct  3 13:05:48 PST: ISAKMP (1365): ID_IPV4_ADDR_SUBNET dst 192.250.3.0/
   255.255.2
55.248 prot 0 port 0
Oct  3 13:05:48 PST: ISAKMP (0:1365): asking for 2 spis from ipsec
Oct  3 13:05:48 PST: IPSEC(key_engine): got a queue event...
Oct  3 13:05:48 PST: IPSEC(spi_response): getting spi 4081056325 for SA
        from 192.232.1.25    to 192.250.3.2      for prot 2
Oct  3 13:05:48 PST: IPSEC(spi_response): getting spi 2776954990 for SA
        from 192.232.1.25    to 192.250.3.2      for prot 3
Oct  3 13:05:48 PST: ISAKMP: received ke message (2/2)
Oct  3 13:05:49 PST: CryptoEngine0: generate hmac context for conn id 1365
```

```
Oct  3 13:05:49 PST: ISAKMP (0:1365): sending packet to 192.232.1.25 (R)
   QM_IDLE

Oct  3 13:05:49 PST: ISAKMP (0:1365): received packet from 192.232.1.25 (R)
   QM_IDLE
Oct  3 13:05:49 PST: CryptoEngine0: generate hmac context for conn id 1365
Oct  3 13:05:49 PST: ipsec allocate flow 0
Oct  3 13:05:49 PST: ipsec allocate flow 0
```

The peer and LNS have agreed upon a transform set. IKE now creates an SA for each direction:

```
Oct  3 13:05:49 PST: ISAKMP (0:1365): Creating IPSec SAs
Oct  3 13:05:49 PST:           inbound SA from 192.232.1.25 to 192.250.3.2
         (proxy 192.232.1.24 to 192.250.3.0)
Oct  3 13:05:49 PST:           has spi 0xF33FFA45 and conn_id 2218 and flags 4
Oct  3 13:05:49 PST:           lifetime of 3600 seconds
Oct  3 13:05:49 PST:           lifetime of 4608000 kilobytes
Oct  3 13:05:49 PST:           outbound SA from 192.250.3.2    to 192.232.1.25
(proxy 192.250.3.0    to 192.232.1.24    )
Oct  3 13:05:49 PST:           has spi -2015188003 and conn_id 2219 and flags 4
Oct  3 13:05:49 PST:           lifetime of 3600 seconds
Oct  3 13:05:49 PST:           lifetime of 4608000 kilobytes
Oct  3 13:05:49 PST: ISAKMP (0:1365): Creating IPSec SAs
Oct  3 13:05:49 PST:           inbound SA from 192.232.1.25 to 192.250.3.2
         (proxy 192.232.1.24 to 192.250.3.0)
Oct  3 13:05:49 PST:           has spi 0xA584F86E and conn_id 2220 and flags 4
Oct  3 13:05:49 PST:           lifetime of 3600 seconds
Oct  3 13:05:49 PST:           lifetime of 4608000 kilobytes
Oct  3 13:05:49 PST:           outbound SA from 192.250.3.2    to 192.232.1.25
(proxy 192.250.3.0    to 192.232.1.24    )
Oct  3 13:05:49 PST:           has spi 155190808 and conn_id 2221 and flags 4
Oct  3 13:05:49 PST:           lifetime of 3600 seconds
Oct  3 13:05:49 PST:           lifetime of 4608000 kilobytes
Oct  3 13:05:49 PST: ISAKMP (0:1365): deleting node 211899060 error FALSE
   reason "quick mode done (await()"
```

Now that the proposal has been accepted, and IKE has finished the negotiations and generated the keying material, IKE notifies IPSec of the new SA:

```
Oct  3 13:05:49 PST: IPSEC(key_engine): got a queue event...
```

The following output pertains to the inbound SA. The connection_ID value in the second shaded line references an entry in the crypto engine connection table:

```
Oct  3 13:05:49 PST: IPSEC(initialize_sas): ,
   (key eng. msg.) dest= 192.250.3.2, src= 192.232.1.25,
     dest_proxy= 192.250.3.0/255.255.255.248/0/0 (type=4),
     src_proxy= 192.232.1.24/255.255.255.248/0/0 (type=4),
```

```
protocol= AH, transform= ah-md5-hmac ,
lifedur= 3600s and 4608000kb,
  spi= 0xF33FFA45(4081056325), conn_id= 2218, keysize= 0, flags= 0x4
```

The following output pertains to the inbound SA. The connection ID value in the second shaded line references an entry in the crypto engine connection table:

```
Oct  3 13:05:49 PST: IPSEC(initialize_sas): ,
  (key eng. msg.) src= 192.250.3.2, dest= 192.232.1.25,
  src_proxy= 192.250.3.0/255.255.255.248/0/0 (type=4),
  dest_proxy= 192.232.1.24/255.255.255.248/0/0 (type=4),
  protocol= AH, transform= ah-md5-hmac ,
  lifedur= 3600s and 4608000kb,
    spi= 0x87E2ABDD(2279779293), conn_id= 2219, keysize= 0, flags= 0x4
Oct  3 13:05:49 PST: IPSEC(initialize_sas): ,
  (key eng. msg.) dest= 192.250.3.2, src= 192.232.1.25,
  dest_proxy= 192.250.3.0/255.255.255.248/0/0 (type=4),
  src_proxy= 192.232.1.24/255.255.255.248/0/0 (type=4),
  protocol= ESP, transform= esp-des esp-md5-hmac ,
  lifedur= 3600s and 4608000kb,
  spi= 0xA584F86E(2776954990), conn_id= 2220, keysize= 0, flags= 0x4
Oct  3 13:05:49 PST: IPSEC(initialize_sas): ,
  (key eng. msg.) src= 192.250.3.2, dest= 192.232.1.25,
  src_proxy= 192.250.3.0/255.255.255.248/0/0 (type=4),
  dest_proxy= 192.232.1.24/255.255.255.248/0/0 (type=4),
  protocol= ESP, transform= esp-des esp-md5-hmac ,
  lifedur= 3600s and 4608000kb,
  spi= 0x9400618(155190808), conn_id= 2221, keysize= 0, flags= 0x4
```

IPSec now installs the SA information into its SA database:

```
Oct  3 13:05:49 PST: IPSEC(create_sa): sa created,
  (sa) sa_dest= 192.250.3.2, sa_prot= 51,
  sa_spi= 0xF33FFA45(4081056325),
    sa_trans= ah-md5-hmac , sa_conn_id= 2218
Oct  3 13:05:49 PST: IPSEC(create_sa): sa created,
  (sa) sa_dest= 192.232.1.25, sa_prot= 51,
  sa_spi= 0x87E2ABDD(2279779293),
    sa_trans= ah-md5-hmac , sa_conn_id= 2219
Oct  3 13:05:49 PST: IPSEC(create_sa): sa created,
  (sa) sa_dest= 192.250.3.2, sa_prot= 50,
  sa_spi= 0xA584F86E(2776954990),
    sa_trans= esp-des esp-md5-hmac , sa_conn_id= 2220
Oct  3 13:05:49 PST: IPSEC(create_sa): sa created,
  (sa) sa_dest= 192.232.1.25, sa_prot= 50,
  sa_spi= 0x9400618(155190808),
    sa_trans= esp-des esp-md5-hmac , sa_conn_id= 2221
Oct  3 13:05:49 PST: IPSEC(add_sa): peer asks for new SAs -- expire current
  in 12 0 sec.,
```

```
(sa) sa_dest= 192.232.1.25, sa_prot= 50,
  sa_spi= 0xE1DAEAC0(3789220544),
  sa_trans= esp-des esp-md5-hmac , sa_conn_id= 2213,
(identity) local= 192.250.3.2, remote= 192.232.1.25,
  local_proxy= 192.250.3.0/255.255.255.248/0/0 (type=4),
  remote_proxy= 192.232.1.24/255.255.255.248/0/0 (type=4)
```

L2TP Dial-Out Debug Output

The following sections show debug output from a successful L2TP dial-out negotiation:

- Dial-Out Debug Example on an LNS
- Dial-Out Debug Example on a LAC

Dial-Out Debug Example on an LNS

To view the following debug output, enable the following commands on the LNS and then initiate an L2TP dial-out call on the LNS:

```
debug vpdn event
debug vpdn error
debug ppp chap
debug ppp negotiation
debug dialer events
```

The following is debug output from successful L2TP dial-out negotiation on an LNS:

```
LNS#
*Apr 22 19:48:32.419:%SYS-5-CONFIG_I:Configured from console by console
*Apr 22 19:48:32.743:%SYS-5-CONFIG_I:Configured from console by console
```

Virtual access interface 1 is created and accesses dialer interface 0.

```
*Apr 22 19:48:33.243:Di0 DDR:dialer_fsm_idle()
*Apr 22 19:48:33.271:Vi1 PPP:Phase is DOWN, Setup
*Apr 22 19:48:33.279:Vi1 PPP:Phase is DOWN, Setup
*Apr 22 19:48:33.279:Virtual-Access1 DDR:Dialing cause ip (s=10.60.1.160,
 d=10.10.1.110)
*Apr 22 19:48:33.279:Virtual-Access1 DDR:Attempting to dial 71014
```

An L2TP session is created and placed in the idle state until an L2TP tunnel can be created.

```
*Apr 22 19:48:33.279:Tnl/Cl 1/1 L2TP:Session sequencing disabled
*Apr 22 19:48:33.279:Tnl/Cl 1/1 L2TP:Session FS enabled
*Apr 22 19:48:33.283:Tnl/Cl 1/1 L2TP:Session state change from idle
 to wait-for-tunnel
*Apr 22 19:48:33.283:Tnl/Cl 1/1 L2TP:Create dialout session
*Apr 22 19:48:33.283:Tnl 1 L2TP:SM State idle
```

The LNS sends an SCCRQ message to the LAC to begin L2TP tunnel negotiation:

```
*Apr 22 19:48:33.283:Tnl 1 L2TP:O SCCRQ
*Apr 22 19:48:33.283:Tnl 1 L2TP:Tunnel state change from idle to wait-ctl-
  reply
*Apr 22 19:48:33.283:Tnl 1 L2TP:SM State wait-ctl-reply
*Apr 22 19:48:33.283:Vi1 VPDN:Bind interface direction=2
```

The LNS receives an SCCRP message from the LAC, the devices authenticate the tunnel, and the LNS sends an SCCN message to the LAC, which completes L2TP tunnel negotiation:

```
*Apr 22 19:48:33.307:Tnl 1 L2TP:I SCCRP from lac_l2x0
*Apr 22 19:48:33.307:Tnl 1 L2TP:Got a challenge from remote peer, lac_l2x0
*Apr 22 19:48:33.307:Tnl 1 L2TP:Got a response from remote peer, lac_l2x0
*Apr 22 19:48:33.311:Tnl 1 L2TP:Tunnel Authentication success
*Apr 22 19:48:33.311:Tnl 1 L2TP:Tunnel state change from wait-ctl-reply
 to established
*Apr 22 19:48:33.311:Tnl 1 L2TP:O SCCCN  to lac_l2x0 tnlid 1
*Apr 22 19:48:33.311:Tnl 1 L2TP:SM State established
```

The LNS sends and OCRQ message to the LAC to initiate L2TP dial-out session negotiation. The LNS then receives an OCRP message from the LAC and replies with an OCCN message, which completes L2TP dial-out session negotiation:

```
*Apr 22 19:48:33.311:L2TP:O OCRQ
*Apr 22 19:48:33.311:Vi1 1/1 L2TP:Session state change from wait-for-tunnel
 to wait-reply
*Apr 22 19:48:33.367:Vi1 1/1 L2TP:I OCRP from lac_l2x0 tnl 1, cl 0
*Apr 22 19:48:33.367:Vi1 1/1 L2TP:Session state change from wait-reply
 to wait-connect
*Apr 22 19:48:33.631:Vi1 1/1 L2TP:I OCCN from lac_l2x0 tnl 1, cl 1
*Apr 22 19:48:33.631:Vi1 1/1 L2TP:Session state change from wait-connect
 to established
*Apr 22 19:48:33.631:Vi1 VPDN:Connection is up, start LCP negotiation now
```

The virtual access interface is now brought up and bound to dialer interface 0:

```
*Apr 22 19:48:33.631:%LINK-3-UPDOWN:Interface Virtual-Access1,
 changed state to up
*Apr 22 19:48:33.631:Vi1 DDR:dialer_statechange(), state=4Dialer
  statechange
 to up Virtual-Access1
*Apr 22 19:48:33.631:Vi1 DDR:dialer_out_call_connected()
*Apr 22 19:48:33.631:Vi1 DDR:dialer_bind_profile() to Di0
*Apr 22 19:48:33.631:%DIALER-6-BIND:Interface Virtual-Access1 bound to
  profile Dialer0Dialer call has been placed Virtual-Access1
```

Dialer interface 0 initiates a dial-out call, and the LNS performs LCP negotiation
with the LAC:

```
*Apr 22 19:48:33.635:Vi1 PPP:Treating connection as a callout
*Apr 22 19:48:33.635:Vi1 PPP:Phase is ESTABLISHING, Active Open
*Apr 22 19:48:33.635:Vi1 LCP:O CONFREQ [Closed] id 1 len 15
*Apr 22 19:48:33.635:Vi1 LCP:    AuthProto CHAP (0x0305C22305)
*Apr 22 19:48:33.635:Vi1 LCP:    MagicNumber 0x50E7EC2A (0x050650E7EC2A)
*Apr 22 19:48:33.663:Vi1 LCP:I CONFREQ [REQsent] id 1 len 15
*Apr 22 19:48:33.663:Vi1 LCP:    AuthProto CHAP (0x0305C22305)
*Apr 22 19:48:33.663:Vi1 LCP:    MagicNumber 0x10820474 (0x050610820474)
*Apr 22 19:48:33.663:Vi1 LCP:O CONFACK [REQsent] id 1 len 15
*Apr 22 19:48:33.663:Vi1 LCP:    AuthProto CHAP (0x0305C22305)
*Apr 22 19:48:33.663:Vi1 LCP:    MagicNumber 0x10820474 (0x050610820474)
*Apr 22 19:48:33.663:Vi1 LCP:I CONFACK [ACKsent] id 1 len 15
*Apr 22 19:48:33.663:Vi1 LCP:    AuthProto CHAP (0x0305C22305)
*Apr 22 19:48:33.663:Vi1 LCP:    MagicNumber 0x50E7EC2A (0x050650E7EC2A)
*Apr 22 19:48:33.663:Vi1 LCP:State is Open
```

LCP negotiation is completed. The LNS and LAC now perform CHAP
authentication:

```
*Apr 22 19:48:33.663:Vi1 PPP:Phase is AUTHENTICATING, by both
*Apr 22 19:48:33.663:Vi1 CHAP:Using alternate hostname lns0
*Apr 22 19:48:33.663:Vi1 CHAP:O CHALLENGE id 1 len 25 from "lns0"
*Apr 22 19:48:33.679:Vi1 CHAP:I CHALLENGE id 1 len 35 from "user0@foo.com0"
*Apr 22 19:48:33.679:Vi1 AUTH:Started process 0 pid 92
*Apr 22 19:48:33.679:Vi1 CHAP:Using alternate hostname lns0
*Apr 22 19:48:33.683:Vi1 CHAP:O RESPONSE id 1 len 25 from "lns0"
*Apr 22 19:48:33.695:Vi1 CHAP:I SUCCESS id 1 len 4
*Apr 22 19:48:33.699:Vi1 CHAP:I RESPONSE id 1 len 35 from "user0@foo.com0"
*Apr 22 19:48:33.699:Vi1 CHAP:O SUCCESS id 1 len 4
*Apr 22 19:48:33.699:Vi1 DDR:dialer_remote_name() for user0@foo.com0
```

PPP negotiation is now complete:

```
*Apr 22 19:48:33.699:Vi1 PPP:Phase is UP
```

The LNS now requests that the LAC connect it to the remote peer at IP address
10.20.1.150:

```
*Apr 22 19:48:33.703:Vi1 IPCP:O CONFREQ [Closed] id 1 len 10
*Apr 22 19:48:33.703:Vi1 IPCP:    Address 10.20.1.150 (0x030614140196)
*Apr 22 19:48:33.703:Vi1 CCP:O CONFREQ [Closed] id 1 len 10
*Apr 22 19:48:33.703:Vi1 CCP:    LZSDCP history 1 check mode SEQ process
 UNCOMPRESSSED (0x170600010201)
*Apr 22 19:48:33.711:Vi1 IPCP:I CONFREQ [REQsent] id 1 len 10
*Apr 22 19:48:33.715:Vi1 IPCP:    Address 10.20.1.120 (0x030614140178)
*Apr 22 19:48:33.715:Vi1 IPCP:O CONFACK [REQsent] id 1 len 10
```

```
*Apr 22 19:48:33.715:Vi1 IPCP:   Address 10.20.1.120 (0x030614140178)
*Apr 22 19:48:33.715:Vi1 CCP:I CONFREQ [REQsent] id 1 len 10
*Apr 22 19:48:33.715:Vi1 CCP:   LZSDCP history 1 check mode SEQ process
UNCOMPRESSSED (0x170600010201)
*Apr 22 19:48:33.715:Vi1 CCP:O CONFACK [REQsent] id 1 len 10
*Apr 22 19:48:33.715:Vi1 CCP:   LZSDCP history 1 check mode SEQ process
UNCOMPRESSSED (0x170600010201)
```

The LNS receives positive acknowledgment that it is connected to 10.20.1.150:

```
*Apr 22 19:48:33.719:Vi1 IPCP:I CONFACK [ACKsent] id 1 len 10
*Apr 22 19:48:33.719:Vi1 IPCP:   Address 10.20.1.150 (0x030614140196)
*Apr 22 19:48:33.719:Vi1 IPCP:State is Open
*Apr 22 19:48:33.719:Vi1 DDR:Dialer protocol up
*Apr 22 19:48:33.719:Dialer0:dialer_ckt_swt_client_connect:incoming
circuit switched call
```

The LNS installs the route to 10.20.1.120, the IP address of the remote peer:

```
*Apr 22 19:48:33.719:Di0 IPCP:Install route to 10.20.1.120
*Apr 22 19:48:33.719:Vi1 CCP:I CONFACK [ACKsent] id 1 len 10
*Apr 22 19:48:33.719:Vi1 CCP:   LZSDCP history 1 check mode SEQ process
UNCOMPRESSSED (0x170600010201)
*Apr 22 19:48:33.719:Vi1 CCP:State is Open
```

Virtual access interface 1 is brought up:

```
*Apr 22 19:48:34.699:%LINEPROTO-5-UPDOWN:Line protocol on Interface
Virtual-Access1, changed state to up
```

Dial-Out Debug Example on a LAC

To view the following debug output, enable the following commands on the LAC and then initiate an L2TP dial-out call on the LNS:

```
debug vpdn event
debug vpdn error
debug dialer events
```

The following is debug output from successful L2TP dial-out negotiation on a LAC:

```
LAC#
*Mar  1 00:05:26.155:%SYS-5-CONFIG_I:Configured from console by console
*Mar  1 00:05:26.899:%SYS-5-CONFIG_I:Configured from console by console
```

The LAC receives an SCCRQ message from the LNS:

```
*Mar  1 00:05:36.195:L2TP:I SCCRQ from lns_l2x0 tnl 1
*Mar  1 00:05:36.199:Tnl 1 L2TP:New tunnel created for remote lns_l2x0,
```

```
      address 10.40.1.150
*Mar  1 00:05:36.203:Tnl 1 L2TP:Got a challenge in SCCRQ, lns_12x0
```

The LAC sends an SCCRP message to the LNS, and then receives an SCCN
message from the LNS. The LAC and LNS complete tunnel authentication,
and the LAC establishes the L2TP tunnel:

```
*Mar  1 00:05:36.207:Tnl 1 L2TP:O SCCRP  to lns_12x0 tnlid 1
*Mar  1 00:05:36.215:Tnl 1 L2TP:Tunnel state change from idle to wait-ctl-
  reply
*Mar  1 00:05:36.231:Tnl 1 L2TP:I SCCCN from lns_12x0 tnl 1
*Mar  1 00:05:36.235:Tnl 1 L2TP:Got a Challenge Response in SCCCN from
  lns_12x0
*Mar  1 00:05:36.239:Tnl 1 L2TP:Tunnel Authentication success
*Mar  1 00:05:36.239:Tnl 1 L2TP:Tunnel state change from wait-ctl-reply to
  established
*Mar  1 00:05:36.243:Tnl 1 L2TP:SM State established
```

The LAC receives an OCRQ message from the LNS, which initiates L2TP
dial-out session negotiation:

```
*Mar  1 00:05:36.251:Tnl 1 L2TP:I OCRQ from lns_12x0 tnl 1
*Mar  1 00:05:36.255:Tnl/Cl 1/1 L2TP:Session sequencing disabled
*Mar  1 00:05:36.259:Tnl/Cl 1/1 L2TP:Session FS enabled
*Mar  1 00:05:36.259:Tnl/Cl 1/1 L2TP:New session created
*Mar  1 00:05:36.263:12C:Same state, 0
*Mar  1 00:05:36.267:DSES 12C:Session create
```

The LAC sends an OCRP message to the LNS:

```
*Mar  1 00:05:36.271:L2TP:Send OCRP
*Mar  1 00:05:36.275:Tnl/Cl 1/1 L2TP:Session state change from idle to
  wait-cs-answer
```

The LAC now dials out to the remote peer and brings up serial interface 0:22:

```
*Mar  1 00:05:36.279:DSES 0x12C:Building dialer map
*Mar  1 00:05:36.283:Dialout 0x12C:Next hop name is 71014
*Mar  1 00:05:36.287:Serial0:23 DDR:rotor dialout [priority]
*Mar  1 00:05:36.291:Serial0:23 DDR:Dialing cause dialer session 0x12C
*Mar  1 00:05:36.291:Serial0:23 DDR:Attempting to dial 71014
*Mar  1 00:05:36.479:%LINK-3-UPDOWN:Interface Serial0:22, changed state to
  up
*Mar  1 00:05:36.519:isdn_call_connect:Calling lineaction of Serial0:22
*Mar  1 00:05:36.519:Dialer0:Session free, 12C
*Mar  1 00:05:36.523::0 packets unqueued and discarded
*Mar  1 00:05:36.527:Se0:22 VPDN:Bind interface direction=1
```

The LAC completes L2TP session negotiation and sends an OCCN message to the LNS, which completes the L2TP dial-out session negotiation:

```
*Mar  1 00:05:36.531:Se0:22 1/1 L2TP:Session state change from wait-cs-
   answer to established
*Mar  1 00:05:36.531:L2TP:Send OCCN
```

The LAC binds the L2TP dial-out session to serial interface 0:22, which is now connected to the remote peer:

```
*Mar  1 00:05:36.539:Se0:22 VPDN:bound to vpdn session
*Mar  1 00:05:36.555:Se0:22 1/1 L2TP:0 FS failed
*Mar  1 00:05:36.555:Se0:22 1/1 L2TP:0 FS failed
*Mar  1 00:05:42.515:%ISDN-6-CONNECT:Interface Serial0:22 is now
connected to 71014
```

INDEX